The Grand Tour

What travel meaneth ... Many do fondly imagine that it is nothing else than a certain gadding about, a vain beholding of sundry places, a transmigration from one country to another ... [The true traveller is he who] whither soever he directeth his journey, travelleth for the greater benefit of his wit, for the commodity of his studies, and the dexterity of his life, who moveth more in mind than body ... *Hermann Kirchner's oration in praise of travel, translated by Thomas Coryate in his* CRUDITIES

The longer any man of candour resides in a foreign country, the greater difficulty he finds in giving a character of its inhabitants. He perceives so many nice varieties, so many exceptions to general rules, as almost destroy his hopes of drawing up one comprehensive description of them: he every day becomes more conscious of the presumption of those who run and read; and, what is worse, write. *Henry Swinburne in his Preface to his* TRAVELS IN THE TWO SICILIES

The Grand Tour
1592–1796

Edited by Roger Hudson

The Folio Society London 1993

Material from James Boswell's journals
is reprinted from *Boswell on the Grand
Tour: Germany and Switzerland, 1764*,
ed. F. A. Pottle, 1953, and *Boswell on
the Grand Tour: Italy, Corsica, and
France, 1764–66*, ed. F. A. Pottle, 1955,
by permission of Yale University and
the Edinburgh University Press.

Material from Robert Adam's papers is
reprinted from documents
GD18/4910, GD18/4763,
GD18/4762, GD18/4803
and GD18/4803, GD18/4769, held in
the Scottish Record Office, by
permission of Sir John Clerk of
Penicuik, Bart, CBE, VRD.

The Maps were drawn by Denys Baker.

The painting reproduced on the
binding is *Hillside with Rome in the
Distance* by Thomas Jones, *c.*1776–83
(*Courtesy of Sotheby's*).

Set in Janson by Selwood Systems;
printed and bound in Hong Kong by
Mandarin Offset Ltd; typography by
Malcolm Harvey Young.

A caricature
by Giovanni Battista Tiepolo

Contents

Illustrations

4

9

Amsterdam
The Hague
Utr

LONDON

Dover

A

Calais
Boulogne
Montreuil

Brussels

Abbeville

Dieppe

R. Seine

Reims

PARIS   R. Marne

Versailles

Châlons-sur-

Fontainebleau

Rennes

Orleans

Blois

Briare

R. Loire

Dij

Nantes

Tours

Nevers

F R A N C E

Moulins

Roanne

Limoges

Lyons

Vienne

Bordeaux

R. Garonne

Ch

Pont St. Esprit

Pont du G

Nîmes

A

Montpellier

A

Marseil

Pont du Gard

Hanover.

•Berlin
Potsdam

Brunswick •Coswig

•Kassel

Cologne

GERMANY

Mainz •Franfurt

•Heidelberg

P R U S S I A

•Leipzig
Dresden

R. Elbe

Prague•

Melk: The Monastery

R. Rhine

Regensberg

AUSTRIA

R. Danube

R. Isar

R. Inn

Passau

Linz

Krems

Vienna

Munich•

Melk

L. Constance

•Salzburg

Baden •Zurich

Innsbruck

WITZERLAND

•Berne

Brenner Pass

Fribourg

Brig. •Simplon Pass

Brenta Canal

DOM OF
inebourg

Milan•

Verona•

Venice

R. Adige

Padua•

•Turin

R. Po

SARDINIA
PIEDMONT

•Genoa

Sestri Levante

Miles
100

0   200

•Nice

Leghorn•

0   100   200   300
Kms

lles

I T A L Y

0   100   200 Miles

0   100   200   300 Kms.

L. Como
R. Adige
Gottolengo
Brescia
VENETO
Milan
Verona
Vicenza
Turin
PIEDMONT
LOMBARDY
Padua
Venice
R. Po
Parma
Modena
Genoa
Bologna
Sestri Levante
PAPAL
Pisa
Florence
R. Arno
TUSCANY
Leghorn
Siena
STATES
Radicofani
CORSICA
Montefiascone
Viterbo
THE
ROME
Tivoli
Frascati
Castel Gandolfo
Manfredonia
KINGDOM
Capua
Cannae
Naples
M.t Vesuvius
Monopoli
SARDINIA
Capri
PUGLIA
Sorrento
Paestum
Francavilla
OF THE
Lecce
TWO
Stromboli I.
Lipari I.
Palermo
Bagheria
Messina
Segesta
Castelvetrano
SICILIES
M.t Etna
Selinunte
Agrigento
Catania

Venice:
The Campanile
and Doge's Palace

Rome: St. Peter's

Introduction

Milordos and Bear Leaders

The Grand Tour in its purest form was the culmination of the rich young eighteenth-century Englishman's education. He was sent to Europe, for years rather than months, in the care of a tutor who was often a clergyman and/or a College Fellow. This tutor or bear leader safeguarded his morals, oversaw his studies and looked after the practicalities of travel and accommodation. Before the Tour by far the greater part of the boy's education would have been in the languages, literature and history of Classical Greece and Rome, and the prime aim now was for him to 'set foot on classic ground', to see the landscapes of antiquity, and to view the ruins and statuary that survived. In practice, for the great majority this meant what could be seen in Italy; visits to Greece remained very much the exception. The Classical heritage *was* Civilisation, to all intents and purposes, for his parents, and they sought to give him at worst a thin coating, at best a thorough marinading, by immersing him at its fount.

Dr James Hay as a bear leader, by Pier Leone Ghezzi. An Italian caricatures a Scottish tutor and his charge touring the country

There were other hopes and expectations, naturally, attached to such expensive and elaborate excursions. Palladian and Baroque architecture and what might be termed post-Raphaelite painting and sculpture were annexed to the Classical corpus. Anything Romanesque or Gothic was excluded – Henry Swinburne thought the magnificent Norman abbey at Monreale in Sicily 'exhibits a very disagreeable specimen of Gothic taste'. William Kent and Thomas Coke, the future 1st Earl of Leicester, did see the Giotto frescoes in the Arena Chapel at Padua and Thomas Patch started the appreciation of Masaccio (p. 133), but they were very much pioneers in bothering with Early-Renaissance art.

The Tourists did not make a blinkered dash to and from Italy. France was universally looked up to as the repository of all that was refined in manners and style, with a court and attached luxury trade that all other countries sought to copy. French had become the *lingua franca* of Europe. Besides this language, 'an easier air in company' was to be acquired in Paris, Vienna, Berlin and the small courts of Germany. As Robert Burns put it:

> *To mak a tour an' take a whirl,*
> *To learn* bon ton, *an' see the worl'.*

As well as book work and art appreciation, there were such accomplishments as fencing, dancing, equitation, music and drawing to be learnt. There were also snuff boxes, tapestries, clocks, watches, and clothes to be bought in Paris; scagliola table-tops or *pietra dura* panels in Florence; coins, cameos, intaglios and prints in Rome. Pompeo Batoni would paint your portrait there with some Classical props from his studio stock (he painted over 150 of the visiting British). Rosalba Carriera would do you in pastel in Venice, with a carnival mask tied to your hat, while Canaletto painted

Charles Sackville, Earl of Middlesex, by the Venetian woman artist Rosalba Carriera. His carnival mask is ready for use

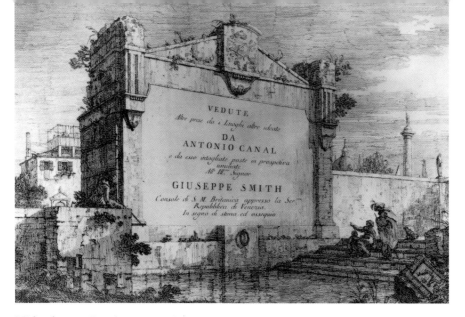

Title plate to Canaletto's set of etchings of Venetian views dedicated to his patron, the British Consul Joseph Smith, whose collection was sold to George III

almost exclusively for English *milordi*. A whole new genre of art was invented for the Tourist trade: ruin scenes painted by Panini and Hubert Robert or drawn and etched by Piranesi. If you wanted a capriccio coastal scene to remind you of the Bay of Naples, Claude Joseph Vernet was your man. An army of copyists would reproduce the paintings of your choice to very high standards. However, if you were after a really outstanding piece of Classical sculpture, an original painting by a High-Renaissance master such as Titian or Raphael, or a good example of the Bolognese school (Domenichino, Reni, Guercino), they were extremely difficult to obtain. Few first-class Classical sculptures found their way to Britain in the eighteenth century (enthusiasts had to make do with casts) and most High-Renaissance and Bolognese paintings were acquired after the French Revolution.

Apart from art, there were famous personages to see or meet – the French royal family at dinner, Bonnie Prince Charlie at his devotions in Rome, Emma Hamilton striking attitudes in Naples, Voltaire at Ferney outside Geneva; and natural phenomena to examine – Vesuvius, Etna, and the glaciers above Chamonix. There were operas to go to, and many English Tourists could speak knowledgeably of what they heard thanks to the regular Italian seasons staged in London. There was the Roman Catholic Church in action, its services, processions, music and relics to be enjoyed with a mixture of guilty fascination and amused superiority. Lastly there was the hope of health for some, from a warmer climate, medicinal waters, or a different diet, and the expectation of excitement for others, from the gaming tables of Paris and Venice, or from the delights of the flesh bestowed by either amateurs or professionals. Some Tourists were single-minded in their efforts to debauch themselves, hence the saying, '*Inglese Italianato è un diavolo incarnato*'.

There were deeper reasons behind the flourishing of Grand Tourism. The parlous state of the English universities was a major factor. Of his time at Oxford Gibbon said, 'I spent fourteen months at Magdalen College: they proved ... the most idle and unprofitable of my whole life.' Many fathers chose not to send their sons at all: in 1733 Christ's College, Cambridge admitted only three freshmen. But if they so decided, the time between school and marriage had to be filled in some other way. With the rising prosperity of the country, as the 'consumer revolution' took a hold, there were the funds available and these, allied to the strengthening taboo on the gently born involving themselves in trade, made the Grand Tour an attractive proposition. The wars of religion that had plagued Europe for a hundred years were dying down by the latter part of the seventeenth century and it was safe for Protestant Englishmen to wander through the largely Catholic Continent.

Sarah, the formidable Duchess of Marlborough, writing to a grandson's bear leader, was down to earth about what was to be expected from the Tour: 'I never thought travelling was of much use but to teach them perfectly the language and to keep them out of harm's way, while they are so young that they cannot keep the best company in England, and to make them see that nothing is so agreeable as England take it altogether.' When Gibbon set out 'the qualifications which I deem the most essential to a traveller', he knew it was a 'sketch of ideal perfection':

He should be endowed with an active, indefatigable vigour of mind and body, which can seize every mode of conveyance, and support with a careless smile every hardship of the road, the weather or the inn. I must stimulate him with a restless curiosity, impatient of ease, covetous of time and fearless of danger; which drives him forth at any hour of the day or night, to brave the flood, to climb the mountain, or to fathom the mine, on the most doubtful promise of entertainment or instruction. The arts of common life are not studied in the closet; with a copious stock of classical and historical learning, my traveller must blend the practical knowledge of husbandry and manufactures; he should be a chemist, a botanist, and a master of mechanics. A musical ear will multiply the pleasures of his Italian tour; but a correct and exquisite eye, which commands the landscape of a country, discerns the merits of a picture, and measures the proportions of a building, is more closely connected with the finer feelings of the mind; and the fleeting image should be fixed and realised by the dexterity of the pencil. I have reserved for the last a virtue which borders on a vice: the flexible temper which can assimilate itself to every tone of society, from the court to the cottage; the happy flow of spirits which can amuse and be amused in every company and situation.

There were few, if any, who lived up to this description. The reality was rather as indicated by Samuel Sharp:

I had always figured to myself, that they were in the highest delight when making the Grand Tour; but I find by experience, that when they are here, they consider it as a kind of apprenticeship for qualifying a gentleman, and would often return abruptly, did they not feel themselves ashamed to indulge the inclination: Indeed, were it not, that in the great cities they meet with numbers of their countrymen, the hours would lie too heavily on their hands; for few men can spend their whole life in the pursuit of virtu, and some have not the qualifications of birth to recommend them to persons of high rank, where only is to be found what little society there is in Italy. It must be confessed, the nobility here are not only polite to Englishmen, but almost proud of their company, provided they come with a testimony that they have blood in their veins, or are gentlemen of large fortunes; yet, upon the whole, their converzationi, *as they are called, grow tiresome, being so little diversified, in comparison of the elegant amusements of London. One may easily conceive how limited a conversation must be, where men dare not speak on the subject, of liberty, politics, or religion; and where no drama is exhibited, and very few writings, except of the most ridiculous, abject, superstitious kind are published; so that a man, in a liberal way of thinking, has no refuge in these conversations but cards, where, Scandal says, there is much foul play; and, probably, Scandal speaks truth; for I have heard of many young gentlemen who have lost considerably, but I never heard of one who carried off his trunk full of sequins* [coins].

Lady Mary Wortley Montagu was equally deflating about the 'boys and governors' after five months in Venice in 1740:

Here are inundations of them broke in upon us this carnival, and my apartment must be their refuge, the greater part of them having kept an inviolable fidelity to the language their nurses taught them. Their whole business abroad (as far as I can perceive) being to buy new clothes, in which they shine in some obscure coffee-house where they are sure of meeting only one another; and after the important conquest of some waiting gentlewoman of an opera queen, who perhaps they remember as long as they live, return to England excellent judges of men and manners. I find the spirit of patriotism so strong in me every time I see them that I look on them as the greatest blockheads in nature; and, to say truth, the compound of booby and petit maître *makes up a very odd sort of animal.*

'Four Learned Milordi', by Joshua Reynolds – a caricature which he painted when a young man in Rome in 1751. From the left: Lord Bruce, John Ward, Lord Milltown and Joseph Henry looking at a print of the *Cloaca Maxima*, the ancient Roman sewer

Alexander Pope can have the last devastating word:

> *Led by my hand, he saunter'd Europe round,*
> *And gather'd ev'ry Vice on Christian ground;*
> *Saw ev'ry Court, heard ev'ry King declare*
> *His royal Sense, of Op'ra's or the Fair;*
> *The Stews and Palace equally explor'd,*
> *Intrigu'd with glory, and with spirit whor'd;*
> *Try'd all* hors-d'œuvres, *all* liqueurs *defin'd,*
> *Judicious drank, and greatly-daring din'd;*
> *Dropt the dull lumber of the Latin store,*
> *Spoil'd his own language, and acquir'd no more;*
> *All Classic learning lost on Classic ground;*
> *And last turn'd* Air, *the Echo of a Sound!*
> *See now, half-cur'd, and perfectly well-bred,*
> *With nothing but a Solo in his head . . .*
>
> The Dunciad, IV

The machinery of modern European tourism – good roads, railways, speedy air travel, hotels, restaurants, travellers' cheques and credit cards – has been in place so long that it requires a conscious effort to imagine a time without it. Eighteenth-century Europe was the equivalent of Third-World territory today, potentially dangerous, certainly uncomfortable; the major cities had a few hotels, but none of the other ingredients was there.

When James Adam, a younger brother of Robert, stayed at Capua between Rome and Naples in 1760, he paid the price for trusting himself to the inn's bed: 'Half an hour after going to bed I was so attacked in flank, front and rear by six batallions of bugs and four squadrons of fleas, exclusive of several companies of *zampones* or *muschetoes*, that I was soon put to flight and obliged to take my night's quarters upon three straw chairs in the middle of the room.' Lord Herbert had the same experience in the same place, perhaps in the same bed, in 1779: 'What a night have I passed, not being able to gett to sleep from Animals crawling continually all over my poor dear Person ... But what were these Animals, why to know that I looked this morning at the Bedstead, and behold I saw some hundreds of Buggs on their march Home, full of Prey, I dare-say ... I was Bitt in three different Places, all three on a very tender part ... which we Britons think the best part of a Bullock to make Steak of ... I deserved it for going to Bed last night without looking, whereas had I proceeded in my customary manner laying myself down on a board, Bench, or table, I should have slept like a Hero.' Other horror stories about accommodation will be found in the main text, and about food too. Restaurants were a late invention of the cooks thrown on their own devices by the fall of the French aristocracy after 1789. Complaints about garlic and the state of the lavatories are shown to have a long history.

Many of the roads were poor, the best being in France and the worst in Germany. Germany also had the worst chaises and carriages. Dr Charles Burney said he did not meet with one 'that had a top, or covering, to protect passengers from heat, cold, wind, or rain in my whole journey: and so violent are the jolts, and so hard are the seats of German post wagons, that a man is rather kicked than carried from one place to another'. It is unsurprising that river transport played such a big part – south down the Rhône from Lyons, along the canal and river systems to the west and south of Venice, east down the Danube to Vienna or north down the Rhine to Holland. When it came to the Alps, there were no roads for wheeled traffic. The first to be opened was that over the Col de Tende between Nice and Turin in the 1780s.

If one chose to 'travel post', this meant hiring either chaise and horses, or horses only if one had a chaise of one's own, at the various post houses on the route. It also meant hiring a postilion to drive the horses, and he might well be struck by lightning. The alternative was to surrender oneself into the hands of a *vetturino* or *voiturin* who, in return for an agreed sum, laid on transport, accommodation and food. Some Tourists took personal servants with them from England. Others hired a *laquais de place* for the duration of their stay in a city. Boswell hired a Swiss called Jacob who accompanied him through Italy and France. Boswell worried Jacob by not maintaining the normal distance:

Disputed with Jacob, who said he knew me perfectly and that it was impossible for servants to live well with me, as I was not, like other gentlemen, content with external acquiescence, but would always show them clearly that they were wrong. He is very right. I am always studying human nature and making experiments on the lowest characters, so that I am too much in the secret with regard to the weakness of man in reality, and my honest, impetuous disposition cannot take up with that eternal repetition of fictitious minutiae by which unthinking men of fashion preserve a great distinction between master and servant. By having Jacob so free with me, I have felt as servants do, and been convinced that the greatest part of them laugh in their sleeve very heartily at the parade of their lords, knowing well that eating, drinking, sleeping and other offices of nature are common to all. Jacob said, 'I believe, Sir, that you have been badly brought up. You have not the manners of a nobleman. Your heart is too open.' I confessed to him that I was two and twenty before I had a servant. Said he, 'The son of a gentleman ought to be accustomed early to command a servant, but reasonably, and never to joke with them; because each must live in his state according to his quality. You, Sir, would live just like a peasant. And you force a servant to speak in a way he shouldn't, because you torment him with questions. You want to get to the bottom of things.'

The grandest travellers took their own artists with them to record the sights, like walking animated cameras; Lord Palmerston took William Pars, William Beckford had J. R. Cozens (as well as a personal physician and a harpsichordist), while Richard Payne Knight took Jakob Philipp Hackert to Sicily.

When abroad, money could be obtained either from the foreign correspondents of one's English banker or by taking bills of exchange, which in theory were negotiable. The other vital documents were letters of introduction, the keys to polite society in France and Italy (as Samuel Sharp implies above), and to the small courts north of the Alps.

The first recognisable Grand Tourists emerged at the end of the sixteenth century, though this is not to say that the Middle Ages were a sedentary time. In 1428, it is recorded that 925 shiploads of pilgrims left England for northern Spain and the shrine of St James of Compostella. The Reformation put an end to the pilgrimage trade; the hostility of Philip II of Spain (who also ruled tracts of the Low Countries and Italy) and the religious wars within France from the 1560s to the 1590s delayed its replacement by the secular Grand Tour. Sir Philip Sidney did go in the 1570s and was honest enough to admit how much fashion had to do with his motives: 'A great number of us never thought in ourselves why we went, but a certain tickling humour to do as other men had done.' Sir Henry Wotton, from a family of royal servants, was sponsored in part by Queen Elizabeth on his Tour in 1589, and was expected to file intelligence reports in return. The two earliest writers included in this book are Fynes Moryson, who left England in 1591, and Thomas Coryate, who set out in 1608. By 1639 Lady Brilliana Harley could write to her son at Oxford: 'I believe that there are but few noblemen's sons in Oxford; for now, for the most part they send their sons into France, when they are very young, there to be bred.' The English Civil War gave some good reasons for absenting themselves for a few years. The young Earl of Devonshire, with Thomas Hobbes as his tutor, stayed away. In 1643 John Evelyn, 'finding it impossible to evade doing very unhandsome things ... obtained a licence of His Majesty ... to travel again'.

By the end of the seventeenth century Grand Tourism was moving into higher gear. Joseph Addison, at the time a bright young Oxford don, went abroad from 1699 to 1703 and the book that resulted, *Remarks On Several Parts Of Italy* (1705), long served as a companion for those on the Tour. (At some point whilst abroad he went on a French excursion with Edward Wortley Montagu, grandson of the Earl of Sandwich, who in 1712 eloped with the brilliant Lady Mary Pierrepont.) Edward Wright, the next of our authors, was bear leader to Lord Parker in the 1720s and his book, *Observations Travelling Through France, Italy, etc*, followed in 1730. Horace Walpole and his friend from Eton and Cambridge, Thomas Gray, were exceptional in that they travelled together without a bear leader, when they set out in 1739. They were also lucky since their tour finished in September 1741, before the War of the Austrian Succession began to impede travellers. Peace with France came again in 1748, but only until 1756 when the Seven Years War started.

After 1763 the Grand Tour was at its height. Paris, Venice and Rome were flooded with English, not merely sprigs of the aristocracy and sons of the very rich, but lesser gentry, literary figures, and the middle-aged, sometimes accompanied by wives and families. The purpose was often less education than entertainment or a search for health. Among the figures going abroad at this time were Hume, Gibbon, Garrick, Adam Smith, Smollett, Sterne and Wilkes. Some of those who wrote books on their Tours were determined not to be over-impressed by what they saw and a new, aggressive, no-nonsense self-confidence is apparent, fuelled no doubt by the British triumphs in the recent war. Tobias Smollett and Samuel

Sharp (both surgeons) are the obvious examples of this trend, which in due course led to a reaction in Laurence Sterne's *Sentimental Journey* and the books of Dr Johnson's expatriate Italian friend Giuseppe Baretti (he went on a French tour with Dr Johnson and Mrs Thrale in 1775).

While the ordinary Tourist now allowed himself greater subjectivity in his outlook and was attracted more by the picturesque if not downright romantic, the focus of interest for the erudite traveller, which had been imperial Rome, shifted southwards and to earlier periods. The discovery outside Naples of Herculaneum in 1738 and Pompeii in 1748, the rediscovery of the ancient Greek temples further south at Paestum and then of similar sites in Sicily, the expeditions to Greece proper mounted by the Dilettanti Society (founded 1732) – all these contributed to the rise of Neoclassicism and to *le goût grec*, the Greek Revival. There was a new admiration for the stoic virtues of republican Rome, and the public nature of the great buildings whose remains could still be seen – the aqueducts, temples, amphitheatres – was applauded. The republican virtues appealed particularly to the Whig magnates of England and the sculpture galleries that they added to their houses were in some sense a defiant political statement against what they saw as the increase in the power of their own Hanoverian kings and the absolutism of the rest of Europe. Historical figures exemplifying a stern public morality, as in the paintings of David, were now of more interest than mythological ones. Voltaire, the *philosophes* and rationalists, in their attacks on intolerance and superstition, had also shaken the moral code based on divinely revealed religion. A new morality had to be constructed and this was one of its building blocks. The other was the new worship of nature, the primitive and the instinctive, the abandonment of the idea of original sin, the raising of the heart and of feelings to an equality with, if not a superiority to, reason – all promoted by the writings of Jean Jacques Rousseau.

The Tourist's route took him first to Paris, then possibly for a few months to a town on the Loire to perfect his French, vital for polite conversation in any other country to which he might go. When he moved on it was normally to Dijon, where one took a boat down the Saône to Lyons. There a choice had to be made between going over the Alps to Turin, or down to a southern French port to take ship for Genoa. If the Alpine route was selected, one headed eastward out of France into Savoy, which was part of the Kingdom of Sardinia. The Mont Cenis Pass led into Piedmont, another part of the same kingdom. The route southwards from Lyons down the Rhône by boat gave the chance to see Classical remains at Arles, Nîmes, and the Pont du Gard before one had entered Italy. There was no corniche road through to Italy, so it was necessary to take a tartine or felucca along the Riviera coast, hoping not to meet any Barbary pirates on the way. Once Genoa was reached it was still best to continue by sea to Leghorn before disembarking for Pisa and Florence.

After Turin, likely stopping places before Venice were Milan, Verona, Vicenza and Padua, unless Europe's pleasure capital was being saved as a reward for the end of the Italian section of the Tour. In the eighteenth century Venice reckoned on 30,000 visitors a year. The road via Bologna reached Florence over the Apennines. There the well-connected Tourist's path would be smoothed by the attentions of the British Envoy to the Grand Ducal court, Sir Horace Mann. Gibbon described him as 'an agreeable man, quiet and polished, but somewhat wrapped up in a round of important trifles'. The high point at Florence was the visit to the Tribuna gallery at the Uffizi palace, where the outstanding Classical sculptures collected by the Medici were on show, including their *Venus*. If the Tour is seen as some kind of aesthetic pilgrimage, then the Tribuna was for most the equivalent of the Kaaba at Mecca.

In Rome, 'so sparsely peopled that one understands it endures only through pure conjugal duty' according to Lady Mary Wortley Montagu, there was no dominating figure such as Sir Horace, but a host of ciceroni (guides) and dealers who battened on Tourists. Thomas Jenkins was involved in a racket selling fake Roman cameos and intaglios. James Byres obtained Poussin's series of paintings, the *Seven Sacraments*, for the Duke of Rutland, circumventing the export ban by substituting copies. He also obtained the famous glass Portland Vase, now in the British Museum. Gavin Hamilton worked as a partner with Piranesi over the excavation and sale of the huge Warwick Vase, and was in league with Bartolomeo Cavaceppi's sculpture workshop to transform Classical sculpture fragments into the complete statues that the Tourist market demanded. Joseph Nollekens, later a most successful sculptor in London, made a good income 'restoring' similar fragments when a young man in Rome.

Naples, in contrast to Rome, was the third largest city in Europe. Sir William Hamilton, the Envoy there, had much of his time taken up by British visitors, but this did not stop him amassing a remarkable collection of Classical remains (including the Warwick Vase, now in the Metropolitan Museum, New York) or becoming the acknowledged expert on Vesuvius. When John Evelyn got to Naples in 1645 he made it the furthest point of his journeyings because he 'had been assured there was little more to be seen in the rest of the civil world ... but plain and prodigal barbarism'. This remained the case for most until the 1760s, though Thomas Coke

James Byres and his family, by Franz Smuglewicz. Byres was a leading art dealer and cicerone in Rome. He acted as guide to Edward Gibbon. Two of his dealing coups are detailed on p. 23

sailed to Sicily from Marseilles in 1716 and Lord Sandwich included it in his Tour from 1737 to 1739, which took in Greece and Egypt as well. By the second half of the eighteenth century, the Swiss glaciers, like Sicily, had been added to the Tourist itinerary. William Windham of Felbrigg Hall in Norfolk pioneered the trip to those above Chamonix with a party of friends in 1741. Both in Switzerland and Germany the Tourist depended much on letters of introduction, either to see Voltaire or Rousseau near Geneva, or to gain access to the German courts, which were the only sources of society and entertainment.

The end of the eighteenth century saw the end of the Grand Tour. The hiatus caused by the French Revolution and Napoleonic wars was soon followed by the spread of railways, hotels and restaurants, which made possible mass tourism and the shorter holiday. There was a change of attitude and taste, too: Victorian earnestness and lust for self-improvement elbowed out the lighter touch of the Georgians; fourteenth- and fifteenth-century paintings and, under the guidance of John Ruskin, Italian Gothic, supplanted the High Renaissance, Palladian and Baroque.

Many of the writers assembled here do not fall within the strict definition of Grand Tourists given at the start of this introduction, being neither that rich nor that young. Several were bear leaders rather than led bears; several were already established literary figures (Tobias Smollett, Arthur Young); many more were subsequently enlisted as such. Sir Horace Mann and, latterly, Lady Mary Wortley Montagu were residents rather than Tourists. In a collection restricted to drawing on the diaries and letters of pure specimens of the Grand Tourist, there would have been far too much of the kind of writing represented by the extracts from lord herbert included here. It is hoped, nevertheless, that a vigorous picture of this historical phenomenon emerges. It was an important one, softening, warming, lighting and civilising the barbarous North, as it did; setting up standards of taste, wit and elegance from which we still benefit and which are encapsulated in the English country house; laying the foundations of the whole travel industry. For a few decades there was an extraordinary convergence and blending among Europe's upper classes and a rich cultural cross-fertilisation. In Vicenza in 1789, Arthur Young was taken to see 'a magazine of earthenware in imitation of Mr Wedgwood. It is surely a triumph of the arts in England to see in Italy Etruscan forms copied from English models. It is a better imitation than many I have seen in France.'

No attempt has been made to regularise spelling, and extracts have been left as first printed. Cuts within extracts are indicated by ellipses. Short annotations are in square brackets in the text, longer ones come as conventional footnotes. The book is organised geographically, following the route most used by the Tourists, each country being divided into cities visited and areas passed through, and these subdivided into sections. An editorial linking passage in italics details the extracts (normally three or four) that make up the succeeding section. Short biographical notes about the writers may be found at the end of the book.

ROGER HUDSON

The title-page to *Coryat's Crudities*, 1611, showing various high and low points on his journey, including his being sick into the English Channel

France

Few writers were as succinct as Edward Gibbon in his Memoirs, *when describing their departure from England: 'A post-chaise conveyed me to Dover, the packet to Boulogne.' Dr Charles Burney was delayed even before he had left the country: 'Having left my sword, that necessary passport for a gentleman on the Continent, I though it of consequence enough to remain at Dover till I recovered it ...' Then he proceeded 'with a fair wind and arrived at Calais without any other accident than the very common one of being intolerably ill during the whole passage'. Thomas Coryate was not going to let go the opportunity his sea-sickness afforded for a few Jacobean flourishes. After embarking at ten in the morning, he arrived in Calais 'about five of the clocke in the afternoone, after I had varnished the exterior parts of the ship with the excrementall ebullitions of my tumultuous stomach, as desiring to satiate the gormandizing paunches of the hungry Haddocks (according as I have hieroglyphically expressed it in the front of my booke) with that wherewith I had superfluously stuffed my selfe at land, having made my rumbling belly their capacious aumbrie [cupboard].'*

The next gauntlet to be run after the Channel was the French Customs. Dr Burney once more:

At Calais the ceremonial of the custom house gives a specimen at once of pride and meanness. The chief *commis*, or clerk there, was sitting in a velvet suit of clothes with every other appurtenance of the dress and appearance of a gentleman, or indeed rather of a man of fashion and quality; who, when he had signed my passport, being asked what there was to pay – '*Ah! monsieur – ça c'est que la politesse*' – and more compliments: and upon giving him a 'pièce de 24 sous', equal to a shilling English, his eyes sparkled, and he seemed as pleased as a man of equal appearance in England would have been with a place at court or a regiment.

Tobias Smollett stayed at Boulogne some time with his family. This allowed him to form typically unflattering conclusions about French society as displayed there.

William Hogarth visited France in 1748 and was briefly arrested as a spy when sketching in Calais. He took his revenge by painting *Calais Gate*. A piece of English beef on its way to the English Inn at Calais attracts the attention of a fat friar and two emaciated French soldiers, and contrasts with the thin French soup. Hogarth sketches on the left while a Scottish Jacobite soldier begs on the right.

The noblesse are vain ... They allow their country-houses to go to decay, and their gardens and fields to waste; and reside in dark holes in the Upper Town of Boulogne, without light, air, or convenience. There they starve within doors, that they may have wherewithal to purchase fine cloaths, and appear dressed once a day in the church, or on the rampart. They have no education, no taste for reading, no housewifery, nor indeed any earthly occupation, but that of dressing their hair, and adorning their bodies. They hate walking, and would never go abroad, if they were not stimulated by the vanity of being seen. I ought to except indeed those who turn devotees, and spend the greatest part of their time with the priest, either at church, or in their own houses. Other amusements they have none in this place, except private parties of card-playing, which are far from being expensive.

Nothing can be more parsimonious than the œconomy of these people: they live upon soupe and bouillé, fish and sallad: they never think of giving dinners, or entertaining their friends; they even save the expence of coffee and tea, though both are very cheap at Boulogne. They presume that every person drinks coffee at home, immediately after dinner, which is always over by one o'clock; and, in lieu of tea in the afternoon, they treat with a

Charles Burney in 1770, sketched possibly at Calais, on his way home from his first Tour

D.ʳ Burney at Calis in the Year 1770

glass of sherbet, or capillaire [an orange-flavoured drink]. In a word, I know not a more insignificant set of mortals than the noblesse of Boulogne; helpless in themselves, and useless to the community; without dignity, sense, or sentiment; contemptible from pride, and ridiculous from vanity ... Considering the vivacity of the French people, one would imagine they could not possibly lead such an insipid life, altogether unanimated by society, or diversion. True it is, the only profane diversions of this place are a puppet-show and a mountebank; but then their religion affords a perpetual comedy.

Their high masses, their feasts, their processions, their pilgrimages, confessions, images, tapers, robes, incense, benedictions, spectacles, representations, and innumerable ceremonies, which revolve almost incessantly, furnish a variety of entertainment from one end of the year to the other. If superstition implies *fear*, never was a word more misapplied than it is to the mummery of the religion of Rome. The people are so far from being impressed with awe and religious terror by this sort of machinery, that it amuses their imaginations in the most agreeable manner, and keeps them always in good humour. A Roman catholic longs as impatiently for the festival of St Suaire, or St Croix, or St Veronique, as a school-boy in England for the representation of punch and the devil; and there is generally as much laughing at one farce as at the other. Even when the descent from the cross is acted, in the holy week, with all the circumstances that ought naturally to inspire the gravest sentiments, if you cast your eyes among the multitude that croud the place, you will not discover one melancholy face: all is prattling, tittering, or laughing; and ten to one but you perceive a number of them employed in hissing the female who personates the Virgin ...

Laurence Sterne, though he wrote his Sentimental Journey *as a direct counterblast to the acerbities of Smollett, admitted that at first he was shocked by the openness of the French approach to the calls of nature.*

Madame de Rambouliet, after an acquaintance of about six weeks with her, had done me the honour to take me in her coach about two leagues out of town. Of all women, Madame de Rambouliet is the most correct; and I never wish to see one of more virtues and purity of heart. In our return back, Madame de Rambouliet desired me to pull the cord. I asked her if she wanted any thing. *Rien que pisser,* said Madame de Rambouliet.

Grieve not, gentle traveller, to let Madame de Rambouliet p—ss on. And, fair mystic nymphs! go each one *pluck your rose,* and scatter them in your path, for Madame de Rambouliet did no more. I handed Madame de Rambouliet out of the coach; and had I been the priest of the chaste Castalia,* I could not have served at her fountain with a more respectful decorum.

Another passage, from Sterne's Tristram Shandy *this time, follows. He sets out his resigned and philosophical attitude towards the inevitable setbacks of travel, and incidentally gets us on the road out of the Channel ports.*

A French postillion has always to alight before he has got three hundred yards out of town.

What's wrong now? – Diable! – a rope's broke! – a knot has slipt! – a staple's drawn! – a bolt's to whittle! – a tag, a rag, a jag, a strap, a buckle, or a buckle's tongue, want altering.

Now true as all this is, I never think myself impowered to excommunicate thereupon either the post-chaise, or its driver – nor do I take it into my head to swear by the living G—, I would rather go a-foot ten thousand times – or that I will be damned, if even I get into another – but I take the matter coolly before me, and consider, that some tag, or rag, or jag, or bolt, or buckle, or buckle's tongue, will ever be awanting, or want altering, travel where I will – so I never chafe, but take the good and the bad as they fall in my road, and get on: – Do so, my lad! said I; he had lost five minutes already, in alighting in order to get at a luncheon of black bread, which he had crammed into the chaise-pocket, and was remounted, and going leisurely on, to relish it the better – Get on, my lad, said I, briskly – but in the most persuasive tone imaginable, for I jingled a four-and-twenty sous piece

* The Castalian spring on Mount Parnassus was the traditional abode of the Muses.

The Customs House at Boulogne, by Thomas Rowlandson

against the glass, taking care to hold the flat side towards him, as he looked back: the dog grinned intelligence from his right ear to his left, and behind his sooty muzzle discovered such a pearly row of teeth, that Sovereignty would have pawned her jewels for them. –

Just heaven! ｛ What masticators! –
         ｛ What bread! –

and so as he finished the last mouthful of it, we entered the town of Montreuil.

Both young Horace Walpole, on his first visit to Paris in April 1739, and Arthur Young, in 1787, were quick to light on a mix of 'parade and poverty' as being a typical phenomenon of the city. Walpole went to see the funeral of the Duc de Tresmes, Governor of Paris and Marshal of France, 'a most vile thing. A long procession of flambeaux and friars; no plumes, trophies, banners, led horses, scutcheons or open chariots ...', as he described it to Richard West, a friend from his schooldays:

HORACE WALPOLE
This goodly ceremony began at nine at night, and did not finish till three this morning; for, each church they passed, they stopped for a hymn and holy water. By and by, some of these choice monks, who watched the body

while it lay in state, fell asleep one night, and let the tapers catch fire of the rich velvet mantle lined with ermine and powdered with gold flower-de-luces, which melted the lead coffin, and burned off the feet of the deceased before it wakened them. The French love show; but there is a meanness reigns through it all. At the house where I stood to see this procession, the room was hung with crimson damask and gold, and the windows were mended in ten or dozen places with paper. At dinner they give you three courses; but a third of the dishes is patched up with salads, butter, puff-paste, or some such miscarriage of a dish. None, but Germans, wear fine clothes; but their coaches are tawdry enough for the wedding of Cupid and Psyche. You would laugh extremely at their signs: some live at the *Y grec*, some at Venus's Toilette, and some at the Sucking Cat. You would not easily guess their notions of honour: I'll tell you one: it is very dishonourable for any gentleman not to be in the army, or in the King's service as they call it, and it is no dishonour to keep public gaming houses: there are at least an hundred and fifty people of the first quality in Paris who live by it. You may go into their houses at all hours of the night, and find hazard, pharaoh, etc. The men who keep the hazard-table at the Duke de Gesvres' pay him twelve guineas each night for the privilege. Even the princesses of the blood are dirty enough to have shares in the banks kept at their houses. We have seen two or three of them; but they are not young, nor remarkable but for wearing their red of a deeper dye than other women, though all use it extravagantly.

ARTHUR YOUNG

This great city appears to be in many respects the most ineligible and inconvenient for the residence of a person of small fortune of any that I have seen; and vastly inferior to London. The streets are very narrow, and many of them crowded, nine-tenths dirty, and all without foot-pavements. Walking, which in London is so pleasant and so clean that ladies do it every day, is here a toil and a fatigue to a man and an impossibility to a well-dressed woman. The coaches are numerous, and, what are much worse, there are an infinity of one-horse cabriolets which are driven by young men of fashion and their imitators, alike fools, with such rapidity as to be real nuisances, and render the streets exceedingly dangerous without an incessant caution. I saw a poor child run over and probably killed, and have been myself many times blackened with the mud of the kennels [gutters] ... To this circumstance also it is owing that all persons of small or moderate fortune are forced to dress in black, with black stockings; the dusky hue of this in company is not so disagreeable a

John Evelyn in 1650
shortly after his return
from the Grand Tour,
by Robert Nanteuil

circumstance as being too great a distinction; too clear a line drawn in company...

To the Benedictine abbey of St Germain, to see pillars of African marble, etc. It is the richest abbey in France: the abbot has 300,000 livres a year. I lose my patience at such revenues being thus bestowed; consistent with the spirit of the tenth century, but not with that of the eighteenth. What a noble farm would the fourth of this income establish! what turnips, what cabbages, what potatoes, what clover, what sheep, what wool! – Are not these things better than a fat ecclesiastic? If an active English farmer was mounted behind this abbot, I think he would do more good to France with half the income than half the abbots of the kingdom with the whole of theirs. Pass the Bastille; another pleasant object to make agreeable emotions vibrate in a man's bosom. I search for good farmers, and run my head at every turn against monks and state prisons.

On his visit to Paris in 1644, John Evelyn already showed that interest in gardens which was to be a distinguishing feature of his life once he returned and settled in England.

I went to see the Count de Liancourt's Palace in the Rue de Seine, which is well built. Towards his study and bedchamber joynes a little garden, which tho' very narrow, by the addition of a well painted perspective is to appearance greatly enlarged; to this there is another part, supported by arches, in which runs a streame of water, rising in the aviary, out of a statue, and seeming to flow for some miles, by being artificially continued in the painting, when it sinkes downe at the wall. It is a very agreeable deceipt. At the end of this garden is a little theatre, made to change with divers pretty seanes, and the stage so ordered that with figures of men and women paynted on light-boards, and cut out, and, by a person who stands under-neath, made to act as if they were speaking, by guiding them, and reciting words in diferent tones as the parts require ...

I went [also] to see more exactly the roomes of the fine Palace of Luxemburge, in the Fauxbourg St Germains, built by Mary de Medices, and I think one of the most noble, entire, and finish'd piles, that is to be seen, taking it with the garden and all its accomplishments. The gallery is of the painting of Rubens, being the history of the Foundresses life, rarely designed; at the end of it is the Duke of Orleans's Library, well furnished with excellent bookes, all bound in maroquin and gilded, the valans of the shelves being of greene velvet fring'd with gold. In the cabinet joyning it are onely the smaler volumes, with 6 cabinets of medails, and an excellent collection of shells, and achates [agates], whereof some are prodigiously rich. This Duke being very learn'd in medails and plants, nothing of that kind escapes him. There are other spacious, noble, and princely furnish'd roomes, which looke towards the gardens, and which are nothing inferior to the rest.

The Court below is formed into a square by a corridor, having over the chiefe entrance a stately cupola, covered with stone; the rest is cloistered and arch'd on pillasters of rustiq worke. The tarrace ascending before the front paved with white and black marble, is balustred with white marble, exquisitely polish'd.

Onely the Hall below is lowe, and the stayrecase somewhat of an heavy designe, but the faciata towards the parterre, which is also arched and vaulted with stone, is of admirable beauty, and full of sculpture.

The Gardens are neere an English mile in compasse, enclos'd with a stately wall, and in a good ayre. The parterre is indeed of box, but so rarely design'd and accurately kept cut, that the embroidery makes a wonderful effect to the lodgings which front it. 'Tis divided into 4 squares, and as many circular knots, having in the centre a noble basin of marble neere 30 feet diameter (as I remember), in which a triton of brasse holds a dolphin that casts a girandola [fountain] of water neere 30 foote high, playing perpetualy, the water being convey'd from Arceuil by an aqueduct of stone, built after the old Roman magnificence. About this ample parterre, the spacious walkes and all included, runs a border of freestone, adorned with pedestalls for potts and statues, and part of it neere the stepps of the terrace, with a raile and balustre of pure white marble.

The walkes are exactly faire, and variously descending, and so justly planted with limes, elms, and other trees, that nothing can be more delicious, especialy that of the hornebeam hedge, which being high and stately, butts full on the fountaine.

Towards the farther end is an excavation intended for a vast fish-pool, but never finish'd. Neere it is an inclosure for a garden of simples [medicinal herbs], well kept, and here the Duke keepes tortoises in greate number, who use the poole of water on one side of the garden. Here is also a conservatory for snow [ice house]. At the upper part towards the Palace is a grove of tall elmes cutt into a starr, every ray being a walk, whose center is a large fountaine.

The rest of the ground is made into severall inclosures (all hedge-worke or rowes of trees) of whole fields, meadowes, boxages, some of them containing divers acres.

Next the streete side, and more contiguous to the house, are knotts in trayle or grasse worke, where likewise runs a fountaine. Towards the grotto and stables, within a wall, is a garden of choyce flowers, in which the Duke spends many thousand pistoles. In sum, nothing is wanting to render this palace and gardens perfectly beautifull and magnificent; nor is it one of the least diversions to see the number of persons of quality, citizens and strangers, who frequent it, and to whom all accesse is freely permitted, so that you shall see some walkes and retirements full of gallants and ladys; in others melancholy fryers; in others studious scholars; in others jolly citizens, some sitting or lying on the grasse, others runing, jumping, some playing at bowles and ball, others dancing and singing; and all this without the least disturbance, by reason of the largeness of the place.

What is most admirable is, you see no gardners or men at worke, and yet all is kept in such exquisite order as if they did nothing else but work; it is so early in the morning, that all is dispatch'd and don without the least confusion...

The next morning I went to the Garden of Monsieur Morine, who from being an ordinary gardner is become one of the most skillful and curious persons in France for his rare collection of shells, flowers, and insects.

His Garden is of an exact oval figure, planted with cypresse cutt flat and set as even as a wall: the tulips, anemonies, ranunculus's, crocus's, etc. are held to be of the rarest, and draw all the admirers of such things to his house during the season. He lived in a kind of Hermitage at one side of his

Louis Gohin and his family, painted by Boilly in 1787: elegant bourgeois prosperity. Gohin invented the colour Prussian blue

garden, where his collection of purselane and coral, whereof one is carved into a large Crucifix, is much esteemed. He had also bookes of prints, by Albert [Dürer], Van Leyden, Calot, etc. His collection of all sorts of insects, especially of Butterflys, is most curious; these he spreads and so medicates that no corruption invading them, he keepes them in drawers, so plac'd as to represent a beautifull piece of tapistre.

One hundred and twenty-one years after Evelyn, English and French tastes in gardens had drifted far apart. In 1765 Horace Walpole said, 'Their gardens are like deserts, with no more verdure or shade: What trees they have are stripped up, and cut away at top; it is quite the massacre of the innocents. Their houses in town are all white and gold and looking-glass.' In December of that year, writing to the same correspondent, the Countess of Suffolk, he gave a vivid description of just such a one. It is followed by a description of a night at the opera, written in the same tone of high camp by Walpole's friend, Thomas Gray, and a visit to the theatre, in which Laurence Sterne seems to have paid rather less attention to the action on stage than to the goings-on in the front of the house.

HORACE WALPOLE

Yesterday I dined at La Borde's, the great banker of the Court. Lord! Madame, how little and poor all your houses in London will look after his!

36

In the first place, you must have a garden half as long as the Mall, and then you must have fourteen windows, each as long as the other half, looking into it, and each window must consist of only eight panes of looking-glass. You must have a first and second ante-chamber, and they must have nothing in them but dirty servants. Next must be the grand cabinet, hung with red damask, in gold frames, and covered with eight large and very bad pictures, that cost four thousand pounds. I cannot afford them you a farthing cheaper. Under these, to give an air of lightness, must be hung bas-reliefs in marble. Then there must be immense *armoires* of tortoise-shells and or-molu, inlaid with medals [Boulle]. And then you may go into the petit-cabinet, and then into the great *salle*, and the gallery, and the billiard-room, and the eating-room; and all these must be hung with crystal lustres and looking-glass from top to bottom, and then you must stuff them fuller than they will hold with granite tables and porphyry urns, and bronzes, and statues, and vases, and the L—d or the devil knows what. But, for fear you should ruin yourself or the nation, the Duchess de Grammont must give you *this*, and Madame de Marseu *that*; and if you have anybody that has any taste to advise you, your eating-room must be hung with huge hunting-pieces in frames of all coloured golds, and at top of one of them you may have a setting-dog, who, having sprung a wooden partridge, it may be flying a yard off against the wainscot. To warm and light this palace it must cost you eight and twenty thousand livres a-year in wood and candles. If you cannot afford that, you must stay till my Lord Clive returns with the rest of the Indies.

THOMAS GRAY
Imagine to yourself for the drama four acts entirely unconnected with each other, each founded on some little history, skilfully taken out of an ancient author, e.g. Ovid's Metamorphoses, etc., and with great address converted into a French piece of gallantry. For instance, that which I saw, called the Ballet de la Paix, had its first act built upon the story of Nereus. Homer having said he was the handsomest man of his time, the poet, imagining such a one could not want a mistress, has given him one. These two come in and sing sentiment in lamentable strains, neither air nor recitative; only, to one's great joy, they are every now and then interrupted by a dance, or (to one's great sorrow) by a chorus that borders the stage from one end to the other, and screams, past all power of simile to represent. The second act was Baucis and Philemon. Baucis is a beautiful young shepherdess, and Philemon her swain. Jupiter falls in love with her, but nothing will prevail upon her; so it is all mighty well, and the chorus sing and dance the praises of Constancy. The two other acts were about Iphis and Ianthe, and the

37

judgment of Paris. Imagine, I say, all this transacted by cracked voices, trilling divisions upon two notes and a half, accompanied by an orchestra of humstrums, and a whole house more attentive than if Farinelli* sung, and you will almost have formed a just notion of the thing. Our astonishment at their absurdity you can never conceive; we had enough to do to express it by screaming an hour louder than the whole dramatis personæ.†

LAURENCE STERNE

At the end of the orchestra, and betwixt that and the first side-box, there is a small esplanade left, where, when the house is full, numbers of all ranks take sanctuary. Though you stand, as in the parterre, you pay the same price as in the orchestra. A poor defenceless being of this order [a dwarf] had got thrust, somehow or other, into this luckless place; the night was hot, and he was surrounded by beings two feet and a half higher than himself. The dwarf suffered inexpressibly on all sides; but the thing which incommoded him most, was a tall corpulent German, near seven feet high, who stood directly betwixt him and all possibility of his seeing either the stage or the actors. The poor dwarf did all he could to get a peep at what was going forwards by seeking for some little opening betwixt the German's arm and his body, trying first one side, then the other; but the German stood square in the most unaccommodating posture that can be imagined, the dwarf might as well have been placed at the bottom of the deepest draw-well in Paris; so he civilly reach'd up his hand to the German's sleeve, and told him his distress. The German turn'd his head back, look'd down upon him as Goliath did upon David, and unfeelingly resumed his posture . . .

The old French officer,‡ seeing me lift up my eyes with an emotion, as I made the apostrophe, took the liberty to ask me what was the matter. I told him the story in three words, and added, how inhuman it was.

By this time the dwarf was driven to extremes, and in his first transports, which are generally unreasonable, had told the German he would cut off his long queue with his knife. The German look'd back coolly, and told him he was welcome, if he could reach it.

An injury sharpen'd by an insult, be it to whom it will, makes every man of sentiment a party: I could have leap'd out of the box to have redressed it. The old French officer did it with much less confusion; for leaning a

* A castrato singer, the most renowned of the eighteenth century, see p. 211.
† Gray to West, April 1739.
‡ Sitting next to Sterne.

A street show in Paris, by Saint-Aubin. It could well be some French adaptation of the Commedia dell'Arte that is being performed

little over, and nodding to a centinel, and pointing at the same time with his finger at the distress, the centinel made his way to it. There was no occasion to tell the grievance – the thing told itself; so thrusting back the German instantly with his musket, he took the poor dwarf by the hand, and placed him before him. This is noble! said I, clapping my hands together. And yet you would not permit this, said the old officer, in England.

In England, dear Sir, said I, *we sit all at our ease.*

The old French officer would have set me at unity with myself, in case I had been at variance, by saying it was a *bon mot*, and as a *bon mot* is always worth something at Paris, he offered me a pinch of snuff.

It was now my turn to ask the old French officer, 'what was the matter?' for a cry of '*Haussez les mains, Monsieur l'Abbé,*' re-echoed from a dozen different parts of the parterre ...

He told me, it was some poor Abbé in one of the upper loges, who he supposed had got planted perdu behind a couple of grissets [sprightly young women], in order to see the opera, and that the parterre espying him, were insisting upon his holding up both his hands during the representation. And can it be supposed, said I, that an ecclesiastic would pick the grissets' pockets? The old French officer smiled, and whispering in my ear, opened a door of knowledge which I had no idea of.

Good God! said I, turning pale with astonishment, is it possible, that a people so smit with sentiment should at the same time be so unclean, and so unlike themselves! *Quelle grossierté!* added I.

There was more to Paris than the sights and shows on offer. Provided one spoke the language and had the right introductions there was the stimulating round of the salons kept by various ladies of intelligence and fashion. Horace Walpole and Laurence Sterne tell how they made their way and how, in Walpole's phrase, 'it is charming to totter into vogue'. First Walpole, writing to his cousin Henry Seymour Conway in October 1765; then Sterne in A Sentimental Journey. *By January 1766, when he wrote to Thomas Gray, Walpole was totally in the swim. Of the ladies he catalogued it was Madame du Deffand whom he most admired and their later correspondence was of great importance to both of them.*

HORACE WALPOLE

For so reasonable a person as I am, I have changed my mind very often about this country. The first five days I was in violent spirits; then came a dismal cloud of whisk [whist] and literature, and I could not bear it. At present I begin, very *Englishly* indeed, to establish a right to my own way. I laugh, and talk nonsense, and make them hear me. There are two or three houses where I go quite at my ease, am never asked to touch a card, nor hold dissertations. Nay, I don't pay homage to their authors. Every woman has one or two planted in her house, and God knows how they water them. The old President Henault is the pagod at Madame du Deffand's, an old blind debauchée of wit, where I supped last night. The President is very near deaf, and much nearer superannuated. He sits by the table: the mistress of the house, who formerly was his, inquires after every dish on the table, is told who has eaten of which, and then bawls the bill of fare of every individual into the President's ears. In short, every mouthful is proclaimed, and so is every blunder I make against grammar. Some that I make on purpose, succeed; and one of them is to be reported to the Queen to-day by Henault, who is her great favourite.

LAURENCE STERNE

There are three epochas in the empire of a French woman: She is coquette, then deist, then *devote*. The empire during these is never lost – she only changes her subjects. When thirty-five years and more have unpeopled her dominions of the slaves of love, she repeoples it with slaves of infidelity, and then with the slaves of the church.

40

'Singing at the Piano', an illustration by Moreau le Jeune to the *Works* of J. J. Rousseau: the essence of the *douceur de vivre* that the Tourist sought in France

Madame de Q—— was vibrating betwixt the first of these epochas: the colour of the rose was shading fast away – she ought to have been a deist five years before the time I had the honour to pay my first visit.

She placed me upon the same sopha with her, for the sake of disputing the point of religion more closely: In short, Madame de V—— told me she believed nothing.

I told Madame de V—— it might be her principle; but I was sure it could not be her interest to level the outworks, without which I could not conceive how such a citadel as hers could be defended – that there was not a more dangerous thing in the world than for a beauty to be a deist; that it was a debt I owed my creed, not to conceal it from her; that I had not been five minutes sat upon the sopha beside her, but I had begun to form designs; and what is it but the sentiments of religion, and the persuasion they had excited in her breast, which could have check'd them as they rose up?

We are not adamant, said I, taking hold of her hand, and there is need of all restraints, till age in her own time steals in and lays them on us. But, my dear lady, said I, kissing her hand, 'tis too, too soon –

I declare I had the credit all over Paris of unperverting Madame de V——. She affirmed to Mons. D—— and the Abbé M——, that in one half-hour I had said more for revealed religion than all their Encyclopedia [published between 1751 and 1772] had said against it. I was lifted directly into Madame de V——'s *Coterie*, and she put off the epocha of deism for two years.

41

The First Lecture at Madame Geoffrin's on Voltaire's tragedy *L'Orphelin de Chine*, by Lemonnier. The play in question was the same that Gibbon saw Voltaire himself perform in 1763 (see p. 240)

HORACE WALPOLE

By what I said of their religious or rather irreligious opinions, you must not conclude their people of quality, atheists – at least not the men – Happily for them, poor souls! they are not capable of going so far into thinking. They assent to a great deal, because it is the fashion, and because they don't know how to contradict. They are ashamed to defend the Roman Catholic religion, because it is quite exploded; but I am convinced they believe it in their hearts. They hate the parliaments and the philosophers, and are rejoiced that they may still idolise royalty ...

The generality of the men, and more than the generality, are dull and empty. They have taken up gravity, thinking it was philosophy and English, and so have acquired nothing in the room of their natural levity and cheerfulness. However, as their high opinion of their own country remains, for which they can no longer assign any reason,* they are contemptuous

* France had been defeated in the Seven Years War which ended in 1763.

and reserved, instead of being ridiculously, consequently pardonably, impertinent. I have wondered, knowing my own countrymen, that we had attained such a superiority. – I wonder no longer, and have a little more respect for English *heads* than I had.

The women do not seem of the same country: if they are less gay than they were, they are more informed, enough to make them very conversable. I know six or seven with very superior understandings; some of them with wit, or with softness, or very good sense.

Madame Geoffrin, of whom you have heard much, is an extraordinary woman, with more common sense than I almost ever met with. Great quickness in discovering characters, penetration in going to the bottom of them, and a pencil that never fails in a likeness – seldom a favourable one. She exacts and preserves, spite of her birth and their nonsensical prejudices about nobility, great court and attention. This she acquires by a thousand little arts and offices of friendship; and by a freedom and severity which seems to be her sole end of drawing a concourse to her; for she insists on scolding those she inveigles to her. She has little taste and less knowledge, but protects artisans and authors, and courts a few people to have the credit of serving her dependants. She was bred under the famous Madame Tencin, who advised her never to refuse any man; for, said her mistress, though nine in ten should not care a farthing for you, the tenth may live to be an useful friend. She did not adopt or reject the whole plan, but fully retained the purport of the maxim. In short, she is an epitome of empire, subsisting by rewards and punishments. Her great enemy, Madame du Deffand … retains all her vivacity, wit, memory, judgment, passions and agreeableness. She goes to operas, plays, suppers, and Versailles; gives suppers twice a week; has everything new read to her; makes new songs and epigrams, ay, admirably, and remembers every one that has been made these fourscore years. She corresponds with Voltaire, dictates charming letters to him, contradicts him, is no bigot to him or anybody, and laughs both at the clergy and the philosophers. In a dispute, into which she easily falls, she is very warm, and yet scarce ever in the wrong: her judgment on every subject is as just as possible; on every point of conduct as wrong as possible: for she is all love and hatred, passionate for her friends to enthusiasm, still anxious to be loved, I don't mean by lovers, and a vehement enemy, but openly. As she can have no amusement but conversation, the least solitude and ennui are insupportable to her, and put her into the power of several worthless people, who eat her suppers when they can eat nobody's of higher rank; wink to one another and laugh at her; hate her because she has forty times more parts – and venture to hate her because she is not rich …

The Duchesse de Choiseul and Madame du Deffand, from a drawing by Carmontelle: two more of the ladies described by Horace Walpole on pp. 43 and 45

Madame de Mirepoix's* understanding is excellent of the useful kind, and can be so when she pleases of the agreeable kind. She has read, but seldom shows it, and has perfect taste. Her manner is cold, but very civil; and she conceals even the blood of Lorrain, without ever forgetting it. Nobody in France knows the world better, and nobody is personally so well with the King. She is false, artful, and insinuating beyond measure when it is her interest, but indolent and a coward. She never had any passion but gaming, and always loses. Forever paying court, the sole produce of a life of art is to get money from the King to carry on a course of paying debts or contracting new ones, which she discharges as fast as she is able ...

Madame de Boufflers, who was in England, is a *savante*, mistress of the Prince of Conti, and very desirous of being his wife. She is two women, the upper and the lower. I need not tell you that the lower is *galante*, and still has pretensions. The upper is very sensible too, and has a measured eloquence that is just and pleasing – but all is spoiled by an unrelaxed attention to applause. You would think she was always sitting for her picture to her biographer.

Madame de Rochfort is different from all the rest. Her understanding is just and delicate; with a finesse of wit that is the result of reflection. Her

*Anne-Marguerite-Gabrielle de Beauvau-Craon (1709–91), who married first Jacques-Henri de Lorraine, Prince de Lixin, and then Charles-Pierre-Gaston-François de Lévis de Lomagne, Duc de Mirepoix, Maréchal de France.

44

manner is soft and feminine, and though a *savante*, without any declared pretensions. She is the *decent* friend of Monsieur de Nivernois, for you must not believe a syllable of what you read in their novels. It requires the greatest curiosity, or the greatest habitude, to discover the smallest connection between the sexes here. No familiarity, but under the veil of friendship, is permitted, and love's dictionary is as much prohibited, as at first sight one should think his ritual was. All you hear, and that pronounced with nonchalance, is, that *monsieur un tel* has had *madame une telle*. The Duc de Nivernois has parts, and writes at the top of the mediocre, but, as Madame Geoffrin says, is *manqué par tout; guerrier manqué, ambassadeur manqué, homme d'affaires manqué*, and *auteur manqué* – no, he is not *homme de naissance manqué*. He would think freely, but has some ambition of being governor to the Dauphin, and is more afraid of his wife and daughter, who are ecclesiastic fagots. The former out-chatters the Duke of Newcastle; and the latter, Madame de Gisors, exhausts Mr Pitt's eloquence in defence of the Archbishop of Paris. Monsieur de Nivernois lives in a small circle of dependent admirers, and Madame de Rochfort is high priestess for a small salary of credit.

The Duchess of Choiseul, the only young one of these heroines, is not very pretty, but has fine eyes, and is a little model in wax-work, which not being allowed to speak for some time as incapable, has a hesitation and modesty, the latter of which the Court has not cured, and the former of which is atoned for by the most interesting sound of voice, and forgotten in the most elegant turn and propriety of expression. Oh! it is the gentlest, amiable, civil, little creature that ever came out of a fairy egg! So just in its phrases and thoughts, so attentive and good-natured! Everybody loves it, but its husband, who prefers his own sister the Duchesse de Grammont, an Amazonian, fierce, haughty dame, who loves and hates arbitrarily, and is detested. Madame de Choiseul, passionately fond of her husband, was the martyr of this union, but at last submitted with a good grace; has gained a little credit with him, and is still believed to idolise him – But I doubt it – she takes too much pains to profess it.

I cannot finish my list without adding a much more common character – but more complete in its kind than any of the foregoing, the Maréchale de Luxembourg. She has been very handsome, very abandoned, and very mischievous. Her beauty is gone, her lovers are gone, and she thinks the Devil is coming. This dejection has softened her into being rather agreeable, for she has wit and good breeding; but you would swear, by the restlessness of her person and the horrors she cannot conceal, that she had signed the compact, and expected to be called upon in a week for the performance ...

You must not attribute my intimacy with Paris to curiosity alone. An accident unlocked the doors for me. That *passe-partout*, called the fashion, has made them fly open – and what do you think was that fashion? – I myself ... I did not come hither to be at the head of a fashion. However, I have been sent for about like an African prince or a learned canary-bird, and was, in particular, carried by force to the Princess of Talmond, the Queen's cousin, who lives in a charitable apartment in the Luxembourg, and was sitting on a small bed hung with saints and Sobieskis,* in a corner of one of those vast chambers, by two blinking tapers. I stumbled over a cat, a foot-stool, and a chamber-pot in my journey to her presence. She could not find a syllable to say to me, and the visit ended with her begging a lap-dog. Thank the Lord! though this is the first month, it is the last week, of my reign; and I shall resign my crown with great satisfaction to a *bouillie* of chestnuts, which is just invented, and whose annals will be illustrated by so many indigestions, that Paris will not want anything else these three weeks.

In 1787, Arthur Young also put himself about in Parisian society, though the circles he moved in tended to be interested in science and its application to agriculture. The speculation on the future of France at dinner then was very accurate of what was to happen in 1789.

Dined to-day with a party whose conversation was entirely political. One opinion pervaded the whole company, that they are on the eve of some great revolution in the government: that everything points to it: the confusion in the finances great; with a *deficit* impossible to provide for without the states-general of the kingdom, yet no ideas formed of what would be the consequence of their meeting: no minister existing, or to be looked to in or out of power, with such decisive talents as to promise any other remedy than palliative ones: a prince on the throne, with excellent dispositions, but without the resources of a mind that could govern in such a moment without ministers: a court buried in pleasure and dissipation; and adding to the distress instead of endeavouring to be placed in a more independent situation: a great ferment amongst all ranks of men, who are eager for some change, without knowing what to look to or to hope for: and a strong leaven of liberty, increasing every hour since the American revolution – altogether form a combination of circumstances that promise e'er long to ferment into motion if some master hand of very superior talents and

* The princess was Polish by birth, as was Louis XV's Queen.

The Oyster Dinner, by de Troy: French aristocratic luxury and conspicuous consumption in 1734. Notice the champagne cork in mid-air

inflexible courage is not found at the helm to guide events, instead of being driven by them ... I meet with so few men that have any just ideas of freedom that I question much the species of this new liberty that is to arise. They know not how to value the privileges of THE PEOPLE: as to the nobility and the clergy, if a revolution added anything to their scale I think it would do more mischief than good.

It was de rigueur *to make the journey out from Paris to Versailles, to view the two sights there – the Palace and the Royal Family. Horace Walpole went in 1739 and again in 1765; his opinion of the place did not mellow between the two visits.*

HORACE WALPOLE

The great front is a lumber of littleness, composed of black brick, stuck full of bad old busts, and fringed with gold rails. The rooms are all small, except the great gallery, which is noble, but totally wainscoted with looking-glass. The garden is littered with statues and fountains, each of which has its tutelary deity. In particular, the elementary God of Fire solaces himself in one. In another, Enceladus, in lieu of a mountain, is overwhelmed with many waters. There are avenues of water-pots, who disport themselves much in squirting up cascadelins. In short, 'tis a garden for a great child. Such was Louis Quatorze, who is here seen in the proper colours, where he commanded in person, unassisted by his armies and generals, and left to the pursuit of his own puerile ideas of glory. [1739]

Versailles, like everything else, is a mixture of parade and poverty, and in every instance exhibits something most dissonant from our manners. In the colonnades, upon the staircases, nay in the antechambers of the royal family, there are people selling all sorts of wares. While we were waiting in the Dauphin's sumptuous bedchamber, till his dressing-room door should be opened, two fellows were sweeping it, and dancing about in sabots to rub the floor.

You perceive that I have been presented. The Queen took great notice of me; none of the rest said a syllable. You are let into the King's [Louis XV] bedchamber just as he has put on his shirt; he dresses and talks good-humouredly to a few, glares at strangers, goes to mass, to dinner, and a-hunting. The good old Queen, who is like Lady Primrose in the face, and Queen Caroline in the immensity of her cap, is at her dressing-table, attended by two or three old ladies, who are languishing to be in Abraham's bosom, as the only man's bosom to whom they can hope for admittance. Thence you go to the Dauphin, for all is done in an hour. He scarce stays a minute; indeed, poor creature, he is a ghost, and cannot possibly last three months. The Dauphiness is in her bedchamber, but dressed and standing; looks cross, is not civil, and has the true Westphalian grace and accents. The four Mesdames, who are clumsy plump old wenches, with a bad likeness to their father, stand in a bed-chamber in a row, with black cloaks and knotting-bags, looking good-humoured, not knowing what to say, and wriggling as if they wanted to make water. [1765]

After Paris had been sampled, it was common to go to a provincial city for a few months to improve one's French. In 1739 Horace Walpole, Henry Seymour Conway, and Thomas Gray went to Reims. Gray describes the slightly stuffy society there.

A view of the chapel at Versailles, by Jacques Rigaud

There is little in it worth a stranger's curiosity, besides the cathedral church, which is a vast Gothic building of a surprising beauty and lightness, all covered over with a profusion of little statues, and other ornaments ... The streets in general have but a melancholy aspect, the houses all old; the public walks run along the side of a great moat under the ramparts, where one hears a continual croaking of frogs; the country round about is one great plain covered with vines, which at this time of the year afford no very pleasing prospect, as being not above a foot high. What pleasures the place denies to the sight, it makes up to the palate; since you have nothing to drink but the best champaigne in the world, and all sort of provisions equally good. As to other pleasures, there is not that freedom of conversation among the people of fashion here, that one sees in other parts of France; for though they are not very numerous in this place, and consequently must live a good deal together, yet they never come to any great familiarity with one another ...

As soon as you enter [an assembly], the lady of the house presents each of you a card, and offers you a party at quadrille; you sit down, and play forty deals without intermission, excepting one quarter of an hour, when every body rises to eat of what they call the *gouter*, which supplies the place of our tea, and is a service of wine, fruits, cream, sweetmeats, crawfish and cheese. People take what they like, and sit down again to play; after that, they make little parties to go to the walks together, and then all the company retire to their separate habitations. Very seldom any suppers or dinners are given; and this is the manner they live among one another; not so much out of any aversion they have to pleasure, as out of a sort of formality they have contracted by not being much frequented by people who have lived at Paris. It is sure they do not hate gaiety any more than the rest of their country-people, and can enter into diversions, that are once proposed, with a good grace enough; for instance, the other evening we happened to be got together in a company of eighteen people, men and women of the best fashion here, at a garden in the town to walk; when one of the ladies bethought herself of asking, Why should not we sup here? Immediately the cloth was laid by the side of a fountain under the trees, and a very elegant supper served up; after which another said, Come, let us sing; and directly began herself: From singing we insensibly fell to dancing, and singing in a round; when somebody mentioned the violins, and immediately a company of them was ordered: Minuets were begun in the open air, and then came country-dances, which held till four o'Clock next morning; at which hour the gayest lady there proposed, that such as were weary should get into their coaches, and the rest of them should dance before them with the music in the van; and in this manner we paraded through all the principal streets of the city, and waked every body in it. Mr Walpole had a mind to make a custom of the thing, and would have given a ball in the same manner next week, but the women did not come into it; so I believe it will drop, and they will return to their dull cards, and usual formalities.

When John Evelyn went to Orleans on the Loire in 1644 he had two unsettling experiences. Fynes Moryson, half a century earlier, was not as lucky as Evelyn, and was robbed when on his way to Châlons-sur-Marne from Lorraine, at the end of the French civil wars of religion, in 1595.

JOHN EVELYN

We had an excellent road, but had like to come short home; for no sooner were we entred two or three leagues into the Forest of Orleans (which extends itself many miles), but the company behind us were set on by rogues, who, shooting from the hedges and frequent covert, slew foure upon the spot. This disaster made such an alarme in Orleans at our arrival, that the Prevost Martial, with his assistants, going in persuite, brought in two whom they had shot, and exposed them in the greate market-place, to see if any would take cognizance of them. I had greate cause to give God thankes for this escape. I lay at the White Lion, where in the night a cat kitten'd on my bed, and left on it a young one having six ears, eight leggs,

Travelling in France, by Thomas Rowlandson: a cumbersome public 'diligence' and a private post-chaise, with its postilion in huge boots

two bodys from the navil downwards, and two tayles. I found it dead, but warm, in the morning when I awaked.

FYNES MORYSON

We [Moryson and his guide] had now scarce entred France, when suddenly the mischiefe fell upon me, which my friends at Metz had foretold me. When I had passed halfe this dayes journey, I met with some dozen horsemen, whose Captaine demaunded of me my name and Countrey. I answered, that I was a Dutch man, and the servant of a Dutch Merchant, who staied for me at Chalons, whither I was then going. He (as it seemed to me) thinking it dishonourable to him, if he should himselfe assault a poore fellow, and a stranger, did let me passe, but before I came to the bottome of the hill, I might see him send two horsemen after me, who wheeling about the mountaines, that I might not know they were of his company, suddenly rushed upon me, and with fierce countenance threatning death, presented their Carbines to my brest. I having no abilitie to defend mee, thought good not to make any the least shew of resistance, so they tooke my sword from my guide, and were content onely to rob me of my money … This I had quilted within my doublet, and when I resolved to goe on foote to Paris, I made me a base cover for my apparrel, which when they

51

perceived, they tooke from me the inward doublet wherein I had quilted the gold, and though they perceived that under my base cover, I had a Jerkin and hose laide with gold lace, yet they were content to take onely the inner doublet, and to leave me all the rest of my apparrell, wherein I doe acknowledge their courtesie, since theeves give all they doe not take ...

One thing in this miserie made me glad. I formerly said, that I sold my horse for 16 French Crownes at Metz, which Crownes I put in the bottome of a wooden box, and covered them with a stinking ointment for scabs. Sixe other French Crownes, for the worst event, I lapped in cloth, and thereupon did wind divers colored threads, wherein I sticked needles, as if I had been so good a husband, as to mend my own clothes. This box and this ball of thread, I had put in my hose, as things of no worth; and when in spoyling me they had searched my pockets, they first tooke the boxe, and smelling the stinke of the ointment, they cast it away on the ground; neither were they so frugall to take my bal of thread to mend their hose, but did tread it likewise under their feet ...

At last we did see the City of Chalons not farre distant, and upon our left hand was a faire spring, which had seven heads, to which wee went to drinke, being both very thirstie. Here I put into the water the hat which the theeves had given me, by unequall exchange for mine, being greasie to the very top, and deepe according to the French fashion, and filling it with water thrice, drunke it up greedily. Then I filled it the fourth time, and broke into it the crummes of the browne loafe, the crust whereof had to that time kept my mouth with some moisture, which I devoured, and thought I had never eaten better brewesse; but three daies sicknesse of vomiting and loosenesse made me repent this intemperance.

Thence wee went to Chalons, where my guide brought mee to a poore Ale-house, and when I expostulated the wrong he did me; he replied, That stately Innes were not for men who had never a penny in their purses: but I told him, that I looked for comfort in that case rather from Gentlemen then Clownes. Whereupon hee willingly obeyed me, and with a dejected and fearefull countenance, brought me to the chiefe Inne, where he ceased not to bewaile my misery, and to recount my Tragedy, as if it had been the burning of Troy, till the very Hoste despairing of my abilitie to pay him, began to looke disdainefully upon me. The next morning when hee being to returne home, and taking his leave of me, I paied him his hire, which he neither asked nor expected, thinking that I had not one penny, and likewise paied my Hoste for my supper and lodging, he first began to talke like a mad man, and comming to himselfe, professed that he knew not how I

Arthur Young in 1794,
by George Dance

should have one pennie, except I were a Jugler, or an Alchumist, or had a familiar spirit. Then confounded betweene wonder and joy, he began to triumph with the servants, and would not depart, till hee had first drunke a quart of Wine.

Arthur Young took a measured view of the strengths and weaknesses of the French inn, while Tobias Smollett was not prepared to let innkeepers put one across him, although he did not always win the rows that ensued.

ARTHUR YOUNG

Having now crossed the kingdom, and been in many French inns, I shall in general observe, that they are on an average better in two respects, and worst in all the rest, than those in England. We have lived better in point of eating and drinking beyond a question than we should have done in going from London to the Highlands of Scotland, at double the expense. But if in England the best of everything is ordered, without any attention to the expense, we should for double the money have lived better than we have done in France; the common cookery of the French gives great advantage. It is true, they roast everything to a chip, if they are not cautioned: but they give such a number and variety of dishes, that if you do not like some, there are others to please your palate. The dessert at a French inn has no rival at an English one; nor are the liqueurs to be despised. We sometimes have met with bad wine, but upon the whole, far better than such port as English inns give. Beds are better in France; in England they

53

are good only at good inns; and we have none of that torment, which is so perplexing in England, to have the sheets aired; for we never trouble our heads about them, doubtless on account of the climate.

After these two points, all is a blank. You have no parlour to eat in; only a room with two, three, or four beds. Apartments badly fitted up; the walls white-washed; or paper of different sorts in the same room; or tapestry so old as to be a fit nidus for moths and spiders; and the furniture such that an English inn-keeper would light his fire with it. For a table, you have everywhere a board laid on cross bars, which are so conveniently contrived as to leave room for your legs only at the end. Oak chairs with rush bottoms, and the back universally a direct perpendicular, that defies all idea of rest after fatigue. Doors give music as well as entrance; the wind whistles through their chinks; and hinges grate discord. Windows admit rain as well as light; when shut they are not easy to open; and when open not easy to shut. Mops, brooms, and scrubbing-brushes are not in the catalogue of the necessaries of a French inn. Bells there are none; the *fille* must always be bawled for; and when she appears, is neither neat, well dressed, nor handsome. The kitchen is black with smoke; the master commonly the cook, and the less you see of the cooking the more likely you are to have a stomach to your dinner; but this is not peculiar to France. Copper utensils always in great plenty, but not always well tinned. The mistress rarely classes civility or attention to her guests among the requisites of her trade.

TOBIAS SMOLLETT

At Brignolles, where we dined, I was obliged to quarrel with the landlady, and threaten to leave her house, before she would indulge us with any sort of flesh-meat. It was a meagre [fast] day, and she had made her provision accordingly. She even hinted some dissatisfaction at having heretics in her house: but, as I was not disposed to eat stinking fish, with ragouts of eggs and onions, I insisted upon a leg of mutton, and a brace of fine partridges, which I found in the larder ...

At a wretched town called Muy, where we dined, I had a warm dispute with our landlord, which, however, did not terminate to my satisfaction. I sent on the mules before, to the next stage, resolving to take post-horses, and bespoke them accordingly of the aubergiste, who was, at the same time, inn-keeper and post-master. We were ushered into the common eating-room, and had a very indifferent dinner; after which, I sent a loui'dore to be changed, in order to pay the reckoning. The landlord, instead of giving the full change, deducted three livres a head for dinner, and sent in the rest of the money by my servant. Provoked more at his ill manners, than at his extortion, I ferretted him out of a bed-chamber, where he had concealed himself, and obliged him to restore the full change, from which I paid him at the rate of two livres a head. He refused to take the money, which I threw down on the table; and the horses being ready, stepped into the coach, ordering the postilions to drive on. Here I had certainly reckoned without my host. The fellows declared they would not budge, until I should pay their master; and as I threatened them with manual chastisement, they alighted, and disappeared in a twinkling.

[Smollett appealed to the consul of the town.] The consul shrugged up his shoulders, and declared it was not in his power. This was a lie, but I perceived he had no mind to disoblige the publican. If the mules had not been sent away, I should certainly have not only payed what I thought proper, but corrected the landlord into the bargain, for his insolence and extortion; but now I was entirely at his mercy, and as the consul continued to exhort me in very humble terms, to comply with his demands, I thought proper to acquiesce. Then the postilions immediately appeared: the crowd seemed to exult in the triumph of the aubergiste; and I was obliged to travel in the night, in very severe weather, after all the fatigue and mortification I had undergone.

[A few paragraphs after the story related above, Smollett had the nerve to deliver the following reflection:] And here, once for all, I would advise every traveller who consults his own ease and convenience … to wink at the imposition of aubergistes on the road, unless it be very flagrant. So sure as you enter into disputes with them, you will be put to a great deal of trouble, and fret yourself to no manner of purpose. I have travelled with œconomists in England, who declared they would rather give away a crown than allow themselves to be cheated of a farthing. This is a good maxim, but requires a great share of resolution and self-denial to put in practice.

Laurence Sterne expressed the same view in Tristram Shandy, *but one suspects he was much less hypocritical than Smollett in doing so.*

I do not think a journey through France and Italy, provided a man keeps his temper all the way, so bad a thing as some people would make you believe: there must be ups and downs, or how the deuce should we get into valleys where Nature spreads so many tables of entertainment. – 'Tis nonsense to imagine they will lend you their voitures to be shaken to pieces for nothing; and unless you pay twelve sous for greasing your wheels, how should the poor peasant get butter to his bread? – We really expect too much – and for the livre or two above par for your suppers and bed – at the

D.ᵒ Stern.
alias
Tristram Shandy.

Nᵒ 20

P. 1769

'Death confronts Laurence Sterne',
an etching by Thomas Patch
executed in 1769, a year after
Sterne's death

most they are but one shilling and ninepence halfpenny – who would embroil their philosophy for it? for heaven's and for your own sake, pay it – pay it with both hands open, rather than leave Disappointment sitting drooping upon the eye of your fair Hostess and her Damsels in the gateway, at your departure – and besides, my dear Sir, you get a sisterly kiss of each of 'em worth a pound – at least I did.

Here is some more of Smollett's intemperate but thoroughly enjoyable invective, part of his sustained assault on the French male.

Woman has been defined a weaker man; but in this country the men are, in my opinion, more ridiculous and insignificant than the women. They certainly are more disagreeable to a rational enquirer, because they are more troublesome. Of all the coxcombs on the face of the earth, a French *petit maitre* is the most impertinent: and they are all *petit maitres*, from the marquis who glitters in lace and embroidery, to the *garçon barbier* [hair-dresser] covered with meal, who struts with his hair in a long queue, and his hat under his arm. I have already observed, that vanity is the great and universal mover among all ranks and degrees of people in this nation; and as they take no pains to conceal or controul it, they are hurried by it into the most ridiculous and indeed intolerable extravagance ...

I shall not even deny, that the French are by no means deficient in natural capacity; but they are at the same time remarkable for a natural levity, which hinders their youth from cultivating that capacity. This is reinforced by the most preposterous education, and the example of a giddy people, engaged in the most frivolous pursuits. A Frenchman is by some Jesuit, or other monk, taught to read his mother tongue, and to say his prayers in a language he does not understand. He learns to dance and to fence, by the masters of those noble sciences. He becomes a compleat connoisseur in dressing hair, and in adorning his own person, under the hands and instructions of his barber and *valet de chambre*. If he learns to play upon the flute or the fiddle, he is altogether irresistible. But he piques himself upon being polished above the natives of any other country by his conversation with the fair sex. In the course of this communication, with which he is indulged from his tender years, he learns like a parrot, by rote, the whole circle of French compliments, which you know are a set of phrases, ridiculous even to a proverb; and these he throws out indiscriminately to all women, without distinction, in the exercise of that kind of address, which is here distinguished by the name of gallantry: it is no more than his making love to every woman who will give him the hearing. It is an exercise, by the repetition of which he becomes very pert, very familiar, and very impertinent. Modesty, or diffidence, I have already said, is utterly unknown among them, and therefore I wonder there should be a term to express it in their language ...

A Frenchman in consequence of his mingling with the females from his infancy, not only becomes acquainted with all their customs and humours; but grows wonderfully alert in performing a thousand little offices, which are overlooked by other men, whose time hath been spent in making more valuable acquisitions. He enters, without ceremony, a lady's bed-chamber, while she is in bed, reaches her whatever she wants, airs her shift, and helps to put it on. He attends at her toilette, regulates the distribution of her patches, and advises where to lay on the paint. If he visits her when she is dressed, and perceives the least impropriety in her *coeffure*, he insists upon adjusting it with his own hands: if he sees a curl, or even a single hair amiss, he produces his comb, his scissars, and pomatum, and sets it to rights with the dexterity of a professed *friseur*. He 'squires her to every place she visits, either on business, or pleasure; and, by dedicating his whole time to her, renders himself necessary to her occasions. This I take to be the most agreeable side of his character: let us view him on the quarter of impertinence. A Frenchman pries into all your secrets with the most impudent and importunate curiosity, and then discloses them without remorse. If you are indisposed, he questions you about the symptoms of your disorder, with more freedom than your physician would presume to use; very often in the grossest terms. He then proposes his remedy (for they are all quacks), he prepares it without your knowledge, and worries you with solicitation to take it, without paying the least regard to the opinion of those whom you have chosen to take care of your health ...

If a Frenchman is admitted into your family, and distinguished by repeated marks of your friendship and regard, the first return he makes for your civilities is to make love to your wife, if she is handsome; if not, to your sister, or daughter, or niece. If he suffers a repulse from your wife, or attempts in vain to debauch your sister, or your daughter, or your niece, he will, rather than not play the traitor with his gallantry, make his addresses to your grandmother; and ten to one, but in one shape or another, he will find means to ruin the peace of a family, in which he has been so kindly entertained ...

Vanity, indeed, predominates among all ranks, to such a degree, that they are the greatest *egotists* in the world; and the most insignificant individual talks in company with the same conceit and arrogance, as a person of the greatest importance. Neither conscious poverty nor disgrace will restrain him in the least either from assuming his full share of the conversation, or making his addresses to the finest lady, whom he has the smallest opportunity to approach: nor is he restrained by any other consideration whatsoever. It is all one to him whether he himself has a wife of his own, or the lady a husband; whether she is designed for the cloister, or pre-ingaged to his best friend and benefactor. He takes it for granted that his addresses cannot but be acceptable; and, if he meets with a repulse, he condemns her taste; but never doubts his own qualifications.

After that wicked but entertaining exhibition of spleen, it is best to turn to Arthur Young for a more levelheaded assessment, which is followed by a warning from the Earl of Cork and Orrery, writing in the 1750s.

A French supper, engraved by Moreau le Jeune

ARTHUR YOUNG

Some of the hotels [town houses] in Paris are immense in size, from a circumstance which would give me a good opinion of the people, if nothing else did, which is the great mixture of families. When the eldest son marries he brings his wife home to the house of his father where is an apartment provided for them; and if a daughter does not wed an eldest son, her husband is also received into the family, in the same way, which makes a joyous number at every table. This cannot altogether be attributed to economical motives, though they certainly influence in many cases, because it is found in families possessing the first properties in the kingdom. It does with French manners and customs, but in England it is sure to fail, and equally so amongst all ranks of people: may we not conjecture with a great probability of truth that the nation in which it succeeds is therefore better tempered? Nothing but good humour can render such a jumble of families agreeable, or even tolerable. In dress they have given the *ton* to all Europe for more than a century; but this is not among any but the highest rank an object of such expense as in England, where the mass of mankind wear much better things (to use the language of common conversation) than in France: this struck me more amongst ladies who, on an average of all ranks, do not dress at one half of the expense of English women. Volatility and changeableness are attributed to the French as national characteristics – but in the case of dress with the grossest exaggeration. Fashions change with ten times more rapidity in England, in form, colour, and assemblage; the vicissitudes of every part of dress are fantastic with us. I see little of this in France; and to instance the mode of dressing the gentlemen's hair, while it has been varied five times at London it has remained the same at Paris.

Nothing contributes more to make them a happy people than the cheerful and facile pliancy of disposition with which they adapt themselves to the circumstances of life: this they possess much more than the high and volatile spirits which have been attributed to them; one excellent consequence is, a greater exemption from the extravagance of living beyond their fortunes than is met with in England ... On comparison with the English, I looked for great talkativeness, volatile spirits, and universal politeness. I think, on the contrary, that they are not so talkative as the English, have not equally good spirits, and are not a jot more polite: nor do I speak of certain classes of people but of the general mass. I think them, however, incomparably better tempered; and I propose it as a question whether good temper be not more reasonably expected under an arbitrary than under a free government?

LORD CORK AND ORRERY

We mistake and misconstrue their faculties. Their gaiety, we imagine, folly: their prudence, we miscall, insincerity: their strength we despise. Our false judgment may, one day or other, cost us dear. The French, (already numerous and prolific,) if they suffered a natural commerce to subsist between their nuns and friars, would swarm and overrun the world.

The normal route to the South of France, 'this clear climate of fantasy and perspiration' as Sterne called it, was by boat down the Rhône from Lyons. Smollett described the process, although he and his family went by land.

Travellers glide down this river with great velocity, passing a great number of towns and villages on each side, where they find ordinaries* every day at dinner and supper. In good weather, there is no danger in this method of travelling, 'till you come to the Pont St Esprit, where the stream runs through the arches with such rapidity, that the boat is sometimes overset. But those passengers who are under any apprehension are landed above-bridge, and taken in again, after the boat has passed, just in the same manner as at London Bridge. The boats that go up the river are drawn against the stream by oxen, which swim through one of the arches of this bridge, the driver sitting between the horns of the foremost beast. We set out from Lyons early on Monday morning, and as a robbery had been a few days before committed in that neighbourhood, I ordered my servant to load my musquetoon with a charge of eight balls. By the bye, this piece did not fail to attract the curiosity and admiration of the people in every place through

* Inns where meals were offered at fixed prices.

which we passed. The carriage no sooner halted, than a crowd immediately surrounded the man to view the blunderbuss, which they dignified with the title of *petit canon*. At Nuys in Burgundy, he fired it in the air, and the whole mob dispersed, and scampered off like a flock of sheep ... In this country I was almost poisoned with garlic, which they mix in their ragouts, and all their sauces; nay, the smell of it perfumes the very chambers, as well as every person you approach. I was also very sick of *beca ficas*, *grieves*, or *thrushes*, and other little birds, which are served up twice a day at all ordinaries on the road. They make their appearance in vine-leaves, and are always half raw, in which condition the French choose to eat them, rather than run the risque of losing the juice by over-roasting.

The douceur de vivre *of the South of France is beautifully summoned up by Laurence Sterne in* Tristram Shandy. *There then follow descriptions of the Classical remains in Nîmes by Arthur Young and of the Pont du Gard by Smollett, foretastes of all that lay ahead in Italy.*

LAURENCE STERNE

I had now the whole south of France, from the banks of the Rhône to those of the Garonne, to traverse upon my mule at my own leisure ...

There is nothing more pleasing to a traveller – or more terrible to travel-writers, than a large rich plain; especially if it is without great rivers or bridges; and presents nothing to the eye, but one unvaried picture of plenty: for after they have once told you, that 'tis delicious! or delightful! (as the case happens) – that the soil was grateful, and that nature pours out all her abundance, etc. ... they have then a large plain upon their hands, which they know not what to do with – and which is of little or no use to them but to carry them to some town; and that town, perhaps of little more, but a new place to start from to the next plain – and so on.

– This is most terrible work; judge if I don't manage my plains better ...

I had not gone above two leagues and a half, before the man with his gun began to look at his priming.

I had three several times loitered terribly behind; half a mile at least every time; once, in deep conference with a drum-maker, who was making drums for the fairs of Baucaira and Tarascone – I did not understand the principles –

The second time, I cannot so properly say, I stopped – for meeting a couple of Franciscans straitened more for time than myself, and not being able to get to the bottom of what I was about – I had turned back with them –

The third, was an affair of trade with a gossip, for a hand-basket of Provence figs for four sous; this would have been transacted at once; but for a case of conscience at the close of it; for when the figs were paid for, it turned out, that there were two dozen of eggs covered over with vine-leaves at the bottom of the basket – as I had no intention of buying eggs – I made no sort of claim of them – as for the space they had occupied – what signified it? I had figs enow for my money –

– But it was my intention to have the basket – it was the gossip's intention to keep it, without which, she could do nothing with her eggs – and unless I had the basket, I could do as little with my figs, which were too ripe already, and most of 'em burst at the side: this brought on a short contention, which terminated in sundry proposals, what we should both do –

– How we disposed of our eggs and figs, I defy you, or the Devil himself, had he not been there (which I am persuaded he was), to form the least probable conjecture ...

As I had made no convention with my man with the gun, as to time – by stopping and talking to every soul I met, who was not in a full trot – joining all parties before me – waiting for every soul behind – hailing all those who were coming through cross-roads – arresting all kinds of beggars, pilgrims, fiddlers, friars – not passing by a woman in a mulberry-tree without commending her legs, and tempting her into conversation with a pinch of snuff – In short, by seizing every handle, of what size or shape soever, which chance held out to me in this journey – I turned my plain into a city – I was always in company, and with great variety too: and as my mule loved society as much as myself, and had some proposals always on his part to offer to every beast he met – I am confident we could have passed through Pall-Mall, or St James's-Street for a month together, with fewer adventures – and seen less of human nature.

O! there is that sprightly frankness, which at once unpins every plait of a Languedocian's dress – that whatever is beneath it, it looks so like the simplicity which poets sing of in better days – I will delude my fancy, and believe it is so.

'Twas in the road betwixt Nismes and Lunel, where there is the best Muscatto wine in all France, and which by the bye belongs to the honest canons of Montpellier – and foul befall the man who has drank it at their table, who grudges them a drop of it.

– The sun was set – they had done their work; the nymphs had tied up their hair afresh – and the swains were preparing for a carousal – my mule made a dead point – 'Tis the fife and tabourin, said I – I'm frightened to death, quoth he – They are running at the ring of pleasure, said I, giving him a prick – By saint Boogar, and all the saints at the backside of the door of purgatory, said he … I'll not go a step further – 'Tis very well, sir, said I – I never will argue a point with one of your family, as long as I live; so leaping off his back, and kicking off one boot into this ditch, and t'other into that – I'll take a dance, said I – so stay you here.

A sun-burnt daughter of Labour rose up from the group to meet me, as I advanced towards them; her hair, which was a dark chestnut approaching rather to a black, was tied up in a knot, all but a single tress.

We want a cavalier, said she, holding out both her hands, as if to offer them – And a cavalier ye shall have; said I, taking hold of both of them.

Hadst thou, Nannette, been arrayed like a duchess! – But that cursed slit in thy petticoat!

Nannette cared not for it.

We could not have done without you, said she, letting go one hand, with self-taught politeness, leading me up with the other.

A lame youth, whom Apollo had recompensed with a pipe, and to which he had added a tabourin of his own accord, ran sweetly over the prelude, as he sat upon the bank – Tie me up this tress instantly, said Nannette, putting a piece of string into my hand – It taught me to forget I was a stranger – The whole knot fell down – we had been seven years acquainted.

The youth struck the note upon the tabourin – his pipe followed, and off we bounded – 'the deuce take that slit!'

The sister of the youth, who had stolen her voice from heaven, sung alternately with her brother – 'twas a Gascoigne roundelay.

> VIVA LA JOIA!
> FIDON LA TRISTESSA!

ARTHUR YOUNG

I viewed the Maison Carrée last night; again this morning, and twice more in the day; it is beyond all comparison the most light, elegant, and pleasing building I ever beheld. Without any magnitude to render it imposing; without any extraordinary magnificence to surprise, it rivets attention. There is a magic harmony in the proportions that charms the eye. One can fix on no particular part of pre-eminent beauty; it is one perfect whole of symmetry and grace. What an infatuation in modern architects that can overlook the chaste and elegant simplicity of taste manifest in such a work and yet rear such piles of laboured foppery and heaviness as are to be met with in France. The temple of Diana, as it is called, and the ancient baths, with their modern restoration, and the promenade, form parts of the same scene, and are magnificent decorations of the city. I was, in relation to the

The Pont du Gard, by Hubert Robert. Smollett said, 'I should take pleasure ... to come hither, in summer, to dine under one of the arches ... on a cold collation'

baths, in ill luck, for the water was all drawn off in order to clean them and the canals. – The Roman pavements are singularly beautiful, and in high preservation ...

[Near] Nismes, meet many merchants returning from the fair; each with a child's drum tied to their cloakbag: my own little girl was too much in my head not to love them for this mark of attention to their children; – but why a drum? – Have they not had enough of the military in a kingdom where they are excluded from all the honours, respect, and emolument that can flow from the sword?

TOBIAS SMOLLETT
About five in the afternoon, I had the first glimpse of the famous Pont du Garde ... I would not willingly pass for a false enthusiast in taste; but I cannot help observing, that from the first distant view of this noble monument, till we came near enough to see it perfectly, I felt the strongest emotions of impatience that I had ever known; and obliged our driver to put his mules to the full gallop, in the apprehension that it would be dark before we reached the place. I expected to find the building, in some measure, ruinous; but was agreeably disappointed, to see it look as fresh as the bridge at Westminster. The climate is either so pure and dry, or the

free-stone, with which it is built, so hard, that the very angles of them remain as acute as if they had been cut last year. Indeed, some large stones have dropped out of the arches; but the whole is admirably preserved, and presents the eye with a piece of architecture, so unaffectedly elegant, so simple, and majestic, that I will defy the most phlegmatic and stupid spectator to behold it without admiration. It was raised in the Augustan age, by the Roman colony of Nismes, to convey a stream of water between two mountains, for the use of that city. It stands over the river Gardon, which is a beautiful pastoral stream, brawling among rocks, which form a number of pretty natural cascades, and overshadowed on each side with trees and shrubs, which greatly add to the rural beauties of the scene ... If I lived at Nismes, or Avignon, I should take pleasure in forming parties to come hither, in summer, to dine under one of the arches of the Pont du Garde, on a cold collation.

At Marseilles, as well as buying 'umbrellas against the heats', John Evelyn visited the galleys in the harbour. These remained a tourist attraction well into the eighteenth century – Smollett visited the King of Sardinia's galleys at Villefranche in 1763 and Boswell went to those in Marseilles in 1765.

JOHN EVELYN

We went to visite the Gallys, being about 25; the Captaine of the Gally Royal gave us most courteous entertainement in his cabine, the slaves in the interim playing both loud and soft musiq very rarely. Then he shew'd us how he commanded their motions with a nod and his whistle, making them row out. The spectacle was to me new and strange, to see so many hundreds of miserably naked persons, having their heads shaven close and having onely high red bonnets, a payre of course canvas drawers, their whole backs and leggs naked, doubly chayn'd about their middle and leggs, in couples, and made fast to their seates, and all commanded in a trise by an imperious and cruell seaman ... I was amaz'd to contemplate how these miserable catyfs lie in their gally crowded together, yet there was hardly one but had some occupation by which, as leisure and calmes permitted, they gat some little monye, insomuch as some of them have, after many yeares of cruel servitude, been able to purchase their liberty. Their rising forward and falling back at their oare is a miserable spectacle, and the noyse of their chaines with the roaring of the beaten waters has something of strange and fearfull to one unaccustom'd to it. They are rul'd and chastiz'd by strokes on their backs and soles of theire feete on the least disorder, and without the least humanity; yet are they chereful and full of knavery.

The boundaries of France in the eighteenth century were not as they are today and Nice, where Smollett spent some time in hopes of improving his health, was part of the Kingdom of Sardinia. Here he runs down the amusements to be found and describes his introduction of bathing to the Riviera.

We have had transient visits of a puppet-shew, strolling musicians, and rope-dancers; but they did not like their quarters, and decamped without beat of drum. In the summer, about eight or nine at night, part of the noblesse may be seen assembled in a place called the Parc; which is, indeed, a sort of a street formed by a row of very paltry houses on one side, and on the other, by part of the town-wall, which screens it from a prospect of the sea, the only object that could render it agreeable. Here you may perceive the noblesse stretched in pairs upon logs of wood, like so many seals upon the rocks by moon-light ... But the Parc is not the only place of public resort for our noblesse in a summer's evening. Just without one of our gates, you will find them seated in ditches on the highway side, serenaded with the croaking of frogs, and the bells and braying of mules and asses continually passing in a perpetual cloud of dust. Besides these amusements, there is a public *conversazione* every evening at the commandant's house called the Government, where those noble personages play at cards for farthings. In carnival time, there is also, at this same government, a ball twice or thrice a week, carried on by subscription. At this assembly every person, without distinction, is permitted to dance in masquerade: but, after dancing, they are obliged to unmask, and if Bourgeois, to retire. No individual can give a ball, without obtaining a permission and guard of the commandant; and then his house is open to all masques, without distinction, who are provided with tickets, which tickets are sold by the commandant's secretary, at five sols a-piece, and delivered to the guard at the door. If I have a mind to entertain my particular friends, I cannot have more than a couple of violins; and, in that case, it is called a *conversazione* ...

The people here were much surprised when I began to bathe in the beginning of May. They thought it very strange, that a man seemingly consumptive should plunge into the sea, especially when the weather was so cold; and some of the doctors prognosticated immediate death. But, when it was perceived that I grew better in consequence of the bath, some of the Swiss officers tried the same experiment, and in a few days, our example was followed by several inhabitants of Nice. There is, however, no convenience for this operation, from the benefit of which the fair sex must be intirely excluded, unless they lay aside all regard to decorum; for the shore is always lined with fishing-boats, and crouded with people.

The Two Gateways to Italy

One of the high points, literally and metaphorically, on the Grand Tour was the crossing of the Alps into Italy, normally by the Mont Cenis Pass. This is in Savoy which, like Nice, at that time was not in France, but was part of the Kingdom of Sardinia. The capital of Savoy is Chambéry, and Lady Mary Wortley Montagu spent a happy winter there in 1741/42, as she described to her friend Lady Pomfret.

Here is the most profound peace and unbounded plenty, that is to be found in any corner of the universe; but not one rag of money. For my part, I think it amounts to the same thing, whether one is obliged to give several pence for bread, or can have a great deal of bread for a penny, since the Savoyard nobility here keep as good tables, without money, as those in London, who spend in a week what would be here a considerable yearly revenue. Wine, which is equal to the best Burgundy, is sold for a penny a quart, and I have a cook for very small wages, that is capable of rivalling Chloé.* Here are no equipages but chairs, the hire of which is about a crown a week, and all other matters proportionable. I can assure you I make the figure of the Duchess of Marlborough, by carrying gold in my purse, there being no visible coin but copper. Yet we are all people that can produce pedigrees to serve for the Order of Malta.† Many of us have travelled, and 'tis the fashion to love reading. We eat together perpetually, and have assemblies every night for conversation. To say truth, the houses are all built after the manner of the old English towns, nobody having had money to build for two hundred years past. Consequently the walls are thick, the roofs low, etc., the streets narrow, and miserably paved.

One of the major additions to the repertoire of human pleasures during the eighteenth century was the enjoyment of mountains. Previously they had been

---

* A famous French cook employed by the Duke of Newcastle.
† Only those able to prove entirely aristocratic forebears going back several generations were eligible to join the Order.

viewed with unrelieved horror; but when he was in Switzerland in 1701 Joseph Addison admitted to 'a sort of agreeable shuddering at this most misshapen scenery'. By the time Thomas Gray and Horace Walpole went to see the monastery of the Grande Chartreuse in Savoy in 1739, there was a definite note of enthusiasm in Gray's description of the landscape on the way.

We proceeded on horses, who are used to the way, to the mountain of the Chartreuse: It is six miles to the top; the road runs winding up it, commonly not six feet broad; on one hand is the rock, with woods of pine-trees hanging over head; on the other, a monstrous precipice, almost perpendicular, at the bottom of which rolls a torrent, that sometimes tumbling among the fragments of stone that have fallen from on high, and sometimes precipitating itself down vast descents with a noise like thunder, which is made still greater by the echo from the mountains on each side, concurs to form one of the most solemn, the most romantic, and the most astonishing scenes I ever beheld: Add to this the strange views made by the craggs and cliffs on the other hand; the cascades that in many places throw themselves from the very summit down into the vale, and the river below; and many other particulars impossible to describe; you will conclude we had no occasion to repent our pains. This place St Bruno chose to retire to, and upon its very top founded the aforesaid Convent, which is the superior of

The Grande Chartreuse, by J. R. Cozens. Gray said of the scenery *en route*, 'Not a precipice, not a torrent, not a cliff, but it is pregnant with religion and poetry'

The Manner of passing Mount Cenis, by George Keate, 1755

the whole [Carthusian] order. When we came there, the two fathers, who are commissioned to entertain strangers, (for the rest must neither speak one to another, nor to any one else) received us very kindly; and set before us a repast of dried fish, eggs, butter, and fruits, all excellent in their kind, and extremely neat. They pressed us to spend the night there, and to stay some days with them; but this we could not do, so they led us about their house, which is, you must think, like a little city; for there are 100 fathers, besides 300 servants, that make their clothes, grind their corn, press their wine, and do every thing among themselves. The whole is quite orderly and simple; nothing of finery, but the wonderful decency, and the strange situation, more than supply the place of it.

The actual crossing of the Mont Cenis Pass often brought some untoward incident: first Horace Walpole, a few weeks after the visit to the Grande Chartreuse, and then Arthur Young, travelling back to Savoy in 1789.

HORACE WALPOLE

So, as the song says, we are in fair Italy! I wonder we are; for, on the very highest precipice of Mount Cenis, the Devil of Discord in the similitude of sour wine had got amongst our Alpine savages, and set them a-fighting, with Gray and me in the chairs: they rushed him by me on a crag where there was scarce room for a cloven foot. The least slip had tumbled us into such a fog, and such an eternity, as we should never have found our way

69

out of again. We were eight days in coming hither from Lyons; the four last in crossing the Alps. Such uncouth rocks and such uncomely inhabitants! my dear West, I hope I shall never see them again! At the foot of Mount Cenis we were obliged to quit our chaise, which was taken all to pieces and loaded on mules; and we were carried in low arm-chairs on poles, swathed in beaver bonnets, beaver gloves, beaver stockings, muffs, and bear-skins. When we came to the top, behold the snows fallen! and such quantities, and conducted by such heavy clouds that hung glouting, that I thought we could never have waded through them. The descent is two leagues, but steep, and rough ... but the dexterity and nimbleness of the mountaineers is inconceivable; they run with you down steeps and frozen precipices, where no man, as men are now, could possibly walk. We had twelve men and nine mules to carry us, our servants and baggage, and were about five hours in this agreeable jaunt!

The day before, I had a cruel accident, and so extraordinary an one, that it seems to touch upon the traveller. I had brought with me a little black spaniel, of King Charles's breed; but the prettiest, fattest, dearest creature! I had let it out of the chaise for the air, and it was waddling along close to the head of the horses, on the top of one of the highest Alps, by the side of a wood of firs. There darted out a young wolf, seized poor dear Tory by the throat, and, before we could possibly prevent it, sprung up the side of the rock and carried him off. The postilion jumped off and struck at him with his whip, but in vain. I saw it and screamed, but in vain; for the road was so narrow, that the servants that were behind could not get by the chaise to shoot him. What is the extraordinary part is, that it was but two o'clock, and broad sunshine. It was shocking to see anything one loved run away with to so horrid a death.

ARTHUR YOUNG

We seated ourselves in machines of four sticks, dignified with the name of *traineau* [sledge]: a mule draws it, and a conductor, who walks between the machine and the animal, serves chiefly to kick the snow into the face of the rider. When arrived at the precipice, which leads down to Lanebourg, the mule is dismissed and the *rammissing* [sliding] begins. The weight of two persons, the guide seating himself in the front, and directing it with his heels in the snow, is sufficient to give it motion. For most of the way he is content to follow very humbly the path of the mules, but now and then crosses to escape a double, and in such spots the motion is rapid enough, for a few seconds, to be agreeable; they might very easily shorten the line one half and by that means gratify the English with the velocity they admire so much. As it is at present, a good English horse would trot as fast as we *rammassed* ... A young Savoyard female, riding her mule, experienced a complete reversal; for attempting to pass my *traineau* her beast was a little restive and, tumbling, dismounted his rider: the girl's head pitched in the snow and sunk deep enough to fix her beauties in the position of a forked post; and the wicked muleteers instead of assisting her laughed too heartily to move: if it had been one of the *ballarini* [ballerinas] the attitude would have been nothing distressing to her.

Mrs Thrale pronounced that, going down the Italian side of the Alps, 'the portion of terror excited either by real or fancied dangers on the way, is just sufficient to mingle with the pleasure and make one feel the full effect of sublimity'. Arthur Young enthused too, but about the prospect of Italy ahead rather than the descent itself: 'The first approach to that country so long and justly celebrated that has produced the men who have conquered, and those who have decorated the world, fills the bosom with too many throbbing feelings to permit a bush, a stone, a clod to be uninteresting. Our percipient faculties are expanded; we wish to enjoy; and then all is attention, and willingness to be pleased.'

    Lord Cork and Orrery (and his party) 'refreshed ourselves and our conductors at the little village called Santa Croce where the principality of Piedmont begins. There we met with three or four persons of our own nation, pursuing their journey into Savoy. They very kindly invited us to drink some wine, of which they were taking frequent draughts, at the same time that they confessed it to be very bad, – but it was wine – and they were true Britons.'

    Once your carriage had been reassembled you could proceed to Turin, capital of Piedmont and residence of the King of Sardinia, the first Italian city encountered by those taking the transalpine route. The alternative route was by sea (there being no corniche road, hugging the Mediterranean) from a Riviera port to Genoa and then on to Leghorn (Livorno). We will see what the British made of Turin first. Gray is flippant and knowing. Lord Cork and Orrery's description of the Court does not make it very alluring. When Gibbon attended it in 1765, on the other hand, he claimed that the princesses were 'the most sociable women I have met ... I chatted for about a quarter of an hour with them ... and grew so very free and easy that I drew out my snuff box, rapped it, took snuff twice (a crime never known before in the presence chamber) ...'

THOMAS GRAY

After eight days journey through Greenland, we arrived at Turin. You approach it by a handsome avenue of nine miles long, and quite strait. The entrance is guarded by certain vigilant dragons, called Douaniers, who mumbled us for some time. The city is not large, as being a place of strength, and consequently confined within its fortifications; it has many beauties and some faults; among the first are streets all laid out by the line, regular uniform buildings, fine walks that surround the whole, and in general a good lively clean appearance: But the houses are of brick plaistered, which is apt to want repairing; the windows of oiled paper, which is apt to be torn; and every thing very slight, which is apt to tumble down. There is an excellent Opera, but it is only in the Carnival: Balls every night, but only in the Carnival: Masquerades, too, but only in the Carnival. This Carnival lasts only from Christmas to Lent; one half of the remaining part of the year is passed in remembering the last, the other in expecting the future Carnival. We cannot well subsist upon such slender diet, no more than upon an execrable Italian Comedy, and a Puppet-Show, called *Rappresentazione d'un' anima dannata*, which, I think, are all the present diversions of the place; except the Marquise de Cavaillac's Conversazione, where one goes to see people play at Ombre and Taroc, a game with 72 cards all painted with suns, and moons, and devils and monks. Mr Walpole has been at court; the family are at present at a country palace, called La Venerie. The palace here in town is the very quintesscence of gilding and looking-glass; inlaid floors, carved pannels, and painting, wherever they could stick a brush.

LORD CORK AND ORRERY

The king of Sardinia is an œconomist. He is served in the most royal, and most frugal manner ... No clock-work ever moved with greater exactness, than this court. Every minute fulfils its destiny, and turns round its own axis with the royal inhabitants of Turin. Already we have beheld, over and over again, the same royal scenes; the same princes, and the same princesses, in the same coaches, taking the air, at the same hour, to the same place. They seem all married to *time*, and I presume that it is a kind of adultery to vary half a dozen minutes from the sun. The three princesses are graceful and genteel. The eldest is very handsome. They were born, I fear, under *Virgo*.

James Boswell was set, as so often, on sex.

Friday, 11 January. This morning I was quite in love with Mme Burgaretta. Billon [a French officer] certainly officiated for me as a genteel pimp. To show how corruption may prevail without shame, thus in gross flattery did I write to him this morning:

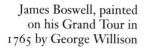
James Boswell, painted on his Grand Tour in 1765 by George Willison

MY DEAR SIR, If you are a man worthy of respect, an obliging man whom one must love; in short, if you have any noble virtue in your soul, arrange for me to see Mme B—— today. You told me yesterday that it will be possible for me to enjoy the favours of that goddess in a very little time. Oh, how adorable she is! I beg of you to be at the coffee-house after the Court. I shall have the honour of finding you there.

Was not this real rascality to prostitute the praises of merit in such a manner? But when a man gives himself up to gross gallantry he must lose much of his delicacy of principle. Billon told me with great simplicity, 'It's a low game.'

Saturday, 12 January. At night I sat a long time in the box of Mme B., of whom I was now violently enamoured. I made my declarations, and was amazed to find such a proposal received with the most pleasing politeness. She however told me, 'It is impossible. I have a lover' (showing him), 'and I do not wish to deceive him.' Her lover was the Neapolitan Minister, Comte Pignatelli, in whose box she sat. He was a genteel, amiable man. He went away, and then I pursued my purpose. Never did I see such dis-simulation, for she talked aloud that I should think no more of my passion, and the *piémontais* around us heard this and said without the least delicacy, 'A traveller expects to accomplish in ten days as much as another will do in a year.' I was quite gone. She then said to me, 'Whisper in my ear,' and told me, 'We must make arrangements,' assuring me that she had talked severely to persuade people that there was nothing between us. She bid me call upon her next day at three. This was advancing with rapidity. I saw she was no very wise personage, so flattered her finely. 'Ah, Madame, I understand you well. This country is not worthy of you. That is true' (like a mere fool). 'You are not loved here as you ought to be.' Billon came and repeated gross bawdy. This was disgusting. When I got home I was so full of my next day's bliss that I sat up all night.

Sunday, 13 January. By want of sleep and agitation of mind, I was quite feverish. At seven I received a letter from Mme —— telling me that people talked of us, and forbidding me to come to her or to think more of the '*plus malheureuse de femmes*'. This tore my very heart. I wrote to her like a madman, conjuring her to pity me. Billon came and went out with me in my coach. He told me I had lost her merely by being an *imprudent* and discovering my attachment to all the world. I had wrought myself up to a passion which I was not master of. I saw he looked upon me as a very simple young man; for amongst the thoroughbred libertines of Turin to have sentiment is to be a child. I changed my lodgings. She wrote to me again. I wrote to her an answer more mad than my former one. I was quite gone. At night I saw her at the opera. We were reserved. But I told her my misery. She said, '*C'est impossible.*' I was distracted. I forgot to mention that I have paid her one visit.

Tuesday, 15 January. Wrote all the morning. After dinner saw the King's palace, where are a number of very excellent pictures. I was shown the King's own apartment. I took up his hat and cane, but found them neither lighter than silk nor heavier than gold. In short, they could not be distinguished from the hat and stick of uncrowned mortals. I was much pleased with his closet, where he had a *prie-dieu* and a good many books of devotion. His Majesty is truly pious.

I then went to Billon's, who had a very pretty girl for me with whom I amused myself. I then went to another ball at the Théâtre de Carignan. I tired much. Billon had promised to have a girl to sleep with me all night at his lodgings. I went there at eleven but did not find her. I was vexed and angry.

Friday, 18 January. I then went to Billon's, where I had a pretty girl. I was disgusted with low pleasure. Billon talked of women in the most indelicate manner. I then went to Mme Burgaretta's, where I found two more swains. She grumbled and complained of a headache; and she dressed before us, changing even her shirt. We indeed saw no harm; but this scene entirely cured my passion for her. Her *femme de chambre* was very clever, and, when the Countess was dressed, carried away her morning clothes in a little barrel.

74

A felucca: the sort of craft a Grand Tourist would have taken from a southern French port to Genoa or Leghorn

We now turn to the other entry to Italy, via Genoa and Leghorn. John Evelyn recounts an incident which illustrates the fiery nature of the Genoese, in the seventeenth century at any rate. A hundred years or so later, Smollett and Mrs Thrale give accounts of the more pacific behaviour of its nobility.

JOHN EVELYN

We pass'd by boate acrosse the harbour. Here I could not but observe the sudden and devilish passion of a seaman, who plying us was intercepted by another who interpos'd his boate before him and tooke us in; for the teares gushing out of his eyes, he put his finger in his mouth and almost bit it off by the joynt, shewing it to his antagonist as an assurance to him of some bloudy revenge if ever he came neere that part of the harbour again. Indeed this beautifull Citty is more stayn'd with such horrid acts of revenge and murthers than any one place in Europ, or haply in the world, where there is a political government, which makes it unsafe to strangers. It is made a gally matter to carry a knife whose point is not broken off.

TOBIAS SMOLLETT

It is not without reason that Genoa is called *La superba*. The city itself is very stately; and the nobles are very proud ... They live with great parsimony in their families; and wear nothing but black in public; so that their expences are but small. If a Genoese nobleman gives an entertainment once a quarter, he is said to live upon the fragments all the rest of the year. I was told that one of them lately treated his friends, and left the entertainment to the care of his son, who ordered a dish of fish that cost a zechine, which is equal to about ten shillings sterling. The old gentleman no sooner saw it appear on the table, than unable to suppress his concern, he burst into tears, and

75

exclaimed, *Ah Figliuolo indegno! Siamo in Rovina! Siamo in precipizio!* Ah Prodigal! ruined! undone!

I think the pride or ostentation of the Italians in general takes a more laudable turn than that of other nations. A Frenchman lays out his whole revenue upon tawdry suits of cloaths, or in furnishing a magnificent *repas* of fifty or a hundred dishes, one half of which are not eatable, nor intended to be eaten. His wardrobe goes to the *fripier*,* his dishes to the dogs, and himself to the devil, and after his decease no vestige of him remains. A Genoese, on the other hand, keeps himself and his family at short allowance, that he may save money to build palaces and churches, which remain to after-ages so many monuments of his taste, piety, and munificence; and in the mean time give employment and bread to the poor and industrious. There are some Genoese nobles who have each five or six elegant palaces magnificently furnished, either in the city, or in different parts of the Riviera. The two streets called *Strada Balbi* and *Strada Nuova*, are continued double ranges of palaces adorned with gardens and fountains: but their being painted on the outside has, in my opinion, a poor effect.†

MRS THRALE

A family coming last night to visit at a house where I had the honour of being admitted as an intimate, gave me another proof of my present state of remoteness from English manners. The party consisted of an old nobleman, who could trace his genealogy unblemished up to one of the old Roman emperors, but whose fortune is now in a hopeless state of decay; his lady, not inferior to himself in birth or haughtiness of air and carriage, but much impaired by age, ill-health, and pecuniary distresses, These had, however, no way lessened her ideas of her own dignity, or the respect of her cavalier servente and her son, who waited on her with an unremitted attention, presenting her their little dirty tin snuff-boxes upon one knee by turns, which ceremony the less surprised me, as having seen her train, made of a dyed and watered lutestring,‡ borne gravely after her upstairs by a footman, the express image of Edgar in the storm scene of *King Lear*, who, as the fool says, 'wisely reserv'd a blanket, else had we all been 'shamed'. Our conversation was meagre, but serious. There was music, and the door being left at jar, as we call it, I watched the wretched servant who stayed in the antechamber, and found that he was listening in spite of sorrow and starving.

---

* Second-hand clothes dealer.
† Addison also criticised these *trompe l'oeil* architectural details.
‡ A glossy silk.

A musical party, by Giuseppe Bonito. The *cicisbeo* is the figure on the right. Boswell regarded them 'as illustrating the last stage of human degradation', doing 'continual duty' for their ladies and enjoying 'only appearances'. One doubts the accuracy of his last claim, as does Lady Mary Wortley Montagu in her description below.

The phenomenon of the cicisbeo, *or* cavaliere servente *as they tended to be called in Venice, was one that fascinated all English writers on eighteenth-century Italy, and during her first visit to Genoa in 1718 Lady Mary Wortley Montagu regaled her sister, Lady Mar, with a full account.*

The ladies affect the French habit and are more genteel than those they imitate. I do not doubt but the custom of *tetis beys* [*cicisbeismo*] has very much improved their airs. I know not whether you have ever heard of those animals. Upon my word, nothing but my own eyes could have convinced [me] there were such upon the earth. The fashion begun here and is now received all over Italy, where the husbands are not such terrible creatures as we represent them. There are none among them such brutes to pretend to find fault with a custom so well established and so politically founded, since I am assured here that it was an expedient first found out by the Senate to put an end to those family hatreds which tore their state to pieces, and to find employment for those young men who were forced to cut one another's throats *pour passer le temps*, and it has succeeded so well that since the institution of *tetis beys* there has been nothing but peace and good humour amongst them. These are gentlemen that devote themselves to the service of a particular lady (I mean a married one, for the virgins are all invisible, confined to convents). They are obliged to wait on her to all public places, the plays, operas, and assemblies (which are called here conversations), where they wait behind her chair, take care of her fan and gloves if she plays, have the privilege of whispers, etc. When she goes out they serve her instead of lackeys, gravely trotting by her chair. 'Tis their business to present against any day of public appearance, not forgetting that of her name. In short, they are to spend all their time and money in her service who rewards them according to her inclination (for opportunity they want none), but the husband is not to have the impudence to suppose 'tis any other than pure platonic friendship. 'Tis true they endeavour to give her a *tetis bey* of their own choosing, but when the lady happens not to be of the same taste (as that often happens) she never fails to bring it about to have one of her own fancy. In former times one beauty used to have eight or ten of these humble admirers, but those days of plenty and humility are no more; men grow more scarce and saucy, and every lady is forced to content herself with one at a time.

Much later in 1752, writing this time to her daughter Lady Bute and admittedly not from Genoa, Lady Mary had more to say on the institution of marriage in Italy.

I cannot let pass in silence the prodigious alteration in regard to our sex. This reformation (or if you please, depravation) begun so lately as the year 1732, when the French overrun this part of Italy [Lombardy], but it has been carried on with such fervour and success that the Italian go far beyond their patterns, the Parisian ladies, in the extent of their liberty. I am not so much surprised at the women's conduct as I am amazed at the change in the men's sentiments. Jealousy, which was once a point of honour amongst them, is exploded to that degree it is the most infamous and ridiculous of all characters, and you cannot more affront a gentleman than to suppose him capable of it.

Divorces are also introduced and frequent enough. They have long been in fashion in Genoa, several of the finest and greatest ladies there having two husbands alive. The constant pretext is impotency, to which the man often pleads guilty, and though he marries again and has children by another wife, the plea remains good by saying he was so in regard to his first; and when I told them that in England a complaint of that kind was esteemed so impudent, no reasonable woman would submit to make it, I was answered we lived without religion, and that their consciences obliged them rather to strain a point of modesty than live in a state of damnation. However, as this method is not without inconvenience (it being impracticable where there is children) they have taken another here: the husband deposes upon oath that he has had a commerce with his mother-in-law, on which the marriage is declared incestuous and nullified, though the children remain legitimate. You will think this hard on the old lady who is scandalised, but it is no scandal at all, nobody supposing it to be true, without circumstances to confirm. But the married couple are set free, to their mutual content, for I believe it would be difficult to get a sentence of divorce if either side made opposition. At least I have heard no example of it.

Genoa offered no easy access to the hinterland and the traveller took ship again for Leghorn further down the thigh of Italy, hugging the coast and probably stopping for the night at small towns such as Sestri Levante, where Smollett encountered an inn that provided him with colourful copy.

The house was tolerable, and we had no great reason to complain of the beds: but, the weather being hot, there was a very offensive smell, which proceeded from some skins of beasts new killed, that were spread to dry on an out-house in the yard. Our landlord was a butcher, and had very much the looks of an assassin. His wife was a great masculine virago, who had all the air of having frequented the slaughter-house. Instead of being welcomed with looks of complaisance, we were admitted with a sort of gloomy condescension, which seemed to say, 'We don't much like your company; but, however, you shall have a night's lodging in favour of the *patron of the gondola*, who is our acquaintance.' In short, we had a very bad supper, miserably dressed, passed a very disagreeable night, and payed a very extravagant bill in the morning, without being thanked for our custom. I was very glad to get out of the house with my throat uncut.

Leghorn served the purpose now served by Pisa airport, as gateway to Tuscany. It is described, first by John Evelyn and then by Joseph Addison.

JOHN EVELYN

Ligorne is the prime Port belonging to all the Duke's territories; heretofore a very obscure Towne, but since Duke Ferdinand has strongly fortified it (after the modern way), has drain'd the marshes by cutting a channell thence to Pisa navigable 16 miles, and has rais'd a Mole, emulating that at

Joseph Addison,
by Kneller

Genoa ... Here, especially in this Piazza, is such a concourse of slaves, Turkes, Mores, and other nations, that the number and confusion is prodigious; some buying, others selling, others drinking, others playing, some working, others sleeping, fighting, singing, weeping, all nearly naked, and miserably chayn'd. Here was a tent, where any idle fellow might stake his liberty against a few crownes, at dice or other hazard, and, if he lost, he was immediately chayn'd and led away to the gallys, where he was to serve a tearm of yeares, but from whence they seldom return'd: many sottish persons in a drunken bravado would try their fortune in this way.

The houses of this neate Towne are very uniforme, and excellently paynted *a fresca* on the outer walls with representations of many of their victories over the Turkes. The houses, though low on account of the earthquakes which frequently happen here (as did one during my being in Italy) are very well built; the Piazza is very fayre and com'odious, and with the Church whose 4 columns at the portico are of black marble polish'd, gave the first hint to the building both of the Church and Piazza in Covent Garden with us, tho' very imperfectly persu'd.

JOSEPH ADDISON
One can scarce imagine how great profits the [Medici] Duke of Tuscany receives from this single place, which are not generally thought so con-

siderable, because it passes for a free port. But it is very well known how the Great Duke, on a late occasion, notwithstanding the privileges of the merchants, drew no small sums of money out of them; though still, in respect of the exorbitant dues that are paid at most other ports, it deservedly retains the name of free. It brings into his dominions a great increase of people from all other nations. They reckon in it near ten thousand Jews, many of them very rich, and so great traffickers, that our English factors complain they have most of our country trade in their hands. 'Tis true the strangers pay little or no taxes directly, but out of everything they buy there goes a large gabel [purchase tax] to the government. The very ice merchant at Leghorn pays above a thousand pounds sterling annually for his privilege, and the tobacco merchant ten thousand. The ground is sold by the Great Duke at a very high price, and houses are every day rising on it. All the commodities that go up into the country, of which there are great quantities, are clogged with impositions as soon as they leave Leghorn. All the wines, oils, and silks, that come down from the fruitful valleys of Pisa, Florence, and other parts of Tuscany, must make their way through several duties and taxes before they can reach the port. The canal that runs from the sea into the Arno gives a convenient carriage to all goods that are to be shipped off ...

It is well known how the Pisans and Florentines long regretted the loss of their ancient liberty, and their subjection to a family that some of them thought themselves equal to, in the flourishing times of their common-wealths. The town of Leghorn has accidentally done what the greatest fetch of politics would have found difficult to have brought about, for it has almost unpeopled Pisa, if we compare it with what it was formerly, and every day lessens the number of the inhabitants of Florence. This does not only weaken those places, but at the same time turns many of the busiest spirits from their old notions of honour and liberty to the thoughts of traffic and merchandise: and as men engaged in a road of thriving are no friends to changes and revolutions, they are at present worn into a habit of sub-jection, and push all their pursuits another way.

The Leaning Tower of Pisa went under several names. Lord Cork and Orrery called it 'the pensile tower' and Fynes Moryson 'the leaning steeple'. Evelyn called it 'the bending tower', and went on:

The Campanile, or Settezonio, built by John Venipont, a German, consists of several orders of pillars, 30 in a row, design'd to be much higher. It stands alone on the right side of the Cathedrall, strangely remarkable for this, that

Robert Adam,
by Willison

the beholder would expect it to fall, being built exceedingly declining, by a rare addresse of the architect; and how it is supported from falling I think would puzzle a good geometrician. The Domo, or Cathedrall, standing neere it, is a superb structure, beautified with 6 columns of greate antiquity; the gates are of brasse, of admirable workmanship. The Cemetere cal'd Campo Santo is made of divers gally ladings of earth formerly brought from Jerusalem, said to be of such a nature as to consume dead bodies in fourty houres. 'Tis cloistred with marble arches; here lies buried the learned Philip Decius who taught in this University. At one side of this Church stands an ample and well-wrought marble vessell which heretofore contain'd the tribute paid yearly by the Citty to Cæsar. It is plac'd, as I remember, on a pillar of opilestone, with divers other antiq urnes. Neere this, and in the same field, is the Baptistry of San Giovanni, built of pure white marble and cover'd with so artificial a cupola that the voice uttered under it seemes to breake out of a cloud. The font and pulpit supported by 4 lyons is of inestimable value for the preciousnesse of the materials.

By 1754, when Robert Adam went to Pisa, the Medicis' long dominance of Florence and Tuscany had ended. So it was a poignant sighting that he reported from the opera there. The particularly Italian custom of mask-wearing (masquerade) allowed the normal formalities of social intercourse to be ignored. (Incidentally, Adam thought the Leaning Tower 'a horrible but an astonishing object'.)

The first time we were at the opera at Pisa we soon cast our eyes towards a very pretty girl dressed in masquerade who went through the whole boxes in the house to pay her respects to the other company, a privilege all Masks have. She sometimes pulled off the mask from her face and showed it, superior in expression, pleasing smiles and agreeable features to any I have seen, whilst its prodigious delicate shape and thoroughbred manner made us cock our ears and make enquiries about her. We soon found her to be of no small rank, being the nearest surviving relation of the Medici family. Her own name, Mary of Medici, but being married to a gentleman of the Customs of Pisa she is now called Signora Gianni.

[The following day they were taken to] what they call the Casino, which is nothing else but a public coffee-house, open from morning to night for the best ranks of people and quality who game, dance or walk about and see others do so. Here we had a particular order to be received at all times we chosed and here we encountered our lovely Signora Gianni. Hope,* who gibbers Italian, was soon in close conversation whilst I stared but could say nothing. Think how I cursed Italian and all foreign languages! We went from there to the opera where Hope asked if we might have the honour of paying her a visit in her own palchetto or box, which she accepted. I went along but uttered not a word. Here again I moralised with some vehemency on the use of different languages and soon concluded it to be a diabolical invention. When she spoke to me in Italian I answered in French, she understanding one word in ten I said and I the same of her conversation. Next night we again met her at the Casino. Hope and I handed her to her coach, a custom in this country, one on each side, and went to the opera with her where we passed the evening very agreeably as I found an abbé who interpreted for me and I made a language of my own, half English, half French and a little sprinkling of Italian – to her great amusement. She had infinite spirit and vivacity, vast good nature, a frolicsome hillicot easy behaviour – will allow you to shake hands with her and in joke will give you a knock on the knee or on the shoulder. And at the same time her character is better than any woman's I have ever yet heard of in Italy, no one having the least thing to say in her dispraise. At the Ball the night after, I had the honour and happiness to dance many minuets with her, as indeed I did with all the Quality of Pisa – some dozens at least.

* Charles Hope, brother of the 2nd Earl of Hopetoun, with whom Adam was travelling.

A typical eighteenth-century 'Italian' opera: a scene from Handel's *Flavio*

Lombardy

Thomas Coryate said the first view of the plain of Lombardy 'did even refocillate my spirits, and tickle my senses with inward joy'. There, Milan was the first objective of the Tourist. In the seventeenth century it was part of the Spanish dominions.

JOHN EVELYN

At approch of the Citty some of our company, in dread of the Inquisition (severer here than in all Spain), thought of throwing away some Protestant books and papers. We ariv'd about 3 in the afternoone, when the officers search'd us thoroughly for prohibited goods, but finding we were onely gentlemen travellers, dismiss'd us for a small reward, and we went quietly to our inn, the Three Kings, where for that day we refreshed ourselves, as we had neede. The next morning ... I went into the Governor's Palace, who was Constable of Castile; tempted by the glorious tapissries and pictures, I adventur'd so far alone, that peeping into a chamber where the greate man was under the barber's hands, he sent one of his Negro's (a slave) to know what I was; I made the best excuse I could, and that I was only admiring the pictures, which he returning and telling his lord, I heard the Governor reply that I was a spie, on which I retir'd with all the speede I could, pass'd the guard of Swisse, got into the streete, and in a moment to my company, who were gone to the Jesuites Church, which in truth is a noble structure, the front especialy, after the moderne ...

We concluded this day's wandring at the Monasterie of Madona della Gratia, and in the Refectorie admir'd that celebrated *Cœna Domini* [Last Supper] of Leonardo da Vinci, which takes up the intire wall at the end, and is the same that the greate Virtuoso Francis I of France was so enamour'd of, that he consulted to remove the whole wall by binding it about with ribs of iron and timber to convey it into France. It is indeede one of the rarest paintings that was ever executed by Leonardo, who was long in the service of that Prince, and so deare to him that the King coming to visite him in his old age and sicknesse, he expired in his armes. This incomparable piece is now exceedingly impair'd.

Thanks to La Scala, Milan is the epicentre of the operatic world and Mrs Thrale gives a lively description of that opera house a few years after its opening in 1778. But first, young William Beckford generalises on opera in Italy.

WILLIAM BECKFORD

Their rage for theatrical spectacles ... [is a] passion they seem to inherit from the antient Romans, and the bequest has lost nothing in their hands. In the fashionable world, the morning is spent in a slovenly dishabille, that prevents their going out, or receiving frequent visits at home. Reading, or work takes up a very small portion of this part of the day; so that it passes away in a yawning sort of nonchalance. People are scarcely wide awake, till about dinner-time. But, a few hours after, the important business of the toilette puts them gently into motion; and, at length, the opera calls them completely into existence. But it must be understood, that the drama, or the music, do not form a principal object of theatrical amusement. Every lady's box is the scene of tea, cards, cavaliers, servants, lap-dogs, abbés, scandal, and assignations; attention to the action of the piece, to the scenes, or even to the actors, male, or female, is but a secondary affair. If there be some actor, or actress, whose merit, or good fortune, happens to demand the universal homage of fashion, there are pauses of silence, and the favourite airs may be heard. But without this cause, or the presence of the sovereign, all is noise, hubbub, and confusion, in an Italian audience. The hour of the theatre, however, with all its mobbing and disturbance, is the happiest part of the day, to every Italian, of whatever station; and the least affluent will sacrifice some portion of his daily bread, rather than not enjoy it.

MRS THRALE

It is now time to talk a little of the theatre, and surely a receptacle so capacious to contain four thousand people, a place of entrance so commodious to receive them, a show so princely, so very magnificent to entertain them, must be sought in vain out of Italy. The centre front box, richly adorned with gilding, arms and trophies, is appropriated to the court, whose canopy is carried up to what we call the first gallery in England; the crescent of boxes ending with the stage consists of nineteen on a side, small boudoirs – for such they seem – and are as such fitted up with silk hangings, girandoles [chandeliers], etc., and placed so judiciously as to catch every sound of the singers if they do but whisper. I will not say it is equally advantageous to the figure as to the voice, no performers looking adequate to the place they recite upon, so very stately is the building itself, being all of stone, with an immense portico, and stairs which for width you might without hyperbole drive your chariot up. An immense sideboard at the first lobby, lighted and furnished with luxurious and elegant plenty, as many people send for suppers to their box and entertain a knot of friends there with infinite convenience and splendour. A silk curtain, the colour of your hangings, defends the closet from intrusive eyes, if you think proper to drop it, and, when drawn up, gives gaiety and show to the general appearance of the whole; while across the corridor leading to these boxes another small chamber, numbered like that it belongs to, is appropriated to the use of your servants, and furnished with every conveniency to make chocolate, serve lemonade, etc.

Can one wonder at the contempt shown by foreigners when they see English women of fashion squeezed into holes lined with dirty, torn red paper, and the walls of it covered with a wretched crimson stuff? Well, but this theatre is built in place of a church, founded by the famous Beatrice di Scala, in consequence of a vow she made to erect one if God would be pleased to send her a son. The church was pulled down and the playhouse erected. The Archduke lost a son that year, and the pious folks cried, 'A judgment!' but nobody minded them, I believe; many, however, that are scrupulous will not go ...

A friend showed me one evening, from my own box at the opera, fifty or a hundred low shopkeepers' wives, dispersed about the pit at the theatre, dressed in men's clothes – '*per disimpegno*', as they call it – that they might be more at liberty forsooth to clap and hiss, and quarrel and jostle, etc. I felt shocked.

Whilst in Milan, Mrs Thrale also allowed herself some thoughts on Italian servants, and on the easy relations between them and their employers. Live-in servants were a rarity.

When evening comes, it is the comicallest sight in the world to see them all go gravely home, and you may die in the night for want of help, though surrounded by showy attendants all day. Till the hour of departure, however, it is expected that two or three of them at least sit in the antechamber, as it is called, to answer the bell, which, if we confess the truth, is no slight service or hardship; for the stairs, high and wide as those of Windsor Palace, all stone too, run up from the door immediately to that apartment, which is very large and very cold, with bricks to set their feet on only, and a brazier filled with warm wood-ashes to keep their fingers from freezing, which in summer they employ with cards, and seem but little inclined to lay them down when ladies pass through to the receiving-room. The strange familiarity this class of people think proper to assume, half-joining in the conversation, and crying '*Oibò!*' [Oh, dear] when the master affirms something they do not quite assent to, is apt to shock one at beginning, the more when one reflects upon the equally offensive humility they show on being first accepted into the family, when it is expected that they receive the new master's or lady's hand in a half-kneeling posture and kiss it, as women under the rank of countess do the Queen of England's when presented at our court. This obsequiousness, however, vanishes completely upon acquaintance, and the footman, if not very seriously admonished indeed, yawns, spits, and displays what one of our travel-writers [Smollett] emphatically terms his flag of abomination [a handkerchief] behind the chair of a woman of quality without the slightest sensation of its impropriety. There is, however, a sort of odd farcical drollery mingled with this grossness which tends greatly to disarm one's wrath; and I felt more inclined to laugh than to be angry one day when, from the head of my own table, I saw the servant of a nobleman who dined with us cramming some chicken patés down his throat behind the door, our own folks humorously trying to choke him by pretending that his lord called him while his mouth was full.

Mrs Thrale,
painted in Italy
on her Tour in 1785

[Later Mrs Thrale remarked on Italian nobles'] amiable carriage towards inferiors, calling their own and their friends' servants by tender names, and speaking to all below themselves with a graciousness not often used by English men or women even to their equals. The pleasure, too, which the high people here express when the low ones are diverted is charming. We think it vulgar to be merry when the mob is so; but if rolling down a hill, like Greenwich, was the custom here as with us, all Milan would run to see the sport, and rejoice in the felicity of their fellow-creatures. When I express my admiration of such condescending sweetness, they reply, '*È un uomo come un altro; è battezzato come noi,*' and the like – 'Why, he is a man of the same nature as we; he has been christened as well as ourselves,' they reply. Yet do I not for this reason condemn the English as naturally haughty above their continental neighbours. Our Government has left so narrow a space between the upper and under ranks of people in Great Britain, while our charitable and truly Christian religion is still so constantly employed in raising the depressed by giving them means of changing their situation, that if our persons of condition fail even for a moment to watch their post, maintaining by dignity what they or their fathers have acquired by merit, they are instantly and suddenly broken in upon by the well-employed talents or swiftly acquired riches of men born on the other side the thin partition; whilst in Italy the gulf is totally impassable, and birth alone can entitle man or woman to the society of gentlemen and ladies.

In 1746 Lady Mary Wortley Montagu, by now a confirmed expatriate in her late fifties, came to live at Brescia and a little later moved about twenty miles south to Gottolengo. She described her rustic idyll to her daughter, Lady Bute, in 1748.

I have been this six weeks, and still am, at my dairy house, which joins to my garden. I believe I have already told you it is a long mile from the castle, which is situate in the midst of a very large village (once a considerable town, part of the walls still remaining) and has not vacant ground enough about it to make a garden, which is my greatest amusement; and it being now troublesome to walk or even go in the chaise till the evening, I have fitted up in this farm-house a room for myself, that is to say, strewed the floor with rushes, covered the chimney with moss and branches, and adorned the room with basins of earthenware (which is made here to great perfection) filled with flowers, and put in some straw chairs and a couch-bed, which is my whole furniture.

This spot of ground is so beautiful I am afraid you will scarce credit the description, which, however, I can assure you shall be very literal, without any embellishment from imagination. It is on a bank forming a kind of peninsula raised from the River Oglio fifty foot, to which you may descend by easy stairs cut in the turf, and either take the air on the river, which is as large as the Thames at Richmond, or by walking an avenue two hundred yards on the side of it you find a wood of a hundred acres, which was already cut into walks and ridings when I took it. I have only added fifteen bowers in different views, with seats of turf. They were easily made, here being a large quantity of underwood and a great number of wild vines which twist to the top of the highest trees, and from which they make a very good sort of wine they call *brusco*. I am now writing to you in one of these arbours, which is so thick shaded the sun is not troublesome even at noon. Another is on the side of the river, where I have made a camp kitchen, that I may take the fish, dress and eat it immediately, and at the same time see the barks which ascend or descend everyday, to or from Mantua, Guastalla or Pontevico, all considerable towns. This little wood is carpeted (in their succeeding seasons) with violets and strawberries, inhabited by a nation of nightingales, and filled with game of all kinds excepting deer and wild boar, the first being unknown here, and not being large enough for the other.

Perhaps I shall succeed better in describing my manner of life, which is as regular as that of any monastery. I generally rise at six, and as soon as I have breakfasted, put myself at the head of my weeder women, and work with them till nine. I then inspect my dairy and take a turn amongst my poultry, which is a very large inquiry. I have at present two hundred chicken, besides turkeys, geese, ducks, and peacocks. All things have hitherto prospered under my care. My bees and silk worms are doubled, and I am told that without accidents my capital will be so in two years' time. At eleven o'clock I retire to my books. I dare not indulge myself in that pleasure above an hour.* At twelve I constantly dine, and sleep after dinner till about three. I then send for some of my old priests and either play at picquet or whist till 'tis cool enough to go out. One evening I walk in my wood, where I often sup, take the air on horseback the next, and go on the water the third. The fishery of this part of the river belongs to me, and my fisherman's little boat (where I have a green lutestring awning) serves me for a barge. He and his son are my rowers, without any expense, he being very well paid by the profit of the fish, which I give him on condition of having everyday one dish for my table. Here is plenty of every sort of freshwater fish excepting salmon, but we have a large trout so like it that I, that have almost forgot the taste, do not distinguish it.

* Her eyesight was bad.

An Italian river landscape by the eighteenth-century Venetian painter Giuseppe Zais, reminiscent of Lady Mary Wortley Montagu's description of her rural retreat near Brescia on the river Oglio

In 1753 Lady Mary regaled her daughter with a story that might have furnished the plot for an extra act of The Marriage of Figaro. *Her view of the Italian servant's lot is rather different to Mrs Thrale's on pp. 87–9.*

I was quietly reading in my closet when I was interrupted by the chambermaid of the Signora Laura Bono, who flung herself at my feet, and in an agony of sobs and tears begged me for the love of the Holy Madonna to hasten to her master's house, where the two brothers would certainly murder one another if my presence did not stop their fury. I was very much surprised, having always heard them spoke of as a pattern of fraternal union. However, I made all possible speed thither, without staying for hoods or attendance. I was soon there (the house touching my garden wall) and was directed to the bedchamber by the noise of oaths and execrations, but on opening the door was astonished to a degree you may better guess than I describe, by seeing the Signora Laura prostrate on the ground, melting in tears, and her husband standing with a drawn stiletto in his hand, swearing she should never see tomorrow's sun. I was soon let into the secret.

The good man, having business of consequence at Brescia, went thither early in the morning, but as he expected his chief tenant to pay his rent that day, he left orders with his wife that if the farmer (who lived two mile off) came himself or sent any of his sons, she should take care to make him very welcome. She obeyed him with great punctuality. The money coming in the hand of a handsome lad of eighteen she did not only admit him to her own table and produced the best wine in the cellar, but resolved to give him *chère entière*. While she was exercising this generous hospitality, the husband met midway the gentleman he intended to visit, who was posting to another side of the country. They agreed on another appointment, and he returned to his own house, where, giving his horse to be led round to the stable by the servant that accompanied him, he opened his door with the *passe-partout* key, and proceeded to his chamber without meeting anybody, where he found his beloved spouse asleep on the bed with her gallant. The opening of the door waked them. The young fellow immediately leaped out of the window, which looked into the garden and was open (it being summer), and escaped over the fields, leaving his breeches on a chair by the bed-side, a very striking circumstance ... As to the poor criminal, she had nothing to say for herself but what I dare swear you will hear from your youngest daughter if ever you catch her stealing of sweet-meats: pray, pray, she would do so no more, and indeed it was the first time.

This last article found no credit with me. I can not be persuaded that any woman who had lived virtuous till forty (for such was her age) could suddenly be endowed with such consummate impudence to solicit a youth at first sight, there being no probability, his age and station considered, that he would have made any attempt of that kind. I must confess I was wicked enough to think the unblemished reputation she had hitherto maintained, and did not fail to put us in mind of, was owing to a series of such frolics; and to say truth, they are the only *amours* that can reasonably hope to remain undiscovered. Ladies that can resolve to make love thus *ex tempore* may pass unobserved, especially if they can content themselves with low life, where fear may oblige their favourites to secrecy. There wants only a very lewd constitution, a very bad heart, and a moderate understanding to make this conduct easy, and I do not doubt it has been practised by many prudes beside her I am now speaking of.

You may be sure I did not communicate these reflections. The first word I spoke was to desire Signor Carlo to sheathe his poniard, not being pleased with its glittering. He did so very readily, begging my pardon for not having done it on my first appearance, saying he did not know what he did; and indeed he had the countenance and gesture of a man distracted. I did not endeavour a defence that seemed to me impossible, but represented to him as well as I could the crime of a murder which, if he could justify before men, was still a crying sin before God, the disgrace he would bring on himself and posterity, and irreparable injury he would do his eldest daughter (a pretty girl of fifteen, that I knew he was extreme fond of). I added that if he thought it proper to part from his lady he might easily find a pretext for it some months hence, and that it was as much his interest as hers to conceal this affair from the knowledge of the world. I could not presently make him taste these reasons, and was forced to stay there near five hours (almost from five to ten at night) before I durst leave them together, which I would not do till he had sworn in the most serious manner he would make no future attempt on her life. I was content with his oath, knowing him to be very devout, and found I was not mistaken ... The lady retains the satisfaction of insulting all her acquaintance on the foundations of a spotless character that only she can boast in the parish, where she is most heartily hated, from these airs of impertinent virtue, and another very essential reason, being the best dressed woman amongst them, though one of the plainest in her figure.

The discretion of the chambermaid in fetching me, which possibly saved her mistress's life, and her taciturnity since, I fancy appears very remarkable to you, and is what would certainly never happen in England. The first part of her behaviour deserves great praise, coming of her own accord and inventing so decent an excuse for her admittance; but her silence may be attributed to her knowing very well that any servant that presumes to talk of his master will most certainly be incapable of talking at all in a short time, their lives being entirely in the power of their superiors. I do not mean by law but by custom, which has full as much force. If one of them was killed it would either never be inquired into at all or very slightly passed over; yet it seldom happens and I know no instance of it, which I think is owing to the great submissions of domestics, who are sensible of their dependence, and the national temper not being hasty and never enflamed by wine, drunkness being a vice abandoned to the vulgar and spoke of with greater detestation than murder, which is mentioned with as little concern as a drinking bout in England, and is almost as frequent. It was extreme shocking to me at my first coming, and still gives me a sort of horror, though custom has in some degree familiarised it to my imagination. Robbery would be pursued with great vivacity and punished with the utmost rigour, therefore is very rare, though stealing is in daily practice; but as all the peasants are suffered the use of firearms the slightest provocation is sufficient to shoot, and they see one of their own species lie dead before them with as little remorse as a hare or a partridge, and when revenge spurs them on, with much more pleasure.

The Rialto bridge, by Canaletto. Gibbon dismissed it merely as 'a fine bridge spoilt by the two rows of houses built upon it'

Veneto

Continuing eastwards at the foot of the mountains, the amphitheatre at Verona was an unmissable sight for those in search of the Classical past, though William Beckford's approach and reactions to it were determinedly in the Romantic mode.

Twilight drawing on, I left my haunt, and stealing downstairs, enquired for a guide to conduct me to the amphitheatre, perhaps the most entire monument of Roman days. The people of the house, instead of bringing me a quiet peasant, officiously delivered me up to a professed antiquary, one of those diligent, plausible young men, to whom, God help me! I have so capital an aversion. This sweet spark displayed all his erudition, and flourished away upon cloacas and vomitoriums [sewers and sick basins] with eternal fluency. He was very profound in the doctrine of conduits, and knew to admiration how the filthiness of all the amphitheatre was disposed of; but perceiving my inattention, and having just grace enough to remark that I chose one side of the street when he preferred the other, and some-times trotted, through despair, in the kennel [gutter], he made me a pretty bow, I tipped him half-a-crown, and seeing the ruins before me, traversed a gloomy arcade and emerged alone into the arena. A smooth turf covers its surface, from which the spacious row of gradines [stepped seats] rises to a majestic elevation. Four arches, with their simple Doric ornament, alone remain of the grand circular arcade which once crowned the highest seats of the amphitheatre; and, had it not been for Gothic violence, this part of the structure would have equally resisted the ravages of time ...

When I paced slowly across it, silence reigned undisturbed among the awful ruins, and nothing moved, save the weeds and grasses which skirt the walls and tremble with the faintest breeze. I liked the idea of being thus shut in on every side by endless gradines, abandoned to a stillness and solitude I was so peculiarly disposed to taste. Throwing myself upon the grass in the middle of the arena, I enjoyed the freedom of my situation, and pursued the last tracks of light, as they faded behind the solitary arches, which rise above the rest. Red and fatal were the tints of the western sky; the wind blew chill and hollow, and something more than common seemed to issue from the withering herbage on the walls. I started up, fled through a dark arcade, where water falls drop by drop; and arrived, panting, in the great square before the ruins.

Then, as now, Tourists tended to pay too little attention to Padua, seduced by the prospect of Venice. Addison visited some of the sights and produced a marvellously economical but telling description of a Palladio church interior.

From Verona to Padua we travelled through a very pleasant country: it is planted thick with rows of white mulberry-trees, that furnish food for great quantities of silk-worms with their leaves, as the swine and poultry consume the fruit. The trees themselves serve, at the same time, as so many stays for their vines, which hang all along like garlands from tree to tree. Between the several ranges lie fields of corn, which, in these warm countries, ripens much better among the mulberry shades than if it were exposed to the open sun ...

St Anthony, who lived about five hundred years ago, is the great saint to whom they here pay their devotions. He lies buried in the church that is dedicated to him at present, though it was formerly consecrated to the blessed Virgin. It is extremely magnificent, and very richly adorned. There are narrow clefts in the monument that stands over him, where good Catholics rub their beads, and smell his bones, which they say have in them a natural perfume, though very like apoplectic balsam; and what would make one suspect that they rub the marble with it, it is observed that the scent is stronger in the morning than at night ...

The church of St Justina, designed by Palladio, is the most handsome, luminous, disencumbered building in the inside that I have ever seen, and is esteemed by many artists one of the finest works in Italy. The long nef consists of a row of five cupolas, the cross one has on each side a single cupola deeper and broader than the others, The martyrdom of St Justina hangs over the altar, and is a piece of Paul Veronese. In the great town-hall of Padua stands a stone superscribed *Lapis Vituperii*. Any debtor that will swear himself not worth five pound, and is set by the bailiffs thrice with his bare buttocks on this stone in a full hall, clears himself of any further prosecution from his creditors; but this is a punishment that nobody has submitted to, these four and twenty years. The university of Padua is of late much more regular than it was formerly, though it is not yet safe walking the streets after sunset.

Thomas Coryate also visited the church of St Anthony and remarked on the tomb in the cloisters of Edward Courtenay, Earl of Devonshire. (This was an ancestor of the boy William Courtenay with whom William Beckford had become infatuated in 1779, the year before he set out on the first of his Grand Tours. Did he see the tomb but choose to pass over it in silence? In 1785 scandal over his association with Courtenay was to force him into exile.) Coryate visited the famous garden maintained by the city of Padua.

It belongeth especially to the Physitians, and is famoused over most places of Christendome for the soveraigne vertue of medicinable hearbes. It is round like a circle, and yeeldeth a passing fruitfull nursery of great variety of hearbes and trees. Amongst the rest I saw a certaine rare tree whereof I have often read both in Virgil and other Authours, but never saw it till then. It is called in Latin Platanus ... in English, we call it the Plane tree. It was of a goodly height. The Poets do faine that Jupiter dallied with Europa under this kinde of tree. And it was in former times so highly esteemed amongst the Romans by reason of the shadow, that they were wont sometimes to nourish the roote of it with wine poured about it. Also I saw a very prety fruit which is esteemed farre more excellent then Apricocks, or any other dainty fruit whatsoever growing in Italy. They call it Pistachi, a fruit much used in their dainty banquets.

Mrs Thrale produced one of her delightful pieces of domestic detail at Padua, set off by the heat. This also caused Thomas Coryate to comment on the prevalence of fans and umbrellas.

MRS THRALE

What an odd thing is custom! Here is weather to fry one in, yet after exercise, and in a state of the most violent perspiration, no consequences follow the use of iced beverages, except the sense of pleasure resulting from them at the moment. Should a Bath belle indulge in such luxury after dancing down forty couple at Mr Tyson's ball, we should expect to hear next day of her surfeit at least, if not of her sudden death. Lying-in ladies take the same liberty with their constitutions, and say that no harm comes of it; and, when I tell them how differently we manage in England, cry, '*Mi pare che dev' essere schiavitù grande in quel paese della benedetta libertá.*'* Fine muslin linen nicely got up is, however, say they, one of the things to be produced only in Great Britain, and much do our Italian ladies admire it,

* 'Methinks there seems to be much slavery required from those who inhabit your fine free country of England.'

though they look very charmingly with much less trouble taken. I lent one lady at some place, I remember, my maid, to show her, as she so much wished it, how the operation of clear-starching was performed; but as soon as it began, she laughed at the superfluous fatigue, as she called it, and her servants crossed themselves in every corner of the room with wonder that such niceties should be required. Well they might! for I caught a great tall fellow ironing his lady's best neck-handkerchief with the warming-pan here at Padua very quietly; and she was a woman of quality, too, and looked as lovely, when the toilette was once performed, as if much more attention had been bestowed upon it.

THOMAS CORYATE

For whereas the fanne consisteth of a painted peece of paper and a little wooden handle; the paper which is fastened into the top is on both sides most curiously adorned with excellent pictures, either of amorous things tending to dalliance, having some witty Italian verses or fine emblemes written under them; or of some notable Italian city with a briefe description thereof added thereunto. These fannes are of a meane price. For a man may buy one of the fairest of them for so much money as countervaileth our English groate. Also many of them doe carry other fine things of a far greater price, that will cost at the least a duckat, which they commonly call in the Italian tongue umbrellaes, that is, things that minister shadow unto them for shelter against the scorching heate of the Sunne. These are made of leather something answerable to the forme of a little canopy, and hooped in the inside with divers little wooden hoopes that extend the umbrella in a pretty large compasse. They are used especially by horsemen, who carry them in their hands when they ride, fastening the end of the handle upon one of their thighes, and they impart so long a shadow unto them, that it keepeth the heate of the sunne from the upper parts of their bodies.

Venice's lack of any Classical remains meant that the educational side of the Grand Tour could be played down for a while and the young milordi were able to enjoy the varied diet of pleasure that the Serenissima was so well equipped and well used to supply. Lady Mary Wortley Montagu pointed out that the cost was very reasonable too: 'As to all the conveniences of life, they are to be had at very easy rates; and for those that love public places, here are two play-houses and two operas constantly performed every night, at exceeding low prices ... It is the fashion for the greatest ladies to walk the streets [still in the 1990s the best way to get around] which are admirably paved; and a mask, price sixpence, with a little cloak and the head of a domino, the genteel dress to carry you everywhere. The greatest equipage

Conversation in the Piazza, by Domenico Tiepolo

is a gondola, that holds eight persons and is the price of an English chair. And it is so much the established fashion for everybody to live their own way that nothing is more ridiculous than censuring the acts of others.' The inhabitants' maturity of outlook was also noted by Mrs Thrale: 'By force of mind and dint of elegance inherent in it [a Venetian] pleases himself first, and finds everybody else delighted of course, nor would quit his own country except for paradise; while an English nobleman clumps his trees and twists his river to comply with his neighbour's taste, when perhaps he had none of his own, feels disgusted with all he has done, and runs away to live in Italy.'

There were dissenting voices; perhaps a place so essentially Romantic rather than Classical was bound to offend Gibbon: 'Old and in general ill built houses, ruined pictures, and stinking ditches dignified with the pompous denomination of Canals; a fine bridge spoilt by two rows of houses upon it, and a large square decorated with the worst architecture I ever yet saw ...' Arthur Young also took exception to an incident at the opera: 'A well-dressed man ... stepped into [the gap between pit and orchestra] and made water with as much indifference as if he had been in the street; and nobody regarded him with any degree of wonder but myself.' But most were determined to enjoy themselves, like William Beckford relishing the all-women orchestra at one of the 'female hospitals': 'Nothing is more common than to see a delicate white hand journeying across an enormous double bass, or a pair of roseate cheeks puffing, with all their efforts, at a French horn. Some that are grown old and Amazonian, who have abandoned their fiddles and their lovers, take vigorously to the kettle drum; and one poor limping lady, who had been crossed in love, now makes an admirable figure on the bassoon.' Boswell may have claimed that he 'was soon wearied of travelling continually by water, shut up in those

A view of Dolo on the Brenta Canal, by Canaletto: the normal route taken by those coming to Venice from Padua

lugubrious gondolas', but Mrs Thrale sensibly took delight in the gondoliers singing Tasso and Ariosto under her window.

Fynes Moryson describes the normal route into Venice and then Coryate gives an 'epitome' of the city.

FYNES MORYSON

Taking boat at the East gate of Paduoa, the same was drawne by horses along the River Brenta; and having shot two or three small bridges, and passed twenty miles, we came to the Village Lizzafusina, where there is a damme to stop the waters of Brenta, lest in processe of time, the passage being open, the Marshes on that side of Venice should be filled with sand or earth, and so a passage made on firme ground to the City; which they are carefull to prevent, and not without just cause, having found safety in their Iles, when Italy was often often overflowed by barbarous people. Besides, they say that this damme was made, lest this fresh-water should bee mingled with their salt waters; since all the Gentlemen of Venice fetch their fresh water by boats from thence, the poorer sort being content with Well water ... We might have had coaches, but since a boat passeth daily too and fro betweene these Cities, most men use this passage as most convenient. For the boat is covered with arched hatches, and there is very pleasant company, so a man beware to give no offence: for otherwise the Lumbards carry shirts of Male, and being armed as if they were in a Camp, are apt to revenge upon shameful advantages. But commonly there is pleasant discourse, and the proverb saith, that the boat shall bee drowned, when it carries neither Monke, nor Student, nor Curtesan (they love them too well to call them whores,) the passengers being for the most part of these kindes.

THOMAS CORYATE

There are reported to be in Venice and the circumjacent islands two hundred Churches in which are one hundred forty three paire of Organs, fifty foure Monasteries, twenty sixe Nunneries, fifty sixe Tribunals or places of judgement, seventeene Hospitals, sixe Companies or Fraternities, whereof I have before spoken; one hundred sixty five marble statues of worthy personages, partly equestriall, partly pedestriall, which are erected in sundry places of the citie, to the honour of those that eyther at home have prudently administred the Commonweale, or abroad valiantly fought for the same. Likewise of brasse there are twenty three, whereof one is that of Bartholomew Coleon.* Also there are twentie seven publique clocks, ten brasen gates, a hundred and fourteen Towers for bels to hang in, ten brasen horses, one hundred fifty five wells for the common use of the citizens, one hundred eighty five most delectable gardens, ten thousand Gondolaes, foure hundred and fifty bridges partly stony, partly timber, one hundred and twenty Palaces, whereof one hundred are very worthy of that name, one hundred seventy foure courts: and the totall number of soules living in the citie and about the same is thought to be about five hundred thousand, something more or lesse.

Evelyn describes a principal street leading to St Mark's (and, like so many modern visitors, comments on the silence); Beckford visits the Doge's Palace at his favourite twilight hour; Mrs Thrale enthuses over the Piazza by night, but has to qualify her remarks by daylight; Samuel Sharp agrees with her qualifications.

JOHN EVELYN

Hence I pass'd thro' the Merceria, which is one of the most delicious streetes in the world for the sweetnesse of it, and is all the way on both sides tapistred as it were with cloth of gold, rich damasks and other silks, which the shops expose and hang before their houses from the first floore,

* The famous equestrian statue in the Campo di SS Giovanni e Paolo, by Verrocchio and Leopardi.

The interior of San Marco, by Canaletto, drawn by him in 1766 'without spectacles', as he labelled it, two years before his death

and with that variety that for neere halfe the yeare spent chiefly in this Citty I hardly remember to have seene the same piece twice expos'd; to this add the perfumes, apothecaries shops, and the innumerable cages of nightingales which they keepe, that entertaine you with their melody from shop to shop, so that shutting your eyes you would imagine yourselfe in the country, when indeede you are in the middle of the Sea. It is almost as silent as the middle of a field, there being neither rattling of coaches nor trampling of horses. This streete, pav'd with brick and exceedingly cleane, brought us thro' an arch into the famous Piazza of St Marc ... And so we entred into St Marc's Church, before which stand two brasse piedestals exquisitely cast and figur'd which beare as many tall masts painted red, on which upon greate festivals they hang flags and streamers. The Church is also Gotic; yet for the preciousnese of the materials being of severall rich marbles, aboundance of porphyrie, serpentine, etc. far exceeding any in Rome, St Peter's hardly excepted. I much admired the splendid historie of our B. Saviour compos'd all of Mosaic over the faciata, below which and over the cheife gate are four horses cast in coper as big as the life, the same that formerly were transported from Rome by Constantine to Byzantium, and thence by the Venetians hither. They are supported by 8 porphyrie columns of very great size and value. Being come into the Church, you see nothing, and tread on nothing, but what is precious. The floore is all inlayed with achats, lazuli's, calcedons, jaspers, porphyries and other rich marbles, admirable also for the work; the walls sumptuously incrusted and presenting to the imagination the shapes of men, birds, houses, flowers, and a thousand varieties. The roofe is of most excellent Mosaic ... In the midst of this rich volto rise five cupolas, the middle very large and sustayn'd by 36 marble columns, eight of which are of precious marbles: under these cupolas is the high altar, on which is a reliquarie of severall sorts of jewells, engraven with figures after the Greeke maner, and set together with plates of pure gold. The altar is cover'd with a canopy of ophit, on which is sculptur'd the storie of the Bible, and so on the pillars, which are of Parian marble, that support it. Behind these are four other columns of transparent and true Oriental alabaster, brought hither out of the mines of Solomon's Temple as they report ...

After all that is said, this Church is in my opinion much too dark and dismal, and of heavy work; the fabric, as is much of Venice both for buildings and other fashions and circumstances, after the Greekes, their next neigh-boures.

WILLIAM BECKFORD

The colossal statues of Mars and Neptune guard the entrance, and have given the appellation of *scala dei giganti* to the steps below, which I mounted not without respect; and, leaning against the balustrades, formed like the rest of the building of the rarest marbles, contemplated the tutelary divinities. My devotions were shortly interrupted by one of the sbirri, or officers of police, who take their stands after sunset before the avenues of the palace, and who told me the gates were upon the point of being closed. So, hurrying down the steps, I left half my vows unpaid and a million of delicate sculptures unexplored; for every pilaster, every frieze, every entablature, is encrusted with porphyry, verde antique, or some other curious marble, carved into as many grotesque wreaths of foliage as we admire in the loggios of Raffaello. The various portals, the strange projections, the length of cloisters; in short, the noble irregularity of these stately piles, delighted mc beyond idea; and I was sorry to be forced to abandon them so soon, especially as the twilight, which bats and owls love not better than I do, enlarged every portico, lengthened every colonnade, and increased the dimensions of the whole, just as imagination dictated. This faculty would have had full scope had I but remained an hour longer. The moon would then have gleamed upon the gigantic forms of Mars and Neptune, and discovered the statues of ancient heroes emerging from the gloom of their niches. Such an interesting assemblage of objects, such regal

The Piazza San Marco, by Canaletto: 'adorned with every excellence of human art and pregnant with pleasure', as Mrs Thrale put it

scenery, with the reflection that many of their ornaments once contributed to the decoration of Athens, transported me beyond myself. The sbirri thought me distracted. True enough, I was stalking proudly about like an actor in an ancient Grecian tragedy, lifting up his hands to the consecrated fánes and images around, expecting the reply of his attendant Chorus, and declaiming the first verses of *Œdipus Tyrannus*.

MRS THRALE

St Mark's Place, lighted up of an evening, adorned with every excellence of human art and pregnant with pleasure, expressed by intelligent countenances sparkling with every grace of nature, the sea washing its walls, the moonbeams dancing on its subjugated waves, sport and laughter resounding from the coffee-houses, girls with guitars skipping about the square, masks and merry-makers singing as they pass you, unless a barge with a band of music is heard at some distance upon the water, and calls attention to sounds made sweeter by the element over which they are brought ...

It is sure there are in this town many astonishing privations of all that are used to make other places delightful ... One has heard of a horse being exhibited for a show there, and yesterday I watched the poor people paying a penny a-piece for the sight of a stuffed one, and am more than persuaded of the truth of what I am told here – that numberless inhabitants live and die in this great capital, nor ever find out or think of inquiring how the milk brought from *terra firma* [the mainland] is originally produced ...

Venetians are something less than cleanly. St Mark's Place is all covered over in a morning with chicken-coops, which stink one to death, as nobody, I believe, thinks of changing their baskets; and all about the ducal palace is made so very offensive by the resort of human creatures for every purpose most unworthy of so charming a place, that all enjoyment of its beauties is rendered difficult to a person of any delicacy.

SAMUEL SHARP
The common people flatter themselves they are the freest state in Europe; and the nasty fellows esteem it a proof they are so, that they can let down their breeches whereever, and before whomsoever they please; accordingly all St Mark's Place, and many parts of that sumptuous marble building, the Doge's palace, are dedicated to *Cloacina*, and you may see the votaries at their devotions every hour of the day, as much whilst the Nobles are going in, and coming out, as at any other time.

Beckford goes on a tour of the Salute, San Giorgio Maggiore and the Redentore churches, before a picnic lunch on the island of the Certosa, the Carthusian monastery. Evelyn visits the Arsenal.

WILLIAM BECKFORD
The sun began to colour the balustrades of the palaces, and the pure exhilarating air of the morning drawing me abroad, I procured a gondola, laid in my provision of bread and grapes, and was rowed under the Rialto, down the grand canal to the marble steps of St Maria della Salute, erected by the Senate in performance of a vow to the Holy Virgin, who begged off a terrible pestilence in 1630. I gazed, delighted with its superb frontispiece and dome, relieved by a clear blue sky ... The great bronze portal opened whilst I was standing on the steps which lead to it, and discovered the interior of the dome, where I expatiated in solitude; no mortal appearing except an old priest who trimmed the lamps and muttered a prayer before the high altar, still wrapt in shadows. The sun-beams began to strike against the windows of the cupola, just as I left the church and was wafted across the waves to the spacious platform in front of St Giorgio Maggiore, by far the most perfect and beautiful edifice my eyes ever beheld. When my first transport was a little subsided, and I had examined the graceful design of each particular ornament, and united the just proportion and grand effect

of the whole in my mind, I planted my umbrella on the margin of the sea, and, reclining under its shade, viewed the vast range of palaces, of porticos, of towers, opening on every side and extending out of sight ... Whilst I remained thus calm and tranquil, I heard the distant buzz of the town. Fortunately some length of waves rolled between me and its tumults; so that I ate my grapes, and read Metastasio,* undisturbed by officiousness or curiosity. When the sun became too powerful, I entered the nef, and applauded the genius of Palladio ...

Gaining my gondola, I arrived, I know not how, at the flights of steps which lead to the Redentore, a structure so simple and elegant, that I thought myself entering an antique temple, and looked about for the statue of the God of Delphi, or some other graceful divinity. A huge crucifix of bronze soon brought me to times present. The charm being thus dissolved, I began to perceive the shapes of rueful martyrs peeping out of the niches around, and the bushy beards of Capuchin friars wagging before the altars. These good fathers had decorated their church according to custom, with orange and citron trees, placed between the pilasters of the arcades; and on grand festivals, it seems, they turn the whole church into a bower, strew the pavement with leaves, and festoon the dome with flowers. I left them occupied with their plants and their devotions.

It was mid-day, and I begged to be rowed to some woody island, where I might dine in shade and tranquillity. My gondoliers shot off in an instant; but, though they went at a very rapid rate, I wished to fly faster, and getting into a bark with six oars, swept along the waters, soon left the Zecca and San Marco behind; and, launching into the plains of shining sea, saw turret after turret, and isle after isle, fleeting before me. A pale greenish light ran along the shores of the distant continent, whose mountains seemed to catch the motion of my boat, and to fly with equal celerity. I had not much time to contemplate the beautiful effects on the waters – the emerald and purple hues which gleamed along their surface. Our prow struck, foaming, against the walls of the Carthusian garden, before I recollected where I was, or could look attentively around me. Permission being obtained, I entered this cool retirement, and putting aside with my hands the boughs of figs and pomegranates, got under an ancient bay-tree on the summit of a little knoll, near which several tall pines lift themselves up to the breezes. I listened to the conversation they held, with a wind just flown from Greece, and charged, as well as I could understand this airy language, with many

* Italian poet and librettist who died in 1782. The libretto of Mozart's *La Clemenza di Tito* is based on one of his plays.

The view from San Giorgio Maggiore, by Canaletto. This is exactly the scene surveyed by Beckford

affectionate remembrances from their relations on Mount Ida. I reposed amidst bay-leaves, fanned by a constant air, till it pleased the fathers to send me some provisions, with a basket of fruit and wine. Two of them would wait upon me, and ask ten thousand questions about Lord George Gordon,* and the American war. I, who was deeply engaged with the winds, and fancied myself hearing these rapid travellers relate their adventures, wished my interrogators in purgatory, and pleaded ignorance of the Italian language. This circumstance extricated me from my difficulties, and procured me a long interval of repose.

JOHN EVELYN

We entred by a strong port always guarded, and ascending a spacious gallery saw armes of back, breast, and head, for many thousands; in another were saddles, over them ensignes taken from the Turks. Another Hall is for the meeting of the Senat; passing a graff [moat] are the smiths forges, where they are continualy at work on ankers and iron work. Neere it is a well of fresh water, which they impute to two rhinoceros's horns which they say lie in it and will preserve it from ever being empoison'd. Then we came to where the carpenters were building their magazines of oares, masts, etc.

---

* The London riots fomented by him took place in 1780.

for an hundred gallys and ships, which have all their aparell and furniture neere them. Then the founderie, where they cast ordinance; the forge is 450 paces long, and one of them has thirteen furnaces. There is one cannon weighing 16,573 lbs. cast whilst Henry III [of France] dined, and put into a gally built, rigg'd, and fitted for launching within that time. They have also armes for 12 galeasses, which are vessels to rowe, of almost 150 foote long and 30 wide, not counting prow or poop, and contain 28 banks of oares, each 7 men, and to carry 1300 men, with 3 masts. In another a magazin for 50 gallys, and place for some hundreds more. Here stands the Bucentaur, with a most ample deck, and so contriv'd that the slaves are not seene, having on the poop a throne for the Doge to sit, when he gos in triumph to espouse the Adriatic. Here is also a gallery of 200 yards long for cables, and over that a magazine of hemp.

Addison scoffs at the plots and libretti of Venetian operas and is patronising about the Commedia dell'Arte. (It is interesting to compare his view of Italian jealousy with Lady Mary Wortley Montagu's a little later in the century, on pp. 77 and 78.) Edward Wright, in the early 1720s, fills in more operatic detail and then describes those peculiar Venetian institutions, the musical 'female hospitals'.

JOSEPH ADDISON

Operas are another great entertainment of this season [Carnival]. The poetry of them is generally as exquisitely ill, as the music is good. The arguments are often taken from some celebrated action of the ancient Greeks or Romans, which sometimes looks ridiculous enough; for who can endure to hear one of the rough old Romans squeaking through the mouth of an eunuch, especially when they may choose a subject out of courts where eunuchs are really actors, or represent by them any of the soft Asiatic monarchs? The opera that was most in vogue during my stay at Venice, was built on the following subject. Cæsar and Scipio are rivals for Cato's daughter. Cæsar's first words bid his soldiers fly, for the enemies are upon them. '*Si leva Cesare, e dice a Soldati. A la fugga. A' lo Scampo.*' The daughter gives the preference to Cæsar, which is made the occasion of Cato's death. Before he kills himself, you see him withdrawn into his library, where, among his books, I observed the titles of Plutarch and Tasso. After a short soliloquy he strikes himself with the dagger that he holds in his hand, but being interrupted by one of his friends, he stabs him for his pains, and by the violence of the blow unluckily breaks the dagger on one of his ribs, so that he is forced to despatch himself by tearing up his first wound. This last circumstance puts me in mind of a contrivance in the opera of St

Commedia dell'Arte players,
by Goya

Angelo, that was acted at the same time. The king of the play endeavours
at a rape, but the poet being resolved to save his heroine's honour, has so
ordered it, that the king always acts with a great case-knife stuck in his
girdle, which the lady snatches from him in the struggle, and so defends
herself ...

The comedies that I saw at Venice, or indeed in any other part of Italy,
are very indifferent, and more lewd than those of other countries. Their
poets have no notion of genteel comedy, and fall into the most filthy double-
meanings imaginable, when they have a mind to make their audience merry.
There is no part generally so wretched as that of the fine gentleman,
especially when he converses with his mistress; for then the whole dialogue
is an insipid mixture of pedantry and romance. But 'tis no wonder that the
poets of so jealous and reserved a nation fail in such conversations on the
stage, as they have no patterns of in nature. There are four standing
characters which enter into every piece that comes on the stage, the Doctor,
Harlequin, Pantaloon, and Coviello [Scaramouche]. The Doctor's character
comprehends the whole extent of a pedant, that, with a deep voice, and a
magisterial air, breaks in upon conversation, and drives down all before
him: everything he says is backed with quotations out of Galen, Hip-
pocrates, Plato, Virgil, or any author that rises uppermost, and all answers
from his companion are looked upon as impertinencies or interruptions.
Harlequin's part is made up of blunders and absurdities; he is to mistake
one name for another, to forget his errands, to stumble over queens [cats?],

A gala concert in Venice, by Francesco Guardi. This shows a female orchestra such as delighted Beckford on p. 99

and to run his head against every post that stands in his way. This is all attended with something so comical in the voice and gestures, that a man, who is sensible of the folly of the part, can hardly forbear being pleased with it. Pantaloon is generally an old cully [dupe], and Coviello a sharper ...

Since I am on this subject, I cannot forbear mentioning a custom at Venice, which they tell me is particular to the common people of this country, of singing stanzas out of Tasso. They are set to a pretty solemn tune, and when one begins in any part of the poet, it is odds but he will be answered by somebody else that overhears him; so that sometimes you have ten or a dozen in the neighbourhood of one another, taking verse after verse, and running on with the poem as far as their memories will carry them.

EDWARD WRIGHT
They have a scandalous custom there, of spitting out of the upper boxes (as well as throwing parings of apples or oranges, etc. upon the company in the pit, a practice frequent enough here,) which they do at random, without any regard where it falls ... Those that make use of books to go along with the performance, have commonly wax-candles in their hands; which are frequently put out by favours from above.

'Tis very usual there to see priests playing in the Orchestra: the famous Vivaldi (whom they call the *Prete rosso*) very well known among us by his concertos, was a topping man among them.*

They are very dextrous at managing machinery of their operas. In one of them Nero presents Tiridates king of Armenia with a Roman show, of which himself makes a part. The emperor with the empress appear in a triumphal chariot, drawn by an elephant. The head, trunk and eyes of the great beast move as if alive, and Tiridates believes he is so. When, all of a sudden, as soon as the emperor and empress are dismounting and have taken their seats, the triumphal chariot is transform'd into an amphitheatre, and fill'd with spectators. The elephant falls all in pieces, and out of his belly come a great number of Gladiators, arm'd with bucklers, which were so many parts of the elephant's sides, so that he seems in a moment to be transform'd into a company of arm'd men, who make a skirmish, all in time to the musick.

There are in Venice four of these female hospitals; the Incurabile, the Pietà, Ospitalletto, and the Mendicanti. Infants are receiv'd into these hospitals; into the Incurabile (originally destin'd to another use) not without a sum given with them; into the Pietà, and the other two, as I take it, without any.

Those who would choose for a wife one that has not been acquainted with the world, go to these places to look for 'em; and they generally take all the care they can, they shall be as little acquainted with the world afterwards. Those put into the Pietà are generally bastards. There are a prodigious number of children taken care of in this hospital: they say they amount sometimes to at least six thousand; and that before the erection of this charity, multitudes us'd to be found which had been thrown into the canals of the city. Every Sunday and holiday there is a performance of musick in the chapels of these hospitals, vocal and instrumental, perform'd by the young women of the place; who are set in a gallery above, and (tho not profess'd) are hid from any distinct view of those below by a lattice of iron-work. The organ-parts, as well as those of the other instruments, are all perform'd by the young women. They have an eunuch for their master, and he composes their musick. Their performance is surprisingly good; and many excellent voices there are among them; and there is somewhat still more amusing, in that their persons are conceal'd from view.

* He held a post at the Ospedale della Pietà.

The Ridotto, by Giovanni Antonio Guardi, where all Venice could gamble, as long as they wore masks

Edward Wright draws a vivid sketch of the Carnival – its dress, gambling at the Ridotto, visiting astrologers, bull-baitings and bull-executions, rope-dancing, human pyramids, mass fisticuffs staged on bridges.

Those times of masking are the dear delight of the Venetians; and the approach of the Carnaval seems to be to them, as the approach of the sun to the Polar Nations after their half year's night. The most common masking dress is a cloak, a Baout, and a white mask: this dress with a hat over all is the general one for both sexes, women as well as men. The Baout is a sort of hood of black silk, which comes round the head, leaving only an opening for the face, with a border of black silk lace which falls about the shoulders. The white mask comes no lower than the bottom of the nose, the Baout covers the rest. Sometimes they have a whole mask painted with the natural colours; in the mouth-part of which the women place a stone-ring, to hold their mask on with, the stone glittering on the outside, as it were to accompany the sparkling of their eyes. As the Carnaval advances, the dress grows more various and whimsical: the women make themselves nymphs and shepherdesses, the men scaramouches and punchinellos, with twenty other fancies, whatever first comes uppermost. For further variety, they sometimes change sexes; women appear in men's habits, and men in women's, and so are now and then pick'd up, to the great disappointment of the lover. In these various disguises they go, not only into assemblies within doors, but publickly all the city over: and during the Carnaval 'tis so much the dress of the season, that whether upon visits, or any other occasion, they go continually in masque.

Their general rendezvous is the Piazza di S. Marco, which, large as it is, is perfectly thronged with them; from thence they march in shoals to the Ridotto, which is not far off. Here none is to enter that shews a human face, except their Excellencies, who keep the bank at the basset-tables [gambling tables]. In other places people *may* mask, but here they *must*: what is a privilege only in other places, is here turned to an obligation; perhaps for the better maintaining that appearance of *equality* which is requisite to the profess'd liberty of the place; That is a reason I have heard given for it: And thus a tinker, by virtue of his masque, may come to a basset-table, and set a ducat with one of the princes of the people. Nothing sure can affect the Stoick more than a nobleman behind one of these basset-tables: they would seem unmoved by their good or bad fortune: but I have sometimes seen the apathy fail a little, and the contrary discover it self in some involuntary contraction of the muscles. All is transacted with a great deal of silence: and I have seen large sums won and lost without a word speaking. Generally he that keeps the bank is the winner; and it may be reasonably concluded, without enquiry into the chances of the game, that the odds lie on the banker's side; since the noblemen secure that privilege to themselves: Tho' 'tis possible for another to keep a bank by proxy, for there are noblemen that will do it for you for ten per cent. of the winnings. The Ridotto makes a pretty odd appearance at first sight. There are seven or eight rooms which I remember, and I believe there are more. The place is dark and silent, a few glimmering tapers with a half light shew a set of beings, stalking along with their pale faces, which look like so many death's heads poking out through black pouches; so that one would almost imagine himself in some enchanted place, or some region of the dead. But there are those to be found there who, if you have a mind, will soon clear your doubts, and let you know they are true flesh and blood. Play and intrigue are the two affairs of the place: he that has more money than he cares for, needs only step aside to a basset-table, where the nobleman who keeps the bank will soon ease him of his superfluous load. Others, who are for forming or carrying on intrigues may without much difficulty find what they seek, and somewhat more perhaps than what they wish. Without doors, puppet-shews, rope-dancers, mountebanks and astrologers are busy at work all the day long. These last dispense destinies thro' a tin trumpet plac'd at the ear of the inquisitive patient; who stands trembling below on the ground, while

A Venetian fortune teller, by Longhi. The tin trumpet, through which they 'dispense destinies', can be seen on the chair

'The Carnival Dance', by Domenico Tiepolo. This fantasy scene provides a magical display of Venetian carnival costumes

the other is exalted on a little sort of stage, and thence in an inclined posture with his mouth at the other end of the trumpet pronounces what *shall or shall not be*.

On *Jovedi Grasso* (the Thursday immediately preceding Lent) all Venice is perfectly in an uproar; the public frenzy, which from the beginning of the Carnaval has had a sort of gradual increase, seems now to be at its utmost height. Now we see a thousand odd disguises, such as each one's caprice suggests; with diversions as boisterous and noisy without doors, as before we had seen quiet and silent within. Young fellows driving bulls all about the town, along those narrow alleys (for most of their streets, as I observed above, are but such) hollowing in such a frantic manner as tho' they were endeavouring to make the beasts they follow as mad as themselves. 'Tis not a very safe curiosity to be in the way of them. Thus they hurry them to the *Campo's* (the more open parts of the city) where they bait them after as extravagant a manner; not tying them to a stake, but dragging them with cords; and sometimes dragg'd by them, as the fury of the beast adds to his strength, while three or four great dogs are set all at once upon them, to catch at their ears, or any part, 'tis all one.

The grand shews are in the Piazzetta, just before the Doge's palace; one of them looks more like an execution than a diversion; or 'tis (if you please)

a pompous piece of butchery. A decollation of three bulls, which are led there in great state, surrounded with the Bombardieri, halberdiers, and a world of other armed attendants; drums beating, and trumpets sounding before them. Those that perform the feat have a great sword of three or four inches broad; some assistants hold the head, and others the tail of the animal; which besides keeping him steady (for there is no block under) puts the parts of the neck to a full stretch, and with one blow the executioner separates the head from the body ...

Another entertainment is what they call the *vola*, or flying. A boy slides down a rope, in a flying posture from the Campanile of S. Mark with a nosegay in his hand, to a window of the Doge's palace, into which he enters, presents the nosegay to his serenity, and up again he mounts like a Ganymede, by the help of a cord, by which he is drawn up the same rope he came down by. Another *vola* they have upwards on the back of a Pegasus, shooting off pistols in the midst of their flight.

But what to me was the most agreeable spectacle, was the Force of Hercules, so call'd, but not very properly; for 'tis a performance rather of flight than strength: I mean the exercise of the young fellows, who build themselves up into a kind of pyramid ... This, when I saw it, was done before the Doge's palace; but 'tis sometimes perform'd in a boat on the

A Festival on the Piazzetta, by Canaletto, showing the ropes for the *vola* and the human pyramid

great canal. On the Sunday following, the Doge's palace was become a perfect amphitheatre for the *Caccia del Tauro*, in plain English a bull-baiting. The poor animal is turned loose into the court of the palace, and an unmerciful number of dogs at once set upon him; you see dogs, bulls, and Barkerolls [gondoliers], all in a heap together, within his Serenity's court; but this is to be taken as another instance of the Venetian liberty, where the meanest of the people may make thus free with their prince ...

And now the fatal day drew near, when the masque, and all its attendant diversions were to be laid aside; for, to the *Piazza di S. Marco* now they come, not to see bull-baiting and rope-dancing, but to be sprinkled by the priest with ashes. *Un gran Passagio*! A great change! as a nobleman of Bologna expressed himself to me upon the occasion. This puts me in mind of a remark I have somewhere read or heard, said to be made by some remote Indian, who was at Venice, during the time of the Carnaval; that the people of Venice, about the beginning of the new year, are seized with a sort of phrenzy or madness: which goes on still increasing, till a certain day, on which a grave person, by sprinkling a sort of powder on their head, brings 'em all to their senses again.

Another entertainment they have, a pretty robust one, which is not annual, nor confin'd to the Carnaval, but exhibited upon some extraordinary occasions, as when a sovereign prince, or great embassador is there; it is the *Guerra de' Pugne*, a pitch'd battle at fisty-cuffs between the Castellani and Nicoloti (inhabitants of the districts – *Sestieri* they call them – di Castello and S. Nicholas). Their Campus Martius is some bridge, generally that of the Carmine, or S. Barnabas: from whence, as there are no battlements, they oft plunge one another into the canal, where ladders are plac'd for them to get out again, and rally. They us'd cudgels heretofore, but that proving often fatal, they were since confin'd to the fist.

Coryate, in spite of his protestations to the contrary, does a marvellous job of advertising for the Venetian prostitutes. But one can rely on Boswell to bring the subject back to earth. His companion, Lord Mountstuart, was the son of Lord Bute and therefore the grandson of Lady Mary Wortley Montagu.

THOMAS CORYATE

It is thought there are of them in the whole City and other adjacent places, as Murano, Malomocco, etc. at the least twenty thousand, whereof many are esteemed so loose, that they are said to open their quivers to every arrow ... [The Venetians] doe graunt large dispensation and indulgence unto them ... For they thinke that the chastity of their wives would be the sooner assaulted, and so consequently they should be capricornified [cuckolded], (which of all the indignities in the world the Venetian cannot patiently endure) were it not for these places of evacuation. But I marvaile how that should be true though these Cortezans were utterly rooted out of

A Venetian courtesan, from *Coryat's Crudities*, 1611: 'the fame of them hath drawn many to Venice'

the City. For the Gentlemen do even coope up their wives alwaies within the walles of their houses for feare of these inconveniences, as much as if there were no Cortezans at all in the City. So that you shall very seldome see a Venetian Gentleman's wife but either at the solemnization of a great marriage, or at the Christening of a Jew, or late in the evening rowing in a Gondola. The second cause is for that the revenues which they pay unto the Senate for their tolleration, doe maintaine a dozen of their galleys, (as many reported unto me in Venice) and so save them a great charge . . .

Their fairest roomes are most glorious and glittering to behold. The walles round about being adorned with most sumptuous tapistry and gilt leather besides you may see the picture of the noble Cortezan most exquisitely drawen. As for her selfe . . . her face is adorned with the quintessence of beauty. In her cheekes thou shalt see the Lilly and the Rose strive for the supremacy, and the silver tramels of her haire displayed in that curious manner besides, her two frisled peakes standing up like prety Pyramides, that they give thee the true *Cos amoris* [the kiss (?) or whetstone (?) of love]. But . . . few of the Cortezans are so much beholding to nature, but that they adulterate their faces, and supply her defect . . . Also the ornaments of her body are so rich, that except thou dost even geld thy affections (a thing hardly to be done) or carry with thee Ulysses hearbe called Moly which is mentioned by Homer, that is, some antidote against those Venereous titillations, shee wil very neare benumme and captivate thy senses . . .

Moreover shee will endevour to enchaunt thee partly with her melodious notes that she warbles out upon her lute, which shee fingers with as laudable a stroake as many men that are excellent professors in the noble science of Musicke; and partly with that heart-tempting harmony of her voice. Also thou wilt finde the Venetian Cortezan (if she be a selected woman indeede) a good Rhetorician, and a most elegant discourser, so that if she cannot move thee with all these foresaid delights, shee will assay thy constancy with her Rhetoricall tongue. And to the end shee may minister unto thee the stronger temptations to come to her lure, shee will shew thee her chamber of recreation, where thou shalt see all manner of pleasing objects, as many faire painted coffers wherewith it is garnished round about, a curious milke-white canopy of needle worke, a silke quilt embrodered with gold: and generally all her bedding sweetly perfumed . . . Moreover I will tell thee this newes which is most true, that if thou shouldest wantonly converse with her, and not give her that *salarium iniquitatis*, which thou hast promised her, but perhaps cunningly escape from her company, shee will either cause thy throate to be cut by her Ruffiano, if he can after catch thee in the City, or procure thee to be arrested (if thou art to be found) and

The Mountebank's platform, a detail from a painting by Carlevaris. 'Oyles, soveraigne waters, amourous songs printed, Apothecary drugs' were sold to the crowds

clapped up in the prison, where thou shalt remaine till thou hast paid her all thou didst promise her.

JAMES BOSWELL

When I got to Venice I had still some small remains of disease, but strange, gay ideas which I had formed of the Venetian courtesans turned my head, and away I went to an opera dancer and took Lord Mountstuart with me. We both had her; and we both found ourselves taken in for the punishment which I had met with at Rome. Pretty doings! Our evil has been recompensed but moderately, but we are as much to blame as if we had suffered most sadly.

Coryate admires the sales techniques of the mountebanks around St Mark's, and warns of Venetian muggers.

While the musicke playes, the principall Mountebanke which is the Captaine and ring-leader of all the rest, opens his truncke, and sets abroach his wares; after the musicke hath ceased, he maketh an oration to the audience of halfe an houre long, or almost an houre. Wherein he doth most hyperbolically extoll the vertue of his drugs and confections, though many of them are very counterfeit and false. Truely I often wondred at many of these naturall Orators. For they would tell their tales with such admirable volubility and plausible grace, even extempore, and seasoned with that singular variety of elegant jests and witty conceits, that they did often strike great admiration into strangers that never heard them before: and by how much the more eloquent these Naturalists are, by so much the greater audience they draw unto them, and the more ware they sell. After the chiefest Mountebankes first speech is ended, he delivereth out his commodities by little and little, the jester still playing his part, and the musitians singing and playing upon their instruments. The principall things that they sell are oyles, soveraigne waters, amorous songs printed, Apothecary drugs, and a Commonweale of other trifles. The head Mountebanke at every time that he delivereth out any thing, maketh an extemporall speech, which he doth eftsoones intermingle with such savory jests (but spiced now and then with singular scurrility) that they minister passing mirth and laughter to the whole company, which perhaps may consist of a thousand people that flocke together about one of their stages ... After they have extolled their wares to the skies, having set the price of tenne crownes upon some one of their commodities, they have at last descended so low, that they have taken for it foure gazets, which is something lesse then a groat ...

There are certaine desperate and resolute villaines in Venice, called Braves, who at some unlawfull times do commit great villainy. They wander abroad very late in the night to and fro for their prey, like hungry Lyons, being armed with a privy coate of maile, a gauntlet upon their right hand, and a little sharpe dagger called a stiletto. They lurke commonly by the water side, and if at their time of the night, which is betwixt eleven of the clocke and two, they happen to meete any man that is worth the rifling, they will presently stabbe him, take away all about him that is of any worth, and when they have throughly pulled his plumes, they will throw him into one of the channels: but they buy this booty very deare if they are after apprehended. For they are presently executed.

Lady Mary Wortley Montagu gives her husband an account of the regatta put on during the visit of the Electoral Prince of Saxony in May 1740. The Saxon royal house were also kings of Poland during the first half of the century.

It is a race of Boats; they are accompany'd by vessells which they call Piotes and Bichones, that are built at the Expence of the nobles and strangers that have a mind to display their magnificence. They are a sort of Machines, adorn'd with all that sculpture and gilding can do to make a shineing appearance. Several of them cost £1,000 sterling and I believe none less than 500. They are row'd by Gondoliers dress'd in rich Habits suitable to

A detail from a painting by Canaletto showing the sort of regatta craft described by Lady Mary Wortley Montagu

what they represent. There was enough of them to look like a little Fleet, and I own I never saw a finer sight. It would be too long to describe every one in particular; I shall only name the principal. The Signora Pisani Mocenigo's represented the chariot of the night, drawn by 4 sea Horses, and showing the rising of the moon accompany'd with stars, the statues on each side representing the hours to the number of 24, row'd by Gondoliers in rich Liveries, which were chang'd 3 times, all of equal richness; and the decorations chang'd also to the dawn of Aurora and the midday Sun, the statues being new dress'd every time, the first in green, the 2nd time red, and the last blue, all equally lac'd with silver, there being 3 Races. Signor Soranzo represented the Kingdom of Poland with all the provinces and Rivers in that Dominions, with a consort of the best instrumental music in rich Polish Habits; the painting and gilding were exquisite in their kinds. Signor [Simoni] Contarini's Piote shew'd the Liberal Arts; Apollo was seated on the stern upon Mount Parnasso, Pegasus behind, and the muses seated round him. Opposite was a figure representing painting, with Fame blowing her Trumpet, and on each side Sculpture and music in their proper dresses. The Procurator Foscarini's was the chariot of Flora, guided by Cupids and adorn'd with all sorts of Flowers, rose trees, etc. [Lady Mary catalogued another eight allegorical Piotes.]

I believe you are allready weary of this description, which can give you but a very imperfect Idea of the show, but I must say one word of the

Bichones, which are less vessels, quite open, some representing Gardens, others apartments, all the oars being gilt either with Gold or Silver, and the Gondoliers' Liverys either velvet or rich silk with a profusion of Lace fringe and Embrodiery.

Edward Wright describes the sombre dress of the eighteenth-century nobles. Evelyn's description of the seventeenth-century ladies' costume shows a considerable change had taken place in the intervening hundred years.

EDWARD WRIGHT

The robe of the nobles is of black cloth, or bays ... 'Tis not much unlike our lawyers gown. In the winter they have one fac'd with furr, and bound with a girdle of the same about their waist. They have no hat, but a woollen cap in the shape of a deep crown of a hat; but they very rarely wear it, otherwise than under their arm: for they wear large full-bottom'd perukes ... The gayer sort of them, especially such as have travell'd, are not at all in love with their dress, but would much rather be equipt with hat and sword, as the gentlemen of other places are, if their laws would allow it; but the power that attends their dress reconciles them pretty well to it ...

The noble ladies are allow'd but little finery any more than the men: they are by their laws to go all in black too: they are to wear no jewels, except the first year after marriage: A gold chain, or some pearl about the wrist, is the chief ornament that's allow'd, and the most ordinary tradesmen's wives make shift to get somewhat of that sort. These laws are very strict, and the noble Ladies do for the most part comply with them; because there is now and then a Superintendant that puts them in execution against all persons; tho' generally the magistrates wink at the noble ladies who happen to transgress.

JOHN EVELYN

The noblemen stalking with their ladys on *choppines*; these are high-heel'd shoes, particularly affected by these proude dames, or, as some say, invented to keepe them at home, it being very difficult to walke with them; whence one being asked how he liked the Venetian dames, replied, that they were *mezzo carne, messo ligno*, half flesh, half wood, and he would have none of them. The truth is, their garb is very odd, as seeming allwayes in masquerade; their other habits also totaly different from all nations. They weare very long crisped haire, of severall strakes and colours, which they make so by a wash, dischevelling it on the brims of a broade hat that has no head, but an hole to put out their heads by; they drie them in the sunn,

Punchinello as dressmaker, one of a series of drawings
by Domenico Tiepolo of Punchinello's activities

as one may see them at their windows. In their tire they set silk flowers and
sparkling stones, their peticoates coming from their very arme-pits, so that
they are neere three quarters and an half apron; their sleeves are made
exceeding wide, under which their shift sleeves as wide, and commonly
tucked up to the shoulder, shewing their naked armes, thro' false sleeves of
tiffany, girt with a bracelet or two, with knots of points richly tagged about
their shoulders and other places of their body, which they usually cover
with a kind of yellow vaile of lawn very transparent. Thus attir'd they set
their hands on the heads of two matron-like servants or old women, to
support them, who are mumbling their beades. 'Tis ridiculous to see how
these ladys crawle in and out of their *gondolas* by reason of their *choppines*, and
what dwarfs they appear when taken downe from their wooden scaffolds; of
these I saw near thirty together, stalking half as high again as the rest of the
world, for courtezans or the citizens may not weare *choppines*.

*Addison and Edward Wright dwell on the ruthlessness and secrecy of the Venetian
State. The carefully induced idleness of the nobility pointed to by Addison is borne
out by Beckford's description of them at the great Casino, though, writing sixty
years after Wright and eighty after Addison, he is dismissive of 'Venetian subtlety
and profound silence'.*

JOSEPH ADDISON
The preservation of the republic is that to which all other considerations
submit. To encourage idleness and luxury in the nobility, to cherish ignorance and licentiousness in the clergy, to keep alive a continual faction in

the common people, to connive at the viciousness and debauchery of convents, to breed dissensions among the nobles of the *terra firma*, to treat a brave man with scorn and infamy; in short, to stick at nothing for the public interest, are represented as the refined parts of the Venetian wisdom.

EDWARD WRIGHT

The Venetians, for the dignity of their government, would represent their Doge as a King, but for the freedom of it, as a King without power; and so indeed he is; for he can't do so much of himself as an English justice of peace: all there is the act of the council: and even by the word Principe the whole aristocracy is understood. He has not the liberty of the meanest subject, for he is not to stir out of Venice without leave. He is liable any night to be surpriz'd in his own chamber; for the inquisitors of state have keys to all his apartments, and may enter them at pleasure: may rifle his cabinets, and tumble over his papers, and he the while lie trembling in his bed, and not dare to ask who's there, or what they are doing.

The inquisitors of state, lately mention'd, are three of the Council of Ten, that formidable Decemvirate, the terror of all the nobles as well as the Doge himself. Their proceedings are secret and active, their judgments rigorous, their sentence irreversible, and the execution of it speedy; so that at the very name of the council of Ten all Venice trembles, from the lowest to the highest. If the guilt of the party be clear to them, they don't stand much upon forms of trial: so that a criminal is often tried and condemn'd, without hearing a word of the process himself, or the event of it, till he is call'd to execution. And the rather, if he be a person of considerable alliance, whose public trial might be apt to make the more noise; in such case, he is perhaps strangled in the *camerotta* [dungeon], or convey'd thence in the dead of night to the canal Orphano, and there drown'd. The manner of which, I have been told, is thus: he is tied down to a plank, which has a weight affix'd sufficient to sink it, and so laid across two Gondola's; the gondola's then separate, and down he goes. This canal Orphano is the deepest part of all the Lagune, and has its name from the many orphans it has made.

WILLIAM BECKFORD

Their great casino, which looks into the piazza, consists of five or six rooms, fitted up in a gay flimsy taste, neither rich nor elegant, where were a great many lights, and a great many ladies negligently dressed, their hair falling very freely about them, and innumerable adventures written in their eyes. The gentlemen were lolling upon the sophas, or lounging about the apartments. The whole assembly seemed upon the verge of gaping, till coffee was carried round. This magic beverage diffused a temporary animation; and, for a moment of two, conversation moved on with a degree of pleasing extravagance; but the flash was soon dissipated, and nothing remained save cards and stupidity. In the intervals of shuffling and dealing, some talked over the affairs of the grand council with less reserve than I expected; and two or three of them asked some feeble questions about the late tumults in London, but mentioned not a syllable of their own commotions. As much, however, through indolence and forgetfulness, I should conjecture, as from any political motive; for I don't believe all those wise stories which some travellers have propagated, of Venetian subtlety and profound silence. They might have reigned during the dark periods of the republic; but, at this moment, the veil is rent in fifty places; and, without any wonderful penetration, the debates of the senate are discoverable ...

It was one o'clock before all the company were assembled, and I left them at three, still dreaming over their coffee and card-tables. Trieze is their favourite game: *uno, due, tre, quatro, cinque, fante, cavallo*, are eternally repeated; the apartments echoed no other sound. No lively people could endure such monotony, yet I have been told the Venetians are remarkably spirited; and so eager in the pursuit of amusement as hardly to allow themselves any sleep. Some, for instance, after declaiming in the senate, walking an hour in the square, and fidgeting about from one casino to another till morning dawns, will get into a gondola, row across the Lagunes, take the post to Mestre or Fusina, and jumble over craggy pavements to Treviso, breakfast in haste, and rattle back again as if the devil were charioteer: by eleven the party is restored to Venice, resumes robe and periwig, and goes to council. This may be very true, and yet I will never cite the Venetians as examples of vivacity. Their nerves unstrung by disease and the consequence of early debaucheries, allow no natural flow of lively spirits, and at best but a few moments of a false and feverish activity. The approaches of rest, forced back by an immoderate use of coffee, render them weak and listless to like any active amusement, and the facility of being wafted from place to place in a gondola, adds not a little to their indolence. In short, I can scarcely regard their Eastern neighbours in a more lazy light.

William Beckford, by Romney

Florence

We can say with Arthur Young, 'I take leave of the Venetian lion; I am tired of it: if the state were to build a pig-sty, I believe they would decorate it with his figure.' The only means of public transport on the first stage south from Venice to Bologna, Florence and Rome was by barge, since the roads across the Po valley were so bad. Arthur Young spares us none of the horrors:

A cabin about ten feet square, round which sat in silence, and the darkness visible of a wretched lamp, a company whose rolling eyes examined, without one word of reception, each passenger that entered. The wind howled and the rain beat in at the hole left for entering ... After a day's spitting of a dozen people, mattresses are spread on the ground, and you rest on them as you can, packed almost like herrings in a barrel; they are then rolled up and tumbled under a bulk, without the least attention which side is given you the night after; add to this the odours of various sorts, easy to imagine. At dinner, the cabin is the kitchen, and the *padrone* the cook; he takes snuff, wipes his nose with his fingers, and the knife with his handkerchief, while he prepares the victuals, which he handles before you, till you are sick of the idea of eating. But on changing the bark to one whose cabin was too small to admit any cookery, he brought his steaks and sausages rolled up in paper, and that in his flag of abomination (as Smollett calls a continental handkerchief), which he spread on his knees as he sat opening the greasy treasure for those to eat out of his lap with their fingers, whose stomachs could bear such a repast ... For myself I walked much of the journey, and especially on the banks of the Po, for the better view of that great river, now rendered immense by the late dreadful floods which have deluged so much of the country.

Bologna does not seem to have drawn out any very arresting descriptions from travellers. The Bolognese school of painters (the Carracci, Domenichino, Guido Reni, Guercino) were the most admired at the time. Apart from their work, just

127

as modern visitors do, Evelyn remarked on the outstanding food – 'This Citty is famous also for sausages; and here is sold great quantities of Parmegiano cheese, with Botargo,* caviare, etc., which makes some of their shops perfume the streetes, with no agreeable smell' – and Gray on the arcades – 'All the streets have porticoes on both sides, such as surround a part of Covent Garden, a great relief in summer-time in such a climate.'

Crossing the Apennines, Beckford indulged in another of his twilight musings. He had decided to walk part of the way up, and met a herd of goats.

Being tired with skipping and butting at me in vain, the whole herd trotted away, and I after them. They led me a dance from crag to crag and from thicket to thicket. It was growing dusky apace, and wreaths of smoke began to ascend from the mysterious depths of the valleys. I was ignorant what monster inhabited such retirements, so gave over my pursuit lest some Polypheme† or other might make me repent it. I looked around, the carriage was out of sight; but hearing the neighing of horses at a distance, I soon came up with them, and mounted another rapid ascent, from whence an extensive tract of cliff and forest land was discernible. The rocks here formed a spacious terrace, along which I continued surveying the distant groves, and marking the solemn approach of night. The sky was hung with storms, and a pale moon seemed to advance with difficulty amongst broken and tempestuous clouds. It was an hour to reap plants with brazen sickles, and to meditate upon revenge. A chill wind blew from the highest peak of the Apennines, inspiring evil, and made a dismal rustle amongst the woods of chesnut that hung on the mountains' side, through which we were forced to pass. I never heard such fatal murmurs, nor felt myself so gloomily disposed. I walked out of the sound of the carriage, where the glimmering moonlight prevailed, and began interpreting the language of the leaves, not greatly to my own advantage or that of any being in the universe. I was no prophet of good, but full of melancholy bodings, and something that bordered on despair. Had I but commanded an oracle, as ancient visionaries were wont, I should have thrown whole nations into dismay. How long I continued in this strange temper I cannot pretend to say, but believe it was midnight before we emerged from the oracular forest, and saw faintly before us the huts of Lognone, where we were to sleep. This blessed hamlet is suspended on the brow of a bleak mountain, and every gust that stirs, shakes the whole village to its foundations. At our approach two hags

---

* A relish made from mullet or tunnyfish roe.
† The giant one-eyed cyclops with a herd of goats, blinded by Odysseus.

Edward Gibbon, drawn in Florence by Thomas Patch while on his Grand Tour in 1764

stalked forth with lanterns and invited us with a grin, which I shall always remember, to a dish of mustard and crows' gizzards, a dish I was more than half afraid of tasting, lest it should change me to some bird of darkness, condemned to mope eternally on the black rafters of the cottage. After repeated supplications we procured a few eggs, and some faggots to make a fire. Its blaze gave me courage to hear the hollow blasts that whistled in the crevices; and pitching my bed in a warm corner I soon fell asleep, and forgot all my cares and inquietudes.

Samuel Sharp was particularly critical of the country inns he found on this stretch of the tour, and his mention of gizzards on the menu shows Beckford was not exaggerating much in the previous extract. Sharp also makes Mrs Thrale's affectionate description of an English inn at Florence quite understandable.

SAMUEL SHARP
No other bed than one of straw, with a matrass of straw, and next to that a dirty sheet, sprinkled with water, and, consequently, damp. The people at inns are so little apprised of an objection to damp sheets, that when you begin to beg they would hang them before the fire, they desire you will feel how wet they are, being prepossessed that you mean they have not been

washed. For a covering you have another sheet, as coarse as the first, and as coarse as one of our kitchen jack-towels, with a dirty coverlet. The bedsted consists of four wooden forms, or benches: An English Peer and Peeress must lye in this manner, unless they carry an upholsterer's shop with them, which is very troublesome. There are, by the bye, no such things as curtains, and hardly, from Venice to Rome, that cleanly and most useful invention, a privy; so that what should be collected and buried in oblivion, is for ever under your nose and eyes. Take along with you, that in all these inns the walls are bare, and the floor has never once been washed since it was first laid ... I must tell you, that they never scour their pewter, and unless you were to see it, you will not conceive how dirty and nauseous it grows in thirty or forty years ... In these inns they make you pay largely, so much a head, and send up ten times as much as you can eat. For example, this is almost constantly the fare – A soop like wash, with pieces of liver swimming in it; a plate full of brains, fried in the shape of fritters; a dish of livers and gizzards; a couple of fowls (always killed after your arrival) boiled to rags, without any the least kind of sauce, or herbage; another fowl, just killed, stewed as they call it; then two more fowls, or a turkey roasted to rags.

MRS THRALE

We arrived late at our inn – an English one they say it is – and many of the last miles were passed very pleasantly by my maid and myself in anticipating the comforts we should receive by finding ourselves among our own country folks. In good time! and by once more eating, sleeping, etc., all in the English way, as her phrase is. Accordingly, here are small, low beds again, soft and clean, and down pillows; here are currant tarts, which the Italians scorn to touch, but which we are happy and delighted to pay not ten, but twenty times their value for, because a currant tart is so much in the English way; it is impossible that bacon should be either wholesome or agreeable; and one eats infinitely worse than one did at Milan, Venice, or Bologna, and infinitely dearer, too; but that makes it still more completely in the English way ...

The sun is so violent that I use no other method of heating up the pinching irons to curl my hair than that of poking them out at a south window with the handles shut in ...

In Italy, so far at least as I have gone, there is no impertinent desire of appearing what one is not – no searching for talk, and torturing expression to vary its phrases with something new and something fine ... We are affected in the house, but natural in the gardens. Italians are natural in

A view of Florence, by Thomas Patch

society, affected and constrained in the disposition of their grounds ...

The clatter made here in the Piazza del Duomo – where you sit in your carriage at a coffee-house door and chat with your friends according to Italian custom, while one eats ice and another calls for lemonade, to while away the time after dinner – the noise made then and there, I say, is beyond endurance.

Our Florentines have nothing on earth to do; yet a dozen fellows crying '*ciambelli!*' (little cakes) about the square, assisted by beggars, who lie upon the church steps and pray, or, rather, promise to pray, as loud as their lungs will let them, for the *anime sante di purgatorio*;* ballad-singers meantime endeavouring to drown these clamours in their own, and gentlemen's servants disputing at the doors whose master shall be first served, ripping up the pedigrees of each to prove superior claims for a biscuit or macaroon – do make such an intolerable clatter among them, that one cannot for one's life hear one another speak.

Today most visitors to Florence head first for the paintings of the Quattrocento, but this was a taste that developed only in the nineteenth century. So it is curious to find a pioneer of the Early Renaissance in Thomas Patch. Sir Horace Mann, the British Envoy to Florence, described Patch's career in a letter to Horace Walpole in 1771. In the eighteenth century the high point of the ducal collection and the

* Holy souls in purgatory.

Zoffany paints Horace Mann (on the right) wearing the Order of the Bath in front of the *Venus de Medici*. Patch (in black) holds Titian's *Venus d'Urbino* next to him

target of every Tourist had become the room called the Tribuna in the Uffizi Gallery. In the 1770s the fashionable artist Johann Zoffany was sent out by George III and Queen Charlotte to paint it (see above). In 1779 Horace Mann wrote to Horace Walpole about the painting, and the gossip to which it gave rise.

About twenty years ago, Patch came a-foot to Italy, went directly to Rome and studied painting under Vernet, whose manner he imitates very well; a specimen of which I will send you in *Due Sopraporte*,* if you give me the measure, or chuse any particular view of Florence. He left Rome many years

---

* Two small rectangular landscapes to go over door frames.

Sir Andrew Fountaine and friends in the Tribune in 1715, by Guilio Pignatta. This Norfolk connoisseur leans against the *Venus Victrix*, which was not included by Zoffany in his painting

ago, on account of some indiscretion about Religion;* but nevertheless, he brought the strongest letters of recommendation hither, from the unprejudiced Prelate Piccolomini, then Governor of Rome, and since Cardinal. I took much to him, and tho' he does not live in my house, he is never out of it a whole day. He has an excellent turn for *Caricatura*, in which the young English often employ him to make Conversation-pieces of any number, for which they then draw lots; but Patch is so prudent as never to caricature any body without his consent.

A year or two ago, Patch took to engraving, of himself, without the least assistance, and by a sort of a Careless manner, is allowed by everybody here to enter into the character of the Author. He was always an adorer of the heads of Masaccio in Carmine,† and both drew them and engraved them himself; and well he did it in time, for about a fortnight ago, the Church was almost consumed by fire, and those paintings so much damaged, that I believe none remain entire ... The loss of Masaccio's paintings will in some measure be repaired by a work Patch has in hand, in which there will be the celebrated pictures of Fra Bartolomeo, at St Mark's,‡ with others of Michel Angelo, Andrea del Sarto, etc., etc., to make up the number of 24.

* In fact for homosexuality.
† In the Brancacci Chapel in Santa Maria del Carmine. They were not as damaged as Mann thought and have recently been restored.
‡ These days it is Fra Angelico's paintings that draw visitors to San Marco.

This is now in hand, and your encouraging and recommending it would be very advantageous to him.

I am glad that you have seen Zoffany and his Portrait of the Tribune. So then it is not true that he was hanged for bigamy, as was reported among the Italians, in spite of all I could say to convince them that with us, though he has two wives, it is not a hanging matter. Your opinion of his laborious performance in all the parts you mention agrees with that of our best judges here; but they found great fault with the perspective which, they say, is all wrong. I know that Zoffany was sensible of it himself, and used to get assistance to correct it; but it was found impossible, and he carried it away as it was. How, or whether, it has been done elsewhere, I know not. I told him of the impropriety of sticking so many figures in it, and pointed out to him, the Great Duke and Dutchess, one or two of their children, if he thought the variety were pictoresk, and Lord Cowper. He told me that the King had expressly ordered my portrait to be there, which I did not believe, but did not object to it; but he made the same merit with all the young travellers then at Florence, some of whom he afterwards rubbed out, such as old Felton Harvey and one of the Queen's Chaplains with a broad black ribbon across his forehead, and filled up their places elsewhere.

If what he said is true, that the Queen sent him to Florence to do that picture, and gave him a large sum for his journey, the impropriety of crowding in so many unknown figures was still greater. But is it true that it is for the Queen's Closet, and that she is to give him three thousand pounds for it? This is asserted, and it got him the name of Her Majesty's Painter; and in that quality he had leave to have any Picture in the Gallery or Palace taken down; for you must have observed that he has transported some from the latter place into *his* Tribune. I should think too the naked Venus which is the principal figure, will not please Her Majesty so much as it did the young men to whom it was shewed. As to the question you make me of my own personage, I can only say that everybody thought it like me, but I suppose Zoffany took pains to lessen my pot-belly and the clumsiness of my figure, and to make me stand in a posture which I never kept to, but then, I remember, that I was sadly tired when I was tortured by him to appear before their Majesties in my best shape and looks.

When Horace Walpole first arrives in Florence in the winter of 1739–40 he is determined to be world-weary in his letter to Richard West. By the end of February his tune has changed. Robert Adam shares his enthusiasm for the Carnival, whose riderless horse races are then described by Mrs Thrale.

Horace Walpole in 1757, an engraving after Reynolds

HORACE WALPOLE

I don't know what volumes I may send you from Rome; from Florence I have little inclination to send you any. I see several things that please me calmly, but *à force d'en avoir vu* I have left off screaming, Lord! this! and Lord! that! To speak sincerely, Calais surprised me more than anything I have seen since. I recollect the joy I used to propose if I could but once see the Great Duke's gallery [the Uffizi]; I walk into it now with as little emotion as I should into St Paul's. The statues are a congregation of good sort of people, that I have a great deal of unruffled regard for ...

The incidents of a week in London would furnish all Italy with news for a twelvemonth. The only two circumstances of moment in the life of an Italian, that ever give occasion to their being mentioned, are, being married, and in a year after taking a cicisbeo. Ask the name, the husband, the wife or the cicisbeo of any person, *et voilà qui est fini*. Thus, child, 'tis dull dealing here!

Well, West, I have found a little unmasqued moment to write to you; but for this week past I have been so muffled up in my domino, that I have not had the command of my elbows. But what have you been doing all the mornings? Could you not write then? – No, then I was masqued too; I have done nothing but slip out of my domino into bed, and out of bed into my domino. The end of the Carnival is frantic, bacchanalian; all the morn one makes parties in masque to the shops and coffee-houses, and all the evening to the operas and balls. *Then I have danced, good gods! how have I danced!* The Italians are fond to a degree of our country dances: *Cold and raw* they only know by the tune; *Blowzybella* is almost Italian, and *Buttered peas* is *Pizelli al buro*. There are but three days more; but the two last are to have balls all the morning at the fine unfinished palace of the Strozzi; and the Tuesday night a masquerade after supper: they sup first, to eat *gras*,* and not encroach upon Ash-Wednesday. What makes masquerading more agreeable here than in England, is the great deference that is showed to the disguised. Here they do not catch at those little dirty opportunities of saying any ill-natured thing they know of you, do not abuse you because they may, or talk gross bawdy to a woman of quality. I found the other day, by a play of Etheridge's, that we have had a sort of Carnival even since the Reformation; 'tis in *She would if She could*, they talk of going a-mumming in Shrove-tide.

After talking so much of diversions, I fear you will attribute to them the fondness I own I contract for Florence; but it has so many other charms, that I shall not want excuses for my taste. The freedom of the Carnival has given me opportunities to make several acquaintances; and if I have not found them refined, learned, polished, like some other cities, yet they are civil, good-natured, and fond of the English. Their little partiality for themselves, opposed to the violent vanity of the French, makes them very amiable in my eyes. I can give you a comical instance of their great prejudice about nobility; it happened yesterday. While we were at dinner at Mr Mann's, word was brought by his secretary, that a cavalier demanded audience of him upon an affair of honour. Gray and I flew behind the curtain of the door. An elderly gentleman, whose attire was not certainly correspondent to the greatness of his birth, entered, and informed the British minister, that one Martin, an English painter, had left a challenge for him at his house, for having said Martin was no gentleman. He would by no means have spoke of the duel before the transaction of it, but that his honour, his blood, his etc. would never permit him to fight with one who was no cavalier; which was what he came to inquire of his excellency. We laughed loud laughs, but unheard: his fright or his nobility had closed his ears. But mark the sequel: the instant he was gone, my very English curiosity hurried me out of the gate St Gallo; 'twas the place and hour appointed. We had not been driving about above ten minutes, but out popped a little figure, pale but cross, with beard unshaved and hair uncombed, a slouched

---

* Ordinary, unrestricted diet was called *gras* (fat), while the fasting diet for Lent was called *maigre* (thin).

hat, and a considerable red cloak, in which was wrapped, under his arm, the fatal sword that was to revenge the highly injured Mr Martin, painter and defendant. I darted my head out of the coach, just ready to say, 'Your servant, Mr Martin,' and talk about the architecture of the triumphal arch that was building there; but he would not know me, and walked off. We left him to wait for an hour, to grow very cold and very valiant the more it grew past the hour of appointment. We were figuring all the poor creature's huddle of thoughts, and confused hopes of victory or fame, of his unfinished pictures, or his situation upon bouncing into the next world. You will think us strange creatures; but 'twas a pleasant sight, as we knew the poor painter was safe. I have thought of it since, and am inclined to believe that nothing but two English could have been capable of such a jaunt. I remember, 'twas reported in London, that the plague was at a house in the city, and all the town went to see it.

ROBERT ADAM
Every mortal masked, from a Marquis to a shoe-black traversing the streets from morning to night. Coaches were filled equally with Princes and Killovy men; Harlequin was postillion, a Devil the coachman, whilst three or four monstrous figures loaded the back of the coach. Then began the Corso. This is a procession of all the equipages in the country and town who go to the great square, ride round making a tour through some of the streets of the town, return to the square again – one set going, another coming – by which means those acquainted with the coach they meet, pop their heads out, say a witty thing and take them in again. This solemn procession, with our best coach etc., we used to parade in for two or three hours, that is from 3 to 6 o'clock, when night called us to other amusements.

Next morning after this series of sports they began anew with greater vigour than ever, and now they went out at ten in the morning. Men, women and children, high and low, met at the Grand Duke's Gallery, the place of rendezvous, where, under cover of the piazzas, they walked up and down for three hours, there being booths for selling all toys, places for all regales and refreshments, and room for much wit and criticism on taste in masking and other things the consequence of this frenzy. In this pleasant entertainment we were occupied till we had just time to get home to dinner, dress and go to the Corso again at three o'clock.

MRS THRALE
After the coaches have paraded up and down some time to show the equipages, liveries, etc., all have on a sudden notice to quit the scene of

action, and all do quit it in such a manner as is surprising. The street is now covered with sawdust, and made fast at both ends; the starting-post is adorned with elegant booths, lined with red velvet, for the court and first nobility; at the other end a piece of tapestry is hung, to prevent the creatures from dashing their brains out when they reach the goal. Thousands and ten thousands of people on foot fill the course, that it is standing wonder to me still that numbers are not killed. The prizes are now exhibited to view, quite in the old classical style; a piece of crimson damask for the winner perhaps, a small silver bason and ewer for the second, and so on, leaving no performer unrewarded. At last come out the *concurrenti* without riders, but with a narrow leathern strap hung across their backs, which has a lump of ivory fastened to the end of it, all set full of sharp spikes like a hedgehog, and this goads them along while galloping worse than any spurs could do, because the faster they run, the more this odd machine keeps jumping up and down and pricking their sides ridiculously enough; and it makes one laugh to see that some of them are provoked by it not to run at all, but set about plunging in order to rid themselves of the inconvenience, instead of driving forward to divert the mob, who leap and shout and caper with delight, and lash the laggers along with great indignation indeed, and with the most comical gestures. I never saw horses in so droll a state of degradation before, for they are all striped or spotted, or painted of some colour to distinguish them each from other; and nine or ten start at a time.

Sir Horace Mann regales Horace Walpole with the hazards and excitements of opera- and ball-going, party-giving and connoisseurship, as well as the problems he faced from English visitors in the 1740s and 1750s. (It was the convention to put the definite article before the names of opera singers.)

We had a strange uproar last Wednesday [1741], at the Burletta; an affair of party. I never saw anything like it before, but have heard of it happening in England. Albergotti [a nobleman] was the hero; he had made his addresses to the Romana, but being ill received, he would not permit the applause the Pit gave her; superior greatly to that which was given to the Cecca, whom really every body did applaud till it was known Albergotti was offended with the notice that was taken of the Romana. Piques of this kind went on for many nights, but were always kept within the bounds of gentle hissing (which may be taken, as 'tis often meant in Italy, for a call of silence, or of attention) and violent clapping; but on the fatal Wednesday night, just when the Romana was at the height of her favourite song, which could hardly be heard for the clapping, she was silenced by a most dreadful

The Trinità Bridge over the Arno, an engraving by Thomas Patch. 'The marble bridge is the resort of everybody, where they hear music, eat iced fruits and sup by moonlight' – Gray

concert of cat-calls, performed by the Lorraine* officers, and their servants. You cannot conceive the damp that was struck all over the theater. The ladies were all offended, and afraid to go home, it having been discovered that the Cat-callers were all armed. Albergotti was not one of them, though publickly known to be the promoter of it. One of the officers called to him from the Pit, and said, '*Marquis, c'est pour vous venger!*' In that the Impresario was affronted, so was his theater. The affair was carried the next morning before the Council, as what might have '*des suites fâcheuses*'; to prevent which it was thought proper to order Albergotti to repair to Arezzo, his native country, there to receive the orders that were to be sent to the Governor.

[July 1742] The Countess del Bellino came here this morning to say how sorry she was she could not come here to-morrow night. I am to have all the town in my garden, and all the musick I can get to entertain them, and *Copiosi rinfreschi* to feed them. I can't tell you their names, and the number, yet, for it is no invitation. The first I spoke to about it was told that other ladies having promised to take the air in my garden, instead of on the Ponte [the Trinità Bridge], she was desired to come too, and so on. Twelve or fourteen have been sent to by Madame Suares who directs, with the same

* The last Medici Grand Duke of Tuscany had been succeeded in 1739 by Francis II of Lorraine, husband of the Empress Maria Theresa of Austria.

message, and to desire they will bring their friends. I, in discourses, have spoke to others; so that I reckon the number will be large ... A great large table is to be placed in the middle of the garden, with many lights, for about 20 Suonatori of diverse sorts. All the alleys will be lined with Chairs and Benches, but no lights in any other parts of the garden, which I am told will please, *per il commodo delle Cicisbeatore*. The Hall is to be well lighted and the whole row of rooms, the windows of which are made into doors so that the walk under the orange trees will receive light from them. This is allowed to be better than sticking a light in every orange tree, or a torch at the end of the walks which, if the wind did not, I should expect would be blown out by those who prefer moonlight to artificial. There's nothing that pleases so much in this country as a Cocchiata [originally a serenade listened to from carriages] in a garden. Everybody is in expectation of it, and I don't doubt but I shall be commended ... If the wind blows, it will drive us all in doors, and then we must ride on each other's backs, for there won't be room for half the company.

[November 1742] I must not conceal to you a strong suspicion of the Dominicallity of your Madonna!* not from the beauty, for nothing can exceed it, but on my unpacking it, I found wrote on the back, Sasso Ferrato;† whose name is not to be found in the *Abecedario Pittorico*, or in any Lives of the Painters that I have seen; but I find his name is well known in Florence as a famous painter of Madonnas. Nunziato Baldocci has one; Marquis Corsi, another. Nobody can tell me where or when he lived; but there is a little place somewhere in Italy, called Sasso Ferrato. I would willingly erase those words, but am afraid that ink or anything else I should use might in time eat into the picture. If I were you, I would line it. The canvass is rather too dry, so that a lining would both preserve it and remove the scandal. I have a little Madonna and Child now in my house which has been called by the same author. It is as much inferior to your's as is possible, but it cannot be denied that there is a great resemblance in the manner of painting.

[1747] You know what a busy time the Carnival is. I partake none of its amusements but the Opera, and yet *that* deranges my whole system. The show at the Via della Pergola is really magnificent. The Tesi has been taken from her involuntary retirement, to act Achilles; and appears with great *eclat*, though she trembled much the first night, believing that her whole

---

*Mann had been helping Walpole to buy a Domenichino.
† Giovanni Battista Salvi, 1609–1685.

future reputation as an Actress was at stake; but she does extremely well and has the *Gloria*, as she calls it, of having restored the Via della Pergola Theater which indeed, by the first Opera produced there, was quite sunk. She rants a little too much whilst she is in woman's cloaths; but, they say, the part requires it ... The *Ladies*, who don't love her, are forced to applaud Putello, who does the part of Ulysses, does it very well, too. He formerly, they say, sung much better; but he lost much of his voice at Naples, so that in his Airs, he is not heard ... Twenty English that are now here, have decided boisterously for Denis,* with all the *Gens d'Armes* and *Cittadinanza*, in opposition to all the Nobility. Judge then, if it is not prudent to be neutral, which however is no easy task!

Those twenty English embarrass me much. It is vastly the mode to entertain. They have separate lodgings and french cooks, and one is tormented to death. Some indeed entertain vastly well, and have their *hors d'œuvres* and *entremets*, in great order. Others who won't give ten zecchins, (about £5) a month to a Cook, do not succeed quite so well, but yet will imitate the fine way. Lord Hobart and I were ready to burst with laughter t'other day, at a noble table, where ten people were set down to a first course of a soup and two *hors d'œuvres* literally consisting of a Mustard pot in a small dish and, opposite to it, a plate of the vile white Radishes. The mustard was to serve for the Bouilli which was to relieve the Soup. I have escaped many dinners by a fever which seized me last Tuesday whilst I was in the hight of my Despatches ... I was blooded the next day, and went to the Opera, with the Princess [Craon]† last night, which unfortunately has exposed me to a great dinner to day. I wish I could give you a description of her setting forth, for it was her first *sortie* after an *epuisement* and an *accablement*‡ of a fortnight. When we thought all was ready to march, she sent Tozzoni into her room for twenty things. Amongst others, he brought her half a hood to hang over her whole face, to keep the air from striking it, and a monstrous fan, or little screen, made of linnen, with a long handle, for a servant to carry at some distance before her, to prevent the air coming with too much force against the covering to her face. I was put into the Coach with her, and was vastly afraid of hurting her, or squeezing her. I was heartily glad when we got to the Theater where, you know, she takes great precautions to arrive as the curtain draws up, as she pleases herself with the notion that it is done to do her honour; – just as she attributed the

---

* A dancer at this opera house.
† Her husband ruled Florence on behalf of Francis of Lorraine. She had been mistress of Leopold, last Duke of Lorraine, and had borne him twenty children.
‡ First outing after exhaustion and prostration.

whole Corso at Rome . . . as coming there to make [her entry] magnificent.

Did I ever tell you that your Princess Griffoni (who often enquires after you) has been abandoned by Manelli [her cicisbeo]. He took the opportunity of his marrying, on a promise to return again, but has not kept his word, and she was sometime without, quite *sconsolata*, till (of very late) Bernardino Riccardi has left his black Frescobaldi, to take to her. Jesus! here is mad Mr St John and Baron Stosch.* The first is come to persuade me to unite the Churches of England and Rome; and the latter to thank me for having sent the corpse of his Brother to be buried at Leghorn.

. . . It was just as I said; Mr St John has been preaching to me for above an hour, to make it clear that nothing is so proper or so easy as to bring about this union; and he is sure if I would but write to King, Lords, and Commons, that they would all agree as to the force of his arguments, and give their consents to put all Dominion under the one or three glorious crowns, so plain a symbol of the Trinity. On his part he will engage to make the Pope accept the laws of England and to prove to him that they are Jesus Christ and the twelve Jurymen his Apostles! Poor man! . . .

[Mann announces the close of the Carnival.] The ashes of Wednesday imbitter the pleasures of the last days; but the last days were rendered lively by a very curious English display. On the night of the 13th, there was a great ball in the Via della Pergola, at which many of the English represented Free Masonry. Their habits were pretty, and Denis, the first dancer, who is a Master Mason, composed a dance on purpose, which succeeded very well. The Italians liked it as a masquerade, which was all they knew of it. They danced it twice, with great applause; but the third time the people were offended that their Tresconi was interrupted, which occasioned some bustle, and had not General Salvi threatened to put all the Fidlers into prison, the Tresconi would have got the better. The Impresarii, I hear, are all offended (for I was not there so late), and Lord March [later the Duke of Queensberry] was so angry with them that he proposed that each of the nine Free Masons should fight an Impresario. They intended to appear in the same habits, at the Ball on Tuesday night, but the fracas has made them alter their minds.

[In 1752 Mann mentions a] roaring, rich West Indian, Young, who talks of his money, and swaggers in his gate as if both his coat pockets were full of it. He buys pictures upon his own judgment, and declares it to be better than any body's. Hugford,† the English painter, allows the assertion, since

* Stosch was in the pay of Britain to spy on the Jacobite Court at Rome.
† Ignacio Hugford, art dealer and cicerone, brother of the Abbot of Vallombrosa who perfected the technique of scagliola, see p. 181.

A Gathering of Dilettanti around the Medici Venus, by Thomas Patch. This statue was regarded in the eighteenth century as the greatest work of art, and first made Gibbon acknowledge 'that the chisel may dispute the pre-eminence with the pencil'. Three of the other sculptures are also in Zoffany's painting on page 132

Young gave him two hundred zecchins for a Danae, which Hugford calls a Titian! The picture is allowed to have merit, but it has been so often washed and retouched that one does not know whose to call it. The great Mengs,* whom Sir Hanbury Williams recommended to me, on Mengs' way to Rome, to work for his master, the King of Poland, not only denys the originality of it, but said it was worth nothing. Mr Young has heard of this, and says that Mengs must be the most D——d ignorant fellow in the world, for said he 'I will assert and lay any man a thousand pounds that it is much better than the Venus in the Tribuna'. You will certainly hear much talk of it when it arrives in England, and probably be tempted to go to see it. In the meantime, speak to Astley about it, who knows the picture extremely well. You may then see Mr Young's Organ, which cost him three thousand pounds, and his electrical instruments which cost forty thousand pounds; but he must retrench, he says, because the late Hurricane did so much harm to his Sugar-canes, that he shan't receive about one third of his Estate; not above £6000 this year.

* Anton Raffael Mengs, one of the earliest Neoclassical painters.

The Grotto Grande in the Boboli Gardens in about 1790, by Bernardo Buontalenti

In spite of Mrs Thrale's aspersions on p. 131 and Smollett's on p. 175, Italian gardens have always been outstanding, particularly in their use of water and statuary, as Edward Wright points out. Florence has many examples, two of which are the Boboli Gardens and, a short distance outside the city, those at the Medici Villa at Pratolino (Villa Demidoff). Beckford visits the former and Evelyn the latter.

EDWARD WRIGHT

The gardens of these villas have in them great numbers of shady tall trees and high hedges, abundance of fountains, and those sorts of water-works which they call *scherzi d'acqua* [sports or plays of water], partly as the contrivance of them is humorous, and the play of fancy, and partly as they are often employ'd to play tricks with the company; but rarely with any other than servants; for, the Italians pique themselves so much upon decorum, that they are cautious of giving such jests as they would not care to take: however, a livery, they think, will bear a shower well enough, which a finer suit would not. But these *scherzi d'acqua* have likewise a real use, for laying the dust, and cooling the air.

The statues in some of these villas are very numerous, and do exceedingly enliven those shady retreats; so that a man can never be said to be alone

144

there, if he can be content with silent company: and a person that is a lover of sculpture, or antiquities in general, may be most agreeably entertain'd in those places, and have abundance of queries answer'd, without a word speaking.

WILLIAM BECKFORD

I returned home and feasted upon grapes and ortolans with great edification: then walked to one of the bridges across the Arno, and surveyed the hills at a distance, purpled by the declining sun. Its mild gleams tempted me to the garden of Boboli, which lies behind the Palazzo Pitti, stretched out on the side of a mountain. I ascended terrace after terrace, robed by a thick underwood of bay and myrtle, above which rise several nodding towers, and a long sweep of venerable wall, almost entirely concealed by ivy. You would have been enraptured with the broad masses of shade and dusky alleys that opened as I advanced, with white statues of fauns and sylvans glimmering amongst them; some of which pour water into sarcophagi of the purest marble, covered with antique relievos. The capitals of columns and ancient friezes are scattered about as seats. On these I reposed myself, and looked up to the cypress groves which spring above the thickets; then, plunging into their retirements, I followed a winding path, which led me by a series of steep ascents to a green platform overlooking the whole extent of wood, with Florence deep beneath, and the tops of the hills which encircle it jagged with pines; here and there a convent, or villa, whitening in the sun. This scene extends as far as the eye can reach. Still ascending I attained the brow of the eminence, and had nothing but the fortress of Belvedere, and two or three open porticos above me. On this elevated situation, I found several walks of trellis-work, clothed with luxuriant vines, that produce, to my certain knowledge, the most delicious clusters. A colossal statue of Ceres, her hands extended in the act of scattering fertility over the country, crowns the summit, where I lingered, to mark the landscape fade, and the bright skirts of the western clouds die gradually away. Then descending alley after alley, and bank after bank, I came to the orangery in front of the palace, disposed in a grand amphitheatre, with marble niches relieved by dark foliage, out of which spring tall aerial cypresses. This spot brought the scenery of an antique Roman garden full into my mind. I expected every instant to be called to the table of Lucullus hard by, in one of the porticos, and to stretch myself on his purple triclinia; but waiting in vain for a summons till the approach of night, I returned delighted with a ramble that had led my imagination so far into antiquity.

JOHN EVELYN

In the grove sits Pan feeding his flock, the water making melodious sound through his pipe; and an Hercules whose club yields a shower of water which falling into a greate shell has a naked woman riding on the backs of dolphins. In another grotto is Vulcan and his family, the walls richly compos'd of corals, shells, coper, and marble figures, with the hunting of several beasts, moving by the force of water. Here, having ben well washed for our curiosity, we went down a large walke, at the sides whereof several slender streams of water gush out of pipes concealed underneath, that interchangeably fall into each others channells, making a lofty and perfect arch, so that a man on horseback may ride under it and not receive one drop of wet. This canopy or arch of water, I thought one of the most surprising magnificencies I had ever seene, and very refreshing in the heate of the sum'er. At the end of this very long walk stands a woman in white marble, in posture of a laundress wringing water out of a piece of linen, very naturally formed, into a vast lavor the work and invention of M. Angelo Buonarotti. Hence we ascended Mount Parnassus, where the Muses plaied to us on hydraulic organs. Neere this is a greate aviarie. All these waters came from the rock in the garden, on which is the statue of a gyant representing the Apennines, at the foote of which stands this villa. Last of all we came to the labyrinth in which a huge colosse of Jupiter throws out a streame over the garden. This is 50 foote in height, having in his body a square chamber, his eyes and mouth serving for windows and dore.

What Horace Walpole (on p. 136) called the 'great prejudice about nobility' of the Florentine upper classes is affirmed by Lord Cork. Samuel Sharp advances reasons for their condition, while Smollett uses their charitable activity as an excuse for a tilt at superstition.

LORD CORK AND ORRERY

The inhabitants of the higher sort are civil, grave, and abstemious. Even an Englishman, conquered by example, drinks no bumpers here. The common people are lazy, proud, and cowardly. Not a grain of Roman spirit remains throughout Tuscany ...

Their good breeding runs into the stiffness of ceremony. They are offended at the least defect in decorum. There are certain established laws in going into a coach, that still puzzle me, and often make me study very heartily which is my right, and which is my left hand. No Florentine ever appears in an undress. The fidlers, the taylors, and the barbers all wear swords. The noblemen (*la nobilità*) stir not to the next door without

'A Punch Party', by Thomas Patch, held at Charles Hadfield's inn, Carlo's, in Florence. Hadfield holds the punch bowl

a numerous attendance of lacqueys, among whom is always a running footman. They are strangers to what the French call EASE; in which point that nation deviates into an extreme, particularly by avoiding cleanliness, and forgetting decorum.

The Florentines affect, and almost reach magnificence. Their equipages are fine, their coaches large, their horses lean; their palaces truly sumptuous. They make few or no entertainments. Neither their dispositions nor revenues will allow of hospitality. They have card-assemblies, in which formality, rather than dignity, or gaiety, presides. I am told they are satyrical. It is certain they are nice observers, and neither defective in judgment or understanding; yet their public amusements and diversions, especially those of the theatre, are the amusements and diversions of children. The practice of religion is outwardly acted by their priests, and indeed by the laiety in the churches. Few traces of it (I speak not of the clergy) are perceptible in their conduct ... Prudence (by an inviolable taciturnity on certain points) added to a most constant attendance at mass, defend the Florentine from the tyranny of the inquisition; which exists, but triumphs not, in this city.

SAMUEL SHARP

At all the houses of the Nobles in Florence, you see an empty flask hanging out, to denote they sell wine by retail; this custom shocks an Englishman, as a practice very derogatory from their dignity, and he cannot but speak of it with surprize. A Florentine cooly and sensibly answers, 'Sir, your Duke of ——, by the interposition of a steward, sells a tree for ten shillings; our Noble, by his porter at the door, sells ten shillings worth of wine; but our noble appears no more in the sale of the wine, than your Duke of ——, in the sale of his tree; different countries have their different modes.' The truth is, that, through all Italy, great part of the rent for estates, is paid in kind, which, joined with a certain exemption from the import on wine, granted to the nobles in Florence, has led them, I believe, into this seeming littleness ...

The Nobles are numerous and poor; indeed, for the same reason; that is to say, because all the children are noble, and because it is a fashion to divide their estates almost equally amongst them: This custom had a very good effect, when it was honourable to be engaged in commerce, as was the case when the trade of Europe was in a manner carried on by the Nobles of Florence, Venice and Lombardy: Every son, by this article, improved his fortune, and enriched his country; but the discovery of the passage to the Indies, by the Cape of Good Hope, putting an end to this monopoly, and to the exorbitant gains attending it, commerce, by degrees, became contemptible, as it grew less profitable; and the Nobility, finding no resources beyond their pitiful incomes, became wretched, at least the greater part of them. I have been credibly informed, that a Noble at Florence, with five hundred pounds a year, is reputed to be in pretty good circumstances; though there are a few, who have some thousands: But poor as the Italian Nobles are, from this circumstance of dividing their estates amongst their sons, they would still be more so, were it a custom for all the sons to marry: But it seems to be a rule established through all Italy, that one or two only of them should marry, the others preserving themselves single, with the view that their estates may revert, and by that means support the dignity of their family.

TOBIAS SMOLLETT

I had occasion to see a procession, where all the noblesse of the city attended in their coaches, which filled the whole length of the great street called the *Corso*. It was the anniversary of a charitable institution in favour of poor maidens, a certain number of whom are portioned* every year. About two hundred of these virgins walked in procession, two and two together, cloathed in violet-coloured wide gowns, with white veils on their heads, and made a very classical appearance. They were preceded and followed by

* Provided with dowries so they could get married.

an irregular mob of penitents in sack-cloth, with lighted tapers, and monks carrying crucifixes, bawling and bellowing the litanies: but the great object was a figure of the Virgin Mary, as big as the life, standing within a gilt frame, dressed in a gold stuff, with a large hoop, a great quantity of false jewels, her face painted and patched, and her hair frizzled and curled in the very extremity of the fashion. Very little regard had been paid to the image of our Saviour on the cross; but when his lady-mother appeared on the shoulders of three or four lusty friars, the whole populace fell upon their knees in the dirt. This extraordinary veneration paid to the Virgin, must have been derived originally from the French, who pique themselves on their gallantry to the fair sex.*

As today, the coldness of Italian winters and the inadequacy of heating arrangements were matter for comment: first Mrs Thrale, then Lord Cork and lastly Robert Adam.

MRS THRALE

Italians seem to me to have no feeling of cold; they open the casements – for windows we have none – now in winter, and cry, 'Che bel freschetto!'† while I am starving outright. If there is a flash of a few faggots in the chimney that just scorches one a little, no lady goes near it, but sits at the other end of a high-roofed room, the wind whistling around her ears, and her feet upon a perforated brass box filled with wood-embers, which the *cavalier servente* pulls out from time to time and replenishes with hotter ashes raked out from between the andirons. How sitting with these fumes under their petticoats improves their beauty of complexion I know not; certain it is they pity us exceedingly for our manner of managing ourselves, and inquire of their countrymen who have lived here awhile how their health endured the burning fossils in the chambers at London.

LORD CORK AND ORRERY

Italy has extremely the advantage of England in point of climate. No damps, no fogs, no vapours, no gloomy suicide-weather, which never fails to render us miserable and melancholy; and for which our chief panacea is wine. The sun appears at noon constantly, and has as much influence in Florence at this time of the year, as he has in London in the celebrated month of May; but the frost has been so powerful, that the Metropolitan of this city

* Horace Mann claimed most of the common people of Florence believed the Trinity to consist of the Father, the Son, and the Madonna.
† 'What a fresh breeze!'

Allen Smith contemplating Florence, by Fabre, 1797. Napoleon's invasion of Italy closed it to the British, but not to Americans like Smith, who was born in South Carolina but spent most of his life in Philadelphia

obtained, about a fortnight ago, a licence from the pope for the common people to eat eggs during the remainder of Lent, the frost having consumed all the garden-stuff.

ROBERT ADAM

What way do you think I have spent these three mornings? I wager you won't guess. Says one, seeing the Venus of Medici, seeing the antique statues and glorious pictures. No! Why, in short – skating on the ice. Never was so cold weather in Scotland as we have had a continuance of here for five or six weeks. The Arno is frozen from one side to the other: the mountains are covered with snow and the poor wretches are starved to death, whilst we, taking advantage of an element unknown to these scorched devils, have scraped together three pairs of skates on which Mr Hope and a very clever fellow, one Wilton a statuary,* and your humble servant have

* The sculptor Joseph Wilton, a protégé of Sir Horace Mann.

crawled, straddled and paddled upon a dubb [pond] without the walls of this town – to no small amusement of the bystanders who have uttered more *Gesu Marias* and other marks of astonishment than can be expressed.

Gray called Florence in summer 'an excellent place to employ all one's animal sensations in, but utterly contrary to one's rational powers'. The Arno came into its own: in Horace Walpole's words it 'is not boated and swelled like the Thames, but 'tis vastly pretty and, I don't know how, being Italian, has something visionary and poetical in its stream'. It was not the Ponte Vecchio that attracted attention, but rather the elegant Ponte a Santa Trinità, which Lord Cork called the most beautiful bridge in the world. Gray in July 1740, and then Horace Mann in 1741, describe the lotus-eating existence, while Samuel Sharp grumbles at the long Italian lunch hour.

THOMAS GRAY

We are settled here with Mr Mann in a charming apartment; the river Arno runs under our windows, which we can fish out of. The sky is so serene, and the air so temperate, that one continues in the open air all night long in a slight nightgown without any danger; and the marble bridge is the resort of every body, where they hear music, eat iced fruits, and sup by moon-light; though as yet (the season being extremely backward every where) these amusements are not begun.

HORACE MANN

There's a very great Cocchiata to night on the Terrass of the Corsini house, *Lung' Arno*. Chains are put up at the ends of the street, to prevent Coaches approaching so that the whole town will be there, or thereabouts, a-foot; 'tis a charming situation, you know, for such a thing; and the night is most favourable, after some of the hottest days, they say, of this or any other summer. Oh, if you were here, I am sure you would be pleased and would be among'st 'em in your long night-gown, till break of day. 'Tis made by 12 Cavalieri, set on foot and managed by Abbate Capponi. It begins at 5 hours.

SAMUEL SHARP

In all the great cities of Italy, several shops are shut up, from twelve to half an hour after one, or longer, so sacred is the ceremony of dining; but, indeed, the languor of trade in Italy is surprising, and the inactivity of the shopkeepers very often borders upon rudeness. Were commerce more brisk, and were there more rivalship amongst the traders, they would not then lie under the odious imputation that they now do, of sharping, not only foreigners, but their countrymen also, if they can ... An English Gentleman, not apprised of the custom, upon his first arrival in Italy, possibly calls his servant, when the man is just sat down to dine; but if he call twenty times, he receives no other answer, than that he is at dinner (*a Tavola, Signore*) which every Italian servant supposes is a sufficient reason that his master should wait, though the business be ever so pressing. In a short time I submitted to this fashion, and at present I do not presume to call up one of our servants at the hour of dining.

Few Tourists seem to have stayed long in Siena. Fynes Moryson calls the scene of the famous Palio horse race 'a most faire marketplace, in the form of an oyster, and lying hollow as the shell thereof is'. Beckford dismisses the startling black-and-white marble duomo as a 'masterpiece of ridiculous taste and elaborate absurdity'. Evelyn is more appreciative and particularly mentions the relics he was shown there: 'an arme of St John the Baptist, wherewith, they say, he baptised our Saviour in Jordan; it was given by the King of Peloponesus to one of the Popes ... They also have St Peter's Sword, with which he smote off the ear of Malchus.' About a hundred years later Horace Walpole makes fun of the whole subject by listing the relics shown to him 'in a small hovel of the Capuchins' at Radicofani, south of Siena: 'a set of gnashing of teeth, the grinders very intire; a bit of the worm that never dies, preserved in spirits; a crow of St Peter's cock, very useful against Easter; the crisping and curling, frizzing and frouncing of Mary Magdalen, which she cut off on growing devout.' It was on the road to Rome, south of Siena, that Smollett ran into trouble in his coach, which he had hired in Florence for seven weeks for 'something less than three guineas and a half'.

At Buon Convento, where the emperor Henry VII [1308–12] was poisoned by a friar with the sacramental wafer, I refused to give money to the hostler, who in revenge put two young unbroke stone-horses [not castrated] in the traces next to the coach, which became so unruly, that before we had gone a quarter of a mile, they and the postilion were rolling in the dust. In this situation they made such efforts to disengage themselves, and kicked with such violence, that I imagined the carriage and all our trunks would have been beaten in pieces. We leaped out of the coach, however, without sustaining any personal damage, except the fright; nor was any hurt done to the vehicle. But the horses were terribly bruised, and almost strangled, before they could be disengaged ...

About half way between Montefiascone and Viterbo, one of our fore-wheels flew off, together with a large splinter of the axle-tree; and if one of

The overthrown coach, a wonderfully lively drawing by Francesco Guardi

the postilions had not by great accident been a remarkably ingenious fellow, we should have been put to the greatest inconvenience, as there was no town, or even house, within several miles. I mention this circumstance, by way of warning, to other travellers, that they may provide themselves with a hammer and nails, a spare iron-pin or two, a large knife, and bladder of grease, to be used occasionally in case of such misfortune.

An English family
sightseeing in
Rome in 1792, by
Archibald Skirving

Rome

Mrs Thrale commended Rome as 'so pregnant with wonders, so productive of reflections', a view conveyed rather more trenchantly by Gibbon to his father in 1764 in the first extract. Smollett follows, with words of warning for young Grand Tourers. The hazards that beset Fynes Moryson at the end of the sixteenth century were of a rather different nature.

EDWARD GIBBON

I am now Dear Sir at Rome. If it was difficult before to give you or Mrs Gibbon any account of what I saw it is impossible here. I have already found such a fund of entertainment for a mind somewhat prepared for it by an acquaintance with the Romans, that I am really almost in a dream. Whatever ideas books may have given us of the greatness of that people, their accounts of the most flourishing state of Rome fall infinitely short of the picture of its ruins. I am convinced there never never existed such a nation and I hope for the happiness of mankind that there never will again. I was this morning upon the top of Trajan's pillar. I shall not attempt a description of it. Only figure to yourself a column 140 foot high of the purest white marble composed only of about 30 blocks and wrought into bas-reliefs with as much taste and delicacy as any chimney piece at Up-Park.*

[Six days after this letter, one of the most famous moments in literary history took place, chronicled by Gibbon in his *Memoirs* some years later.] It was on the fifteenth of October in the gloom of evening, as I sat musing on the Capitol, while the barefooted fryars were chanting their litanies in the temple of Jupiter,† that I conceived the first thought of my history. My

---

* In Sussex. Sir Matthew Fetherstonhaugh, the owner, was a family friend of the Gibbons'.
† Actually in Santa Maria in Aracoeli, on the site of the temple of Juno.

The arrival of a young traveller (on the left) in the Piazza di Spagna during the Roman Carnival, by David Allan, 1775

original plan was confined to the decay of the City; my reading and reflection pointed to that aim; but several years elapsed, and several avocations intervened, before I grappled with the decline and fall of the Roman Empire.

TOBIAS SMOLLETT

Our young gentlemen who go to Rome will do well to be upon their guard against a set of sharpers, (some of them of our own country,) who deal in pictures and antiques, and very often impose upon the uninformed stranger, by selling him trash, as the productions of the most celebrated artists. The English are more than any other foreigners exposed to this imposition. They are supposed to have more money to throw away; and therefore a greater number of snares are layed for them. This opinion of their superior wealth they take a pride in confirming, by launching out into all manner of unnecessary expence: but, what is still more dangerous, the moment they set foot in Italy, they are seized with the ambition of becoming connoisseurs in painting, musick, statuary, and architecture; and the adventurers of this country do not fail to flatter this weakness for their own advantage. I have seen in different parts of Italy, a number of raw boys, whom Britain seemed to have poured forth on purpose to bring her national character into

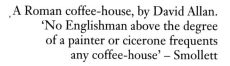

A Roman coffee-house, by David Allan.
'No Englishman above the degree
of a painter or cicerone frequents
any coffee-house' – Smollett

contempt: ignorant, petulant, rash, and profligate, without any knowledge or experience of their own, without any director to improve their understanding, or superintend their conduct. One engages in play with an infamous gamester, and is stripped perhaps in the very first partie: another is poxed and pillaged by an antiquated cantatrice: a third is bubbled by a knavish antiquarian; and a fourth is laid under contribution by a dealer in pictures. Some turn fiddlers, and pretend to compose: but all of them talk familiarly of the arts, and return finished connoisseurs and coxcombs, to their own country. The most remarkable phænomenon of this kind, which I have seen, is a boy of seventy-two, now actually travelling through Italy, for improvement, under the auspices of another boy of twenty-two.

When you arrive at Rome, you receive cards from all your country-folks in that city: they expect to have the visit returned next day, when they give orders not to be at home; and you never speak to one another in the sequel. This is a refinement in hospitality and politeness, which the English have invented by the strength of their own genius, without any assistance either from France, Italy, or Lapland. No Englishman above the degree of a painter or cicerone frequents any coffee-house at Rome; and as there are no public diversions, except in carnival-time, the only chance you have for seeing your compatriots, is either in visiting the curiosities, or at a conversazione. The Italians are very scrupulous in admitting foreigners, except those who are introduced as people of quality: but if there happens to be any English lady of fashion in Rome, she generally keeps an assembly, to which the British subjects resort.

FYNES MORYSON

We returned to Rome, where that I might stay with more security, to see the antiquities thereof, it hapned very fitly, that the Cardinall Allan an Englishman, having used to persecute the English comming thither, and therefore being ill spoken of by them, had changed his mind, since the English had overthrowne the Spanish Navy, in the yeere 1588, and there was now small hope of reducing England to papistry, and therefore to gaine his Countrey-mens love, did not onely mislike that they should be intrapped at Rome, but did himselfe protect them, though suspected for religion, so they would seeke his favour.

I presently went to the said Cardinall, and after the fashion, having kissed the hemme of his vesture, I humbly desired, that according to this his curtesie, for which hee was much honoured in England, hee would receive mee into his protection, till I might view the antiquities of Rome. He being of a goodly stature and countenance with a grave looke and pleasant speech had me rest secure, so I could commaund my tongue, and should abstaine from offence. Onely for his duties sake, hee said, that he must advise me, and for the love of his Countrey intreate me, that I would be willing to heare those instructions for religion here, which I could not heare in England. I submitted my selfe to these conditions, and when (after due reverence made) I would have gone away, the English Gentlemen and Priests there present, overtooke me in the next roome ... All commended my judgement, in comming to the Cardinall, and inquiring after my lodging, promised to be my guides in Rome, and for Countries sake, to doe me all good offices, and so after mutuall salutations, I went from them. I well knew, that such guides would be very troublesome to me, for they (according to the manner) disputing of Religion, I must either seeme to consent by silence, or maintaine arguments ful of danger in that place, besides that to gratifie them for their courtesie, I must needes have runne into extraordinary expences. Therefore having told them my lodging, I presently changed it and tooke a chamber in a vitling house, in the Market-place, close under the Popes Pallace, where I thought they, or any else would least seeke mee, and so being free from that burthen, and yet secure

A capriccio interior decorated with paintings of the Classical remains in Rome, by Panini. The Pantheon and the Colosseum can be seen centre right

in the Cardinals promised protection, I began boldly, (yet with as much hast as I possibly could make) to view the Antiquities of Rome.

We accompany Boswell and his cicerone or guide, Colin Morrison, first to the Colosseum and then to the Palatine Hill where, overcome by enthusiasm, Boswell starts spouting Latin. Then we visit the Colosseum again, followed by the Forum, with William Beckford, avid as always for the picturesque if not downright romantic.

JAMES BOSWELL

We entered the famous Colosseum, which certainly presents a vast and sublime idea of the grandeur of the ancient Romans. It is hard to tell whether the astonishing massiveness or the exquisite taste of this superb building should be more admired. A hermit has a little apartment inside. We passed through his hermitage to climb to where the seats and corridors of the theatre once were; Mr Morison gave me a clear picture of all this. It was shocking to discover several portions of this theatre full of dung. It is rented to people who use it in this fashion [keep cattle in it] ... We climbed the Palatine hill where the magnificent Palace of the emperors stood. Since

159

it has suffered many changes, we must believe that the ruins we now see date from the time of Domitian ... We saw a superb hall from which one can judge the grandeur of this imperial mansion, and we went down to see the baths, where one can yet see on the ceiling fragments of stucco-work painted and gilded in a very elegant manner. We walked to where the house of Cicero had stood. A statue there resembles him a great deal. Struck by these famous places, I was seized with enthusiasm. I began to speak Latin. Mr Morison replied. He laughed a bit at the beginning. But we made a resolution to speak Latin continually during this course of antiquities. We have persisted, and every day we speak with greater facility, so that we have harangued on Roman antiquities in the language of the Romans themselves.

WILLIAM BECKFORD

I absolutely will have no antiquary to go prating from fragment to fragment, and tell me, that were I to stay five years at Rome, I should not see half it contained. The thought alone of so much to look at, is quite distracting, and makes me resolve to view nothing at all in a scientific way, but struggle and wander about, just as the spirit chuses. This evening, it led me to the Coliseo, and excited a vehement desire in me to break down and pulverise the whole circle of saints' nests and chapels, which disgrace the arena. You recollect, I dare say, the vile effect of this holy trumpery, and would join with all your heart in kicking it into the Tyber. A few lazy abbots were at their devotion before them, such as would have made a lion's mouth water, fatter, I dare say, than any saint in the whole martyrology, and ten times more tantalising. I looked first, at the dens where wild beasts used to be kept, to divert the magnanimous people of Rome with devastation and murder; then, at the tame cattle before the altars. Heavens! thought I to myself, how times are changed! Could ever Vespasian have imagined his amphitheatre would have been thus inhabited? I passed on, making these reflections, to a dark arcade, overgrown with ilex. In the openings which time and violence have made, a distant grove of cypresses discover themselves, springing from heaps of mouldering ruins, relieved by a clear transparent sky, strewed with a few red clouds. This was the sort of prospect I desired, and I sat down on a shattered frieze to enjoy it ...

The cool breeze of the evening played in the beds of canes and oziers, which flourished under the walls of the Coliseo. A cloud of birds were upon the wing to regain their haunts in its crevices; and, except the sound of their flight, all was silent, for happily no carriages were rattling along. I observed the palace and obelisk of Saint John of Lateran, at a distance; but

The Forum at Rome, by van Swanevelt. A weekly livestock market took place there which is why it was called the 'Campo Vaccino', the cattle field

it was too late to take a nearer survey; so, returning leisurely home, I traversed the Campo Vaccino [the Forum], and leaned a moment against one of the columns which supported the temple of Jupiter Stator. Some women were fetching water from the fountain hard by, whilst another group had kindled a fire under the shrubs and twisted fig-trees which cover the Palatine hill. Innumerable vaults and arches peep out of the vegetation. It was upon these, in all probability, the splendid palace of the Cæsars was raised. Confused fragments of marble, and walls of lofty terraces, are the sole traces of its antient magnificence. A wretched rabble were roasting their chesnuts, on the very spot, perhaps, where Domitian convened a senate, to harangue upon the delicacies of his entertainment. The light of the flame cast upon the figures around it, and the mixture of tottering wall with foliage impending above their heads, formed a striking picture, which I staid contemplating from my pillar till the fire went out, the assembly dispersed, and none remained but a withered hag, raking the embers and muttering to herself. I thought also it was high time to retire, lest the unwholesome mists, which were streaming from the opening before the Coliseo, might make me repent my stay.

St Peter's extracts praise for its proportions from Addison, whilst Gray regales his mother with a highly-coloured account of the Good Friday ceremonies there in April 1740 and Charles Burney goes into the mysteries surrounding Allegri's famous Miserere. *Lastly Gibbon, in* The Decline and Fall, *admits that the beauty of eighteenth-century Rome owes much to the corruption and nepotism of papal rule.*

JOSEPH ADDISON

St Peter's seldom answers expectation at first entering it, but enlarges itself on all sides insensibly, and mends upon the eye every moment. The proportions are so very well observed, that nothing appears to an advantage, or distinguishes itself above the rest. It seems neither extremely high, nor long, nor broad, because it is all of them in a just equality. As on the contrary, in our Gothic cathedrals, the narrowness of the arch makes it rise in height, or run out in length; the lowness often opens it in breadth, or the defectiveness of some other particular makes any single part appear in great perfection. Though every thing in this church is admirable, the most astonishing part of it is the cupola. Upon my going to the top of it, I was surprised to find that the dome, which we see in the church, is not the same that one looks upon without-doors, the last of them being a kind of case to the other, and the stairs lying betwixt them both, by which one ascends into the ball.

THOMAS GRAY

To-day I am just come from paying my adoration at St Peter's to three extraordinary reliques, which are exposed to public view only on these two days in the whole year, at which time all the confraternities in the city come in procession to see them. It was something extremely novel to see that vast church, and the most magnificent in the world, undoubtedly, illuminated (for it was night) by thousands of little crystal lamps, disposed in the figure of a huge cross at the high altar, and seeming to hang alone in the air. All the light proceeded from this, and had the most singular effect imaginable as one entered the great door. Soon after came one after another, I believe, thirty processions, all dressed in linen frocks, and girt with a cord, their heads covered with a cowl all over, only two holes to see through left. Some of them were all black, others red, others white, others party-coloured; these were continually coming and going with their tapers and crucifixes before them; and to each company, as they arrived and knelt before the great altar, were shown from a balcony at a great height, the three wonders, which are, you must know, the head of the spear that

St Peter's, by Panini. 'Your eye is filled so equally and regularly, that nothing appears stupendous' – Smollett

wounded Christ; St Veronica's handkerchief, with the miraculous impression of his face upon it; and a piece of the true cross, on the sight of which the people thump their breasts, and kiss the pavement with vast devotion. The tragic part of the ceremony is half a dozen wretched creatures, who with their faces covered, but naked to the waist, are in a side-chapel disciplining themselves with scourges full of iron prickles; but really in earnest, as our eyes can testify, which saw their backs and arms so raw we should have taken it for a red satin doublet torn, and shewing the skin through, had we not been convinced of the contrary by the blood which was plentifully sprinkled about them.

CHARLES BURNEY
This piece, which, for upwards of a hundred and fifty years, has been annually performed in Passion Week at the Pope's chapel, on Wednesday and Good Friday, and which, in appearance, is so simple as to make those, who have only seen it on paper, wonder whence its beauty and effect could arise, owes its reputation more to the manner in which it is performed,

Pope Benedict XIV visiting the Trevi Fountain, by Panini. 'Artificial rivers ...
discharge into basins a flood of salubrious and refreshing waters' – Gibbon

than to the composition: the same music is many times repeated to different
words, and the singers have, by tradition, certain customs, expressions, and
graces of convention, which produce great effects; such as swelling and
diminishing the sounds altogether; accelerating or retarding the measure
at some particular words, and singing some entire verses quicker than
others ...

However, some of the great effects produced by this piece, may, perhaps,
be justly attributed to the time, place and solemnity of the ceremonials,
used during the performance: the Pope and conclave are all prostrated on
the ground; the candles of the chapel, and the torches of the balustrade,
are extinguished, one by one; and the last verse of this psalm is terminated
by two choirs; the Maestro di Cappella beating time slower and slower, and
the singers diminishing or rather *extinguishing* the harmony, by little and
little, to a perfect point.

It is likewise performed by select voices, who have frequent rehearsals,
particularly on the Monday in Passion Week, which is wholly spent in
repeating and polishing the performance.

This composition used to be held so sacred, that it was imagined excommunication would be the consequence of an attempt to transcribe it.* Padre

* Mozart in this actual year (1770) had astounded Rome by writing down the *Miserere*
from memory, after hearing it once performed. He was only fourteen at the time.
Mendelssohn performed a similar feat in 1830.

Martini told me there were never more than two copies of it made by authority, one of which was for the late King of Portugal, and the other for himself: this last he permitted me to transcribe at Bologna, and Signore Santarelli favoured me with another copy from the archives of the Pope's chapel.

EDWARD GIBBON

The beauty and splendour of the modern city may be ascribed to the abuses of the government, to the influence of superstition. Each reign (the exceptions are rare) has been marked by the rapid elevation of a new family, enriched by the childless pontiff at the expense of the church and country. The palaces of these fortunate nephews are the most costly monuments of elegance and servitude: the perfect arts of architecture, painting and sculpture, have been prostituted in their service; and their galleries and gardens are decorated with the most precious works of antiquity. The ecclesiastical revenues were more decently employed by the popes themselves in the pomp of the Catholic worship; but it is superfluous to enumerate their pious foundations since these lesser stars are eclipsed by the sun of the Vatican, by the dome of St Peter, the most glorious structure that ever has been applied to the use of religion. The fame of Julius II, Leo X and Sixtus V, is accompanied by the superior merit of Bramante and Fontana, of Raphael and Michael Angelo; and the same munificence which had been displayed in palaces and temples was directed with equal zeal to revive and emulate the labours of antiquity. Prostrate obelisks were raised from the ground; of the eleven aqueducts of the Caesars and consuls three were restored; the artificial rivers were conducted over a long series of old or of new arches, to discharge into marble basins a flood of salubrious and refreshing waters; and the spectator impatient to ascend the steps of St Peter's, is detained by a column of Egyptian granite, which rises between two lofty and perpetual fountains to the height of one hundred and twenty feet.

Every winter Rome had its Carnival before the start of Lent, like Florence and Venice. Robert Adam was there in 1756.

You dine about one o'clock and after dinner you mask and go out in your coach to the parade of coaches in the great street [the Corso]. There you have two rows of coaches – one going and the other coming – for near a mile of the way, with every person masked – noblemen driving their coaches or rather landaus, all spread open, full of fine dressed ladies with masks

The start of the Carnival in Rome, by David Allan

over their eyes and noses. Each coach carries its basket with confections and as soon as they discover the others passing them, skirmish with these confetti as a sign of their knowing them. The street is as straight as a line and the windows all have balconies and all these balconies are hung with tapestry and full of quality, gentry and artists who also salute their acquaintances by the assaulting sweetmeats. About five at night, the coaches stop and array themselves on each side of the street, leaving an avenue in the middle for the Barbes or race-horses, who run from one end of the street to the other without anybody on their backs, and are sometimes a dozen, sometimes more and sometimes fewer. They have instruments fixt about them that hurt them immensely and make them run like mad creatures.

What adds to the beauty of the show is that the footwalks on each side of the street have two rows of chairs, one raised above the other like the busking of a green-house, which are full of very handsome women and of all kinds, who love to spy into the manner of one another without being known; so that a princess and a country girl will be sat next one another. Upon twenty-four [six] striking the Corso finishes and the coaches withdraw. People then think of operas and plays at which they pass their time till near twelve at night. After that all go to the Festina or Masquerade where they divert themselves dancing till five, six and seven in the morning . . .

166

The start of the riderless horse race, by David Allan, signalled by the firing of the mortars

Tomorrow night I shall be dressed in a white sack, tied about the middle, an immense wig of horse-hair which covers half my back, and a most ugly mask face. I went to the Corso one afternoon with my coachman and Donald and the other servant all dressed as Harlequins, I in my black domino and a lady and gentleman in the coach with me, the lady in men's clothes ...

Our Carnival is finished [March 25] and very happily, without colds or other inconveniences. I exhibited in character of Signor Pulcinello most notably. Kept up dumb show with Sir William Stanhope, Abbé Grant* and many others, as well as English and Italian acquaintances, who could not for their souls find out who I was. Some said I was a woman disguised; others said I was an Italian and a third that I was some Prince or Cardinal who did not choose to make himself known. But all in vain. Abbé Grant searched through all the rooms to find me out, as he wanted me to dance: took everybody by the sleeve who had a black domino with red ribbons, calling him Mr Adams and swearing it was strange what had become

---

* Stanhope was brother of the Earl of Chesterfield, the famous letter writer, while Peter Grant was for many years the Scottish Catholic Agent in Rome and a great oiler of the wheels of expatriate society there.

The Young Pretender, Bonnie Prince
Charlie, by Blanchet, 1737–8

Prince Henry Benedict, Cardinal York,
by Blanchet, 1737–8

of me that night – whilst I was at his elbow the whole time without his once dreaming of my appearance in so grotesque a form. And next day, though I told him everything he had said, he would not believe I was there.

The last day of the Corso was very fine. Everybody was there parading with their finest equipages, and there were several cars dressed up, one full of Bacchantes all dressed with habits covered with vine leaves and bunches of grapes, each holding a bough in his hand. Festoons of grapes formed a canopy over them and upon the top of all was a Silenus bestriding a hogshead, crowned with vines and with two Bacchantes supporting him. They eat and drank away very merrily and had music alongst with them, there being at least twenty-five persons in the car, drawn by six horses with each a little Bacchante on his back. After it turned night each of these people held a wax taper in his hand which made a very fine illumination. It was dressed up in amphitheatrical form and I'm convinced the Silenus was twenty feet from the ground. There was another car of Pulcinellos with immense wigs, but none of them as curious as what I have described, which was at the expense of the Princess Borghese.

The Old Pretender and his sons, the Young Pretender and Cardinal York, were among the curiosities of Rome. Gray was intrigued by them in 1740, claiming that all English letters entering and leaving Rome were seen by them. By the 1760s Samuel Sharp is telling of the withdrawal of papal support and seediness taking over. In 1778 and 1779 Henry Swinburne sent some unflattering descriptions of the Stuart brothers back to his own brother in Northumberland.

THOMAS GRAY

[May] I have more time than I thought, and I will employ it in telling you about a Ball that we were at the other evening. Figure to yourself a Roman villa; all its little apartments thrown open, and lighted up to the best advantage. At the upper end of the gallery, a fine concert, in which La Diamantina, a famous virtuosa, played on the violin divinely, and sung angelically; Giovannino and Pasqualini (great names in musical story) also performed miraculously. On each side were ranged all the secular grand monde of Rome, the Ambassadors, Princesses, and all that. Among the rest Il Serenissimo Pretendente (as the Mantova gazette calls him) displayed his rueful length of person, with his two young ones, and all his ministry around him. '*Poi nacque un grazioso ballo*,'* where the world danced, and I sat in a corner regaling myself with iced fruits, and other pleasant rinfrescatives . . .

[July] A great ball given by Count Patrizii . . . at which the Pretender and his two sons were present. They are good fine boys, especially the younger, who has the more spirit of the two, and both danced incessantly all night long. For him, he is a thin ill-made man, extremely tall and aukward, of a most unpromising countenance, a good deal resembling King James II, and has extremely the air and look of an idiot, particularly when he laughs or prays. The first he does not often, the latter continually.

SAMUEL SHARP

The Pope and his Council have come to a resolution, upon the death of the Pretender,† to have no more concern in this business, and not only do not acknowledge the title of the present Pretender, but have forbidden all the Princes and Cardinals here to visit him; so that he sees only two or three friends, and leads a recluse and melancholy life. We this morning saw him at St Peter's church; he came thither, attended by three Gentlemen, and seven servants, to pay his devotions; there was hardly one in the church but ourselves, so that we had the opportunity of examining his person and behaviour very minutely. When I first saw him on his knees, I felt some compunction, which went off by degrees, as I became more certain, from his gestures, of the extreme bigotry and superstitious turn of his mind. After he had prayed at one altar, (for it was not to hear mass) he walked to another, and prayed a second time, kneeling in both places on the hard pavement. I never saw any one more stedfast in prayer than he appeared, not allowing his eyes to wander one moment from either the altar, the

* Then an elegant ball began.
† James Stuart, the Old Pretender, died in 1766.

'A Sporting Contest on the Tiber', by Claude Joseph Vernet: water jousting in front of the Castel Sant' Angelo

ground, or the book in his hand. During this transaction, reason superseded my pity, and I felt a kind of exultation in reflecting we were not under the dominion of a Prince so fond of images and hierarchy. Now I have seen him before the Virgin Mary, I can believe all that was said of his gross attachment to Popery when he was with us in 1745. His revenues are said to be very straight, not exceeding four thousand pounds a year. His stature is very elegant, but his face is a little bloated and pimpled, as if he had drunk too much, a vice laid to his charge, but, perhaps, without good grounds.

HENRY SWINBURNE

Cardinal York was officiating in the church [at Frascati outside Rome, where he was bishop] when we went in, and immediately sent to tell the ladies they must pull off their hats, or else go out. This peremptory order of the ex-prince could not very easily be complied with, according to the present mode of ladies' hats being fastened on the cushion by long pins, etc., unless His Royal Highness had provided a perruquier [hairdresser] to extricate them. They therefore refused to obey. Many messages passed and repassed. Mrs Swinburne sent him word that she had not heard mass, and left the omission on his conscience. He is an ugly foolish-looking, long-visaged fellow, very like his grandfather [James II], full of pride, and just such another obstinate bigot.

Abbé Grant told us a comical story of Cardinal York and Cardinal de

Bernis. They were sitting together one day, when the floor of the room gave way, and partly fell in. Frightened to death and thinking themselves on the verge of eternity, they both called with a loud voice, the one, '*Eccelenza! assoluzione in articulo mortis!*' the other '*Altessa reale! assoluzione in articulo mortis!*'* However, their fears were groundless – I do not mean to pun – for the floor did not fall a great way, and they met with no hurt.

We went to the opera [in Florence] where, for the first time, I beheld the poor unhappy representative of the Stuart race in the Count d'Albanie [Bonnie Prince Charlie]. He goes regularly to the theatre, and always falls asleep in a corner of his box, at the end of the first act, being generally intoxicated. His face is red and his eyes are fiery, otherwise he is not an ill-looking man. The Countess is not handsome, being black and sallow, with a pug nose. She always wears a hat. Alfieri, the Piedmontese [the poet, her lover], is a constant attendant in her box.

In 1740, in various letters to Richard West and Henry Seymour Conway, Walpole contrasts the present decay with the past glories of the city.

HORACE WALPOLE

[16 April] I am very glad that I see Rome while it yet exists: before a great number of years are elapsed, I question whether it will be worth seeing. Between the ignorance and poverty of the present Romans, everything is neglected and falling to decay; the villas are entirely out of repair, and the palaces so ill kept, that half the pictures are spoiled by damp. At the Villa Ludovisi is a large oracular head of red marble, colossal, and with vast foramina [openings] for the eyes and mouth: – the man that showed the palace said it was *un ritratto della famiglia* [a family portrait]. The Cardinal Corsini has so thoroughly pushed on the misery of Rome by impoverishing it, that there is no money but paper to be seen. He is reckoned to have amassed three millions of crowns. You may judge of the affluence the nobility live in, when I assure you, that what the chief princes allow for their eating is a testoon a day; eighteen pence: there are some extend their expense to five pauls, or half a crown: Cardinal Albani is called extravagant for laying out ten pauls for his dinner and supper. You may imagine they never have any entertainments: so far from it, they never have any company. The princesses and duchesses particularly lead the dismalest of lives. Being the posterity of Popes, though of worse families than the ancient nobility,

* 'Grant me final absolution of my sins.'

The Theatre of Marcellus, an etching by Piranesi showing its real appearance

they expect greater respect than my ladies the countesses and marquises will pay them; consequently they consort not, but mope in a vast palace with two miserable tapers, and two or three monsignori, whom they are forced to court and humour, that they may not be entirely deserted. Sundays they do issue forth in a vast unwieldy coach to the Corso.

In short, child, after sunset one passes one's time here very ill; and if I did not wish for you in the mornings, it would be no compliment to tell you that I do in the evening. Lord! how many English I could change for you, and yet buy you wondrous cheap! And then French and Germans I could fling into the bargain by dozens. Nations swarm here. You will have a great fat French cardinal garnished with thirty abbés roll into the area of St Peter's, gape, turn short, and talk of the chapel of Versailles. I heard one of them say t' other day, he had been at the *Capitale*. One asked of course how he liked it – *Ah! il y a assez de belles choses.*

[23 April] I am far gone in medals, lamps, idols, prints, etc. and all the small commodities to the purchase of which I can attain; I would buy the Coliseum if I could: judge. My mornings are spent in the most agreeable manner; my evenings ill enough. Roman conversations (conversaziones) are dreadful things! such untoward mawkins as the princesses! and the princes are worse.

[7 May] I am persuaded that in an hundred years Rome will not be worth seeing; 'tis less so now than one would believe. All the public pictures are decayed or decaying; the few ruins cannot last long; and the statues and private collections must be sold, from the great poverty of the families. There are now selling no less than three of the principal collections, the

The Theatre of Marcellus, an etching by Piranesi showing how he imagined it once more reduced to a ruin

Barberini, the Sacchetti, and Ottoboni: the latter belonged to the Cardinal who died in the Conclave.* I must give you an instance of his generosity, or rather ostentation. When Lord Carlisle was here last year, who is a great virtuoso, he asked leave to see the Cardinal's collection of cameos and intaglios. Ottoboni gave leave, and ordered the person who showed them to observe which my Lord admired most. My Lord admired many: they were all sent him the next morning. He sent the Cardinal back a fine gold repeater; who returned him an agate snuff-box, and more cameos of ten times the value. *Voilà qui est fini!* Had my Lord produced more golden repeaters, it would have been begging more cameos.

Edward Wright talks of Roman interior decor in general. In 1764 Smollett criticises the gardens of the Villa Borghese for being insufficiently English, while in 1779 the young Lord Herbert adopts a very down-to-earth approach in his description of the villa's decoration and sculpture collection.

EDWARD WRIGHT

The windows of their palaces have not sashes, to slide up or down, but all the parts of them are made to open, by way of casement, from bottom to top: neither do they use wainscot, their rooms being generally either painted in fresco, or plain plaister-walls, cover'd over with pictures, or hung with tapestry, velvet, or damask, as in England and other places. But what looks the most oddly to a stranger, is, to see a room hung perhaps with velvet or

* The College of Cardinals met in 1740 to elect a new Pope, Benedict XIV.

173

The Bishop of Derry and his granddaughter in the Borghese Gardens, by Gavin Hamilton. The Gardens are those run down by Smollett. The Bishop (also Earl of Bristol) was nearly killed on Vesuvius in 1766

the richest arras, a velvet bed perfectly emboss'd with high-rais'd gold-embroidery, the chairs, cabinets, glasses, and all the rest of the furniture suitable, set out in the most costly manner; the porphyry tables supported by carv'd-work in various figures, richly gilt; and after all this, a plain brick floor. For though it may be true, as they say, that marble would be too cold in winter, and boards inconvenient in summer, because subject to cracking or breeding of vermin, one would think they might have some fine sort of tile, of a better shape and consistence too than those plain bricks are. Their furniture is sometimes fancied after an extraordinary manner, some of the ornaments having been design'd by the best masters, (Carlo Maratti, and others of the first rate) as the frames of their chairs, tables, stands, and ornaments about their beds and elsewhere. They have indeed sometimes so much of the grand gusto in them, or to speak more plainly, are so incumber'd with finery, that they are much fitter to be look'd at than us'd. It is the general custom to have curtains to draw over the doors; and that not only in the palaces, but in the meaner houses too.

TOBIAS SMOLLETT
In a fine extensive garden or park, an Englishman expects to see a number of groves and glades, intermixed with an agreeable negligence, which seems

to be the effect of nature and accident. He looks for shady walks encrusted with gravel; for open lawns covered with verdure as smooth as velvet, but much more lively and agreeable; for ponds, canals, basins, cascades, and running streams of water; for clumps of trees, woods, and wildernesses, cut into delightful alleys, perfumed with honey-suckle and sweet-briar, and resounding with the mingled melody of all the singing birds of heaven: he looks for plats of flowers in different parts to refresh the sense, and please the fancy; for arbours, grottos, hermitages, temples, and alcoves, to shelter him from the sun, and afford him means of contemplation and repose; and he expects to find the hedges, groves, and walks, and lawns kept with the utmost order and propriety. He who loves the beauties of simple nature, and the charms of neatness, will seek for them in vain amidst the groves of Italy. In the garden of the Villa Pinciana [Borghese], there is a plantation of four hundred pines, which the Italians view with rapture and admiration: there is likewise a long walk of trees, extending from the garden-gate to the palace; and plenty of shade, with alleys and hedges in different parts of the ground: but the groves are neglected; the walks are laid with nothing but common mould or sand, black and dusty; the hedges are tall, thin and shabby; the trees stunted; the open ground, brown and parched, has scarce any appearance of verdure. The flat, regular alleys of evergreens are cut into fantastic figures; the flower gardens embellished with thin cyphers and flourished figures in box, while the flowers grow in rows of earthen-pots, and the ground appears as dusky as if it was covered with the cinders of a blacksmith's forge. The water, of which there is great plenty, instead of being collected in large pieces, or conveyed in little rivulets and streams to refresh the thirsty soil, or managed so as to form agreeable cascades, is squirted from fountains in different parts of the garden, through tubes little bigger than common glyster-pipes.* It must be owned indeed that the fountains have their merit in the way of sculpture and architecture; and that here is a great number of statues which merit attention: but they serve only to encumber the ground, and destroy that effect of rural simplicity, which our gardens are designed to produce.

LORD HERBERT

Over the door facing the entrance is an Equestrian Statue of Curtius leaping into the Gulph, (which Gulph by the by is in reality a Marsh, which at the time did exist). The Man is said to be very fine, and I believe he is, but with respect to the Animal he is upon, he is more like any other four legged

---

* A clyster-pipe, used to inject liquid into the intestines.

Piranesi's Egyptian designs for the English Coffee House in Rome, 'a filthy vaulted room', according to Thomas Jones, the Welsh landscape painter who was in Rome in the 1770s and 80s.

Animal than a Horse. It resembles more as to the Body, the figure of an Ass, but the position of his fore leggs was never resembled. The Sealing is painted by a Roman whose name I do not know, but the whole has a good effect. The sides of the Apartments do not correspond to the top, they are in the same manner as the English Coffee House, very proper for the English Coffee House, but very improper for a House belonging to the Prince Borghese, who has such an innumerable quantity of antique things. There are several fine Busts and Statues in this and in every corner of the House too numerous to be either mentioned or recollected. The second room is more unfinished than the Hall, the Scaffolding was all up, the richness of Marbles is inconceivable. In this Room is quantity of Alabaster Verd Antique, etc., etc. In the Hall which I before mentioned are six very fine Columns of Porphyry, but it is a pity that all these valuable things are disposed of with so little taste. The Prince says he has none, but he might at least apply to some one that had, as I should do in the same case. In the third Room we saw an innumerable quantity of other Busts and Statues, kept there till their places are settled; the Black Marble Statue supposed to be in a Vause of Blood generally called Seneca dying. Many Authors particularly French, mention what expression they found in it of a dying man, all of which I take to be false as the figure is not that of a dying Seneca or of any other dying man, but of an attendant to the Baths; much the same figure was found about 18 Months ago. The finest Bust is that of Lucus Verus; but besides the superb one there are several Copies, five I think in all. The fighting Gladiator, at least it is generally so called, is the finest

176

The Gardens of the Villa d'Este at Tivoli, by Fragonard, who was at the French Academy in Rome from 1751–61

Statue, but it was intended for some ancient Hero. The position of it is not natural, if you try to putt yourself in the same, you will most likely have the satisfaction of measuring your length on the Floor. The Hermaphrodite is also exceedingly fine, though the figure in its proportions is entirely Female, that is generally reckoned the fault of it. Note ... The Matress of the Hermaphrodite is reckoned fine, by Bernini. The parts of G. [genitals] is the only thing that distinguishes the Male part of the Character, all the rest being that of a beautiful Woman.

Frascati, Castel Gandolfo and Tivoli were places of summer retreat near Rome. The gardens of the Villa d'Este, the falls and ruins at Tivoli, more painted than any other scenes in the Roman landscape, are described by Gray in a letter to Richard West in May 1740.

We shall proceed to the garden, containing two millions of superfine laurel hedges, a clump of cypress trees, and half the river Teverone, that pisses

The Falls of Tivoli, by Fragonard. 'It is the most noble sight in the world' – Gray

into two thousand several chamber-pots. Finis. – Dame Nature desired me to put in a list of her little goods and chattels, and, as they were small, to be very minute about them. She has built here three or four little mountains, and laid them out in an irregular semi-circle; from certain others behind, at a greater distance, she has drawn a canal, into which she has put a little river of hers, called Anio; she has cut a huge cleft between the two innermost of her four hills, and there she has left it to its own disposal; which she has no sooner done, but, like a heedless chit, it tumbles headlong down a declivity fifty feet perpendicular, breaks itself all to shatters, and is converted into a shower of rain, where the sun forms many a bow, red, green, blue and yellow. To get out of our metaphors without any further trouble, it is

178

the most noble sight in the world. The weight of that quantity of waters, and the force they fall with, have worn the rocks they throw themselves among into a thousand irregular craggs, and to a vast depth. In this channel it goes boiling along with a mighty noise till it comes to another steep, where you see it a second time come roaring down (but first you must walk two miles farther) a greater height than before, but not with that quantity of waters; for by this time it has divided itself, being crossed and opposed by the rocks, into four several streams, each of which, in emulation of the great one, will tumble down too; and it does tumble down, but not from an equally elevated place; so that you have at one view all these cascades intermixed with groves of olive and little woods, the mountains rising behind them, and on the top of one (that which forms the extremity of one of the half-circle's horns) is seated the town itself. At the very extremity of that extremity, on the brink of the precipice, stands the Sybils' temple, the remains of a little rotunda, surrounded with its portico, above half of whose beautiful Corinthian pillars are still standing and entire; all this on one hand. On the other, the open Campagna of Rome, here and there a little castle on a hillock, and the city itself on the very brink of the horizon, indistinctly seen (being 18 miles off) except the dome of St Peter's; which, if you look out of your window, wherever you are, I suppose, you can see. I did not tell you that a little below the first fall, on the side of the rock, and hanging over that torrent, are little ruins which they shew you for Horace's house.

The Temple of the Sybil at Tivoli, by Piranesi: one of the most painted buildings in the world

179

A capriccio of Roman buildings, by Hubert Robert, who catered for the French enthusiasm for antiquity

Edward Wright investigates Roman church interiors, Dr Burney sees a young girl enter a convent, and we end with Samuel Sharp meeting the Holy Father himself.

EDWARD WRIGHT

The modern churches, and those especially which are dedicated to modern saints, are adorn'd most. That of S. Catherine of Siena is a perfect cabinet for neatness: nothing is to be seen in it, but carv'd-work and stucco gilt, marble and painting. They have a piece of good husbandry, whereby they make a little marble go a great way, only by incrustation, as they call it, or cementing thin flakes of it upon the wall they would cover. The same method was in use among the ancients, as we have seen in some old ruins. They cut it sometimes to not above a quarter of an inch thickness, and dispose the veins so, as to answer one another, as the joiners here do in their cabinets and other works of wallnut-tree, which they call fineering. Thus, tho' there be a great deal of labour in the workmanship, a small quantity (comparatively) spreads over a whole church; and has the same effect to the eye, as if the wall were all of solid marble. And it is necessary they should husband it thus in their finest works, where they employ such sorts of marble as are not the growth of Italy, and are scarce (if at all) now to be had, except in the ruins of old temples, palaces, baths, sepulchres, and other antique monuments; for the adorning of which, Egypt and India were ransack'd, while the Romans were masters of the world. Another art they

The companion capriccio, by Hubert Robert

have, of imitating marble so, that the difference is hardly to be perceived. It is done with what they call *scagliola*, which is not unlike what I have seen here in England called spar, and by some, *mater metallorum*, which is found in the lead-mines. With this material, burnt and powder'd, and made into a paste or plaister, and so mixt up with proper colours, they imitate marble to a great nicety; and with this mixture, in several variations, some of the churches are incrusted, and make much the same appearance as if they were incrusted with real marble ...

They have no pews in their churches, and 'tis a great advantage to the prospect within them, that they have not: for by this means, at the entrance, you have one clear uninterrupted view quite to the farther end. The people kneel upon the bare marble; only ladies of the first quality, and ambassadors ladies, have cushions. They seldom have preaching on a Sunday, except it be some extraordinary festival. Lent is the great time for that performance; and then they fill the middle of the church with benches, and stretch a canopy of canvas quite over preacher and people, a little higher than the pulpit, partly for warmth, and partly to assist the voice of the preacher, more than what the canopy of the pulpit alone could do.

Their pulpits are some of them perfect galleries, or indeed stages; on which many of them act their parts extremely well, and persuade their audience that they are in very good earnest themselves. Their action is what we should be apt to call overdone, but 'tis what the people there are us'd to, and expect; and the preachers find their account in it. They'll walk

The Earl of Northampton, by Pompeo Batoni – one of over 150 British visitors to Rome whom Batoni painted

sometimes from one end of the pulpit to the other, in much commotion, their eyes perfectly sparkling, and tears flashing in them, to produce the same effect in their audience ... The lowness of the parapet, or desk-part of the pulpit, shews their action to the more advantage: they'll sometimes lean over, strip their sleeve up to the elbow, and shake their fist at the people; sometimes snatch a little crucifix, which is always ready within reach, and shake that at them, and make appeals to it, and expostulations between it and the people.

CHARLES BURNEY

When the cardinal was robed, the noviciate was led into the chapel by a lady of the first rank in Rome, and brought to the altar in exceeding high dress. Her hair was of a beautiful light brown, and curled *en tête de mouton* all over her head. Her gown was of the richest embroidered, and, I believe, embossed blue and silver, I ever saw. She had on a large stage hoop, and a great quantity of diamonds; the train of her robe dragged full two yards on

The Piazza di Spagna, by Panini. 'Here most of the English reside' – Smollett

the ground; she seemed rather a pretty sort of young person than a beauty. When she first appeared, she looked very pale, and more dead than alive; she made a most profound reverence to the cardinal, who was seated on the steps of the altar in his mitre and all his rich vestments, ready to receive her. She threw herself upon her knees at the foot of the altar, and remained in that posture some time, while other parts of the ceremony were adjusting; then she walked up to the cardinal, who said, *Figlia mia, che domandate?* My child, what is your request? She said, that she begged to be admitted into that convent as a sister of the order of St Ursula: Have you well, said the cardinal, considered of what you ask? She answered, cheerfully, that she had; and was well informed of all she was about to do. Then she kneeled down again, and kissed the cardinal's hands, and received from him a little crucifix, which she also kissed; after which she retired again to the foot of the altar, where she threw herself on her knees, while the cardinal said mass, which was sung at the same time in the organ loft. After this, there was a sermon in the Italian language, and that being over, the cardinal led the nun-elect into the convent, where she was divested of all her gorgeous attire and worldly vanities, and had her hair cut off. She then came to the gate in her religious dress, to receive the white veil, with which she was invested by the lady abbess, the cardinal and the other assistants standing by.

After this there was more pretty music badly performed. The organ, by executing all the symphonies and accompaniments, overpowered the violins, and had a bad effect, though neatly played.

When her veil was on, the new sister came to the convent door, to receive

The Piazza Navona, by Panini. The square was flooded twice a week during the summer 'to refresh the air'

the congratulations of her friends and of the company; but first, with a lighted taper in her hand, she went round the convent to salute all the nuns, who had likewise tapers in their hands. When she was at the door, with the veil and crown on, but her face uncovered, I, among the rest, went close to her, and found she was much prettier than I had before imagined. She had a sweet mouth, and the finest teeth in the world, with lively sparkling eyes, and a genteel shaped visage; she would, anywhere else, have been styled a very pretty woman; but here, so circumstanced, a beauty. At the altar she changed countenance several times, first pale, then red, and seemed to pant, and to be in danger of either bursting into tears, or fainting; but she recovered before the ceremony was ended, and at the convent door assumed an air of great cheerfulness; talked to several of her friends and acquaintance, and seemed to give up the world very heroically. And thus ended this human sacrifice!

SAMUEL SHARP

The churches at Rome are so splendid and rich, that they have destroyed my appetite for that pursuit [church viewing]; besides, to use a metaphysical expression, the association of ideas spoils my relish for these gaudy and sumptuous objects, as I cannot look on their golden altars, and their fat priests, without reflecting on their deserted Campania, and starving laity; however I must mention, that as all ranks of men are allowed to wear a churchman's habit, and many do, a stranger is not to imagine that every person he sees with a band, etc. is an Ecclesiastick: there are multitudes in this dress at Rome, who have not the least connection with the church.

The Pope [Clement XIII, 1758–69] is said to be a good natured old man, and, I think, I can read that character in his countenance and gestures: When he returned to Rome for the winter, from his palace in the country, my company and I met him in the skirts of the town, and having no scruples of conscience to pay the same devoirs that others do here to a Prince of the country, and the head of the church, we threw ourselves on our knees, evidently to his great satisfaction; for, I assure you his eyes sparkled. We made a small groupe at a distance from any croud: I could see he was gathering himself into an attitude to give us an extraordinary benediction as he approached us, perceiving we were English; and I flatter myself to this moment, that he felt an inward joy, when he extended his hands, and poured out the blessing on to many wretched Hereticks. I will not say we are the better for his Holiness, but, to use the Catholick argument, we are certainly not the worse.

The Castel Sant' Angelo, by J. R. Cozens: a watercolour painted perhaps when he travelled with Beckford

The Bay of Naples, by Claude Joseph Vernet, 'where the renowned of ancient Rome enjoyed the luxury of glorious retreat and the true flow of soul' – Boswell

Naples

Most travellers going south from Rome along the Appian Way were soon seduced by the sensual delights and the animation of Naples: witness Gray writing to his mother in June 1740, Boswell to John Johnston in March 1765, and Mrs Thrale in January 1786.

THOMAS GRAY

Our journey hither was through the most beautiful part of the finest country in the world; and every spot of it, on some account or other, famous for these three thousand years past. The season has hitherto been just as warm as one would wish it; no unwholesome airs, or violent heats, yet heard of: The people call it a backward year, and are in pain about their corn, wine, and oil; but we, who are neither corn, wine, nor oil, find it very agreeable … The minute one leaves his Holiness's dominions, the face of things begins to change from wide uncultivated plains to olive groves and well-tilled fields of corn, intermixed with ranks of elms, every one of which has its vine twining about it, and hanging in festoons between the rows from one tree to another. The great old fig-trees, the oranges in full bloom, and myrtles in every hedge, make one of the delightfullest scenes you can conceive; besides that, the roads are wide, well-kept, and full of passengers, a sight I have not beheld this long time. My wonder still increased upon entering the city, which I think, for number of people, outdoes both Paris and London. The streets are one continued market, and thronged with populace so much that a coach can hardly pass. The common sort are a jolly lively kind of animal, more industrious than Italians usually are; they work till evening; then take their lute or guitar (for they all play) and walk about the city, or upon the sea-shore with it, to enjoy the fresco. One sees their little brown children jumping about stark-naked, and the bigger ones dancing with castanets, while others play on the cymbal to them. Your maps will show you the situation of Naples; it is on the most lovely bay in the world, and one of the calmest seas: It has many other beauties besides those

Thomas Gray,
painted in 1747
by Ecchardt

of nature. We have spent two days in visiting the remarkable places in the country round it, such as the bay of Baiæ, and its remains of antiquity; the lake Avernus and the Solfatara, Charon's grotto, etc. We have been in the Sybil's cave and many other strange holes under ground; but the strangest hole I ever was in, has been to-day at a place called Portici [Herculaneum], where his Sicilian Majesty has a country-seat. About a year ago, as they were digging, they discovered some parts of ancient buildings above thirty feet deep in the ground: Curiosity led them on, and they have been digging ever since; the passage they have made, with all its turnings and windings, is now more than a mile long.

JAMES BOSWELL

If a man's mind never failed to catch the spirit of the climate in which he breathes, I ought now to write you a most delicious letter, for Naples is indeed a delicious spot; *praeter omnes ridet.** I have been near three weeks here and have been constantly employed in seeing the classical places all around. Is it possible to conceive a richer scene than the finest bay diversified with islands and bordered by fields where Virgil's Muses charmed the creation, where the renowned of ancient Rome enjoyed the luxury of

* 'Which smiles beyond all others' (Horace, *Odes*, II. vi. 13–14).

glorious retreat and the true flow of soul* which they valued as much as triumphs? But, my dear friend, modern Naples has nothing of the ancient Parthenope except its heat and its idleness. The people are the most shocking race: eaters of garlic and catchers of vermin, an exercise which they scruple not to perform on the public streets . . .

The warmth of the air here has extracted the vicious humours from my blood and covered my chin and neck with a prodigious scurvy which plagues me much. But as it probably has saved me a fever, I do not complain, though almost certain that no woman under fifty would give me a kiss without being paid for it, as you have been paid for being the *doer* of some old lady. Go on and prosper.

MRS THRALE

Here are the most excellent, the most incomparable fish I ever eat; red mullets, large as our maycril, and of singularly high flavour; besides the calamaro, or ink-fish [squid], a dainty worthy of imperial luxury; almond and even apple-trees in blossom, to delight those who can be paid for coarse manners and confined notions, by the beauties of a brilliant climate. Here are all the hedges in blow as you drive towards Pozzuoli, and a snow of white May-flowers clustering round Virgil's tomb. So strong was the sun's heat this morning, even before eleven o'clock, that I carried an umbrella to defend me from his rays, as we sauntered about the walks, which are spacious and elegant, laid out much in the style of St James's Park, but with the sea on one side of you, the broad street, called Chiaja, on the other. What trees are planted there, however, either do not grow up so as to afford shade, or else they cut them, and trim them about to make them in pretty shapes forsooth, as we did in England half a century ago.

The Kingdom of the Two Sicilies – Naples and Sicily – was in fact ruled by the Spanish. Addison explains one method of diverting the Neapolitans from revolt. Beckford is not prepared totally to condemn King Ferdinand IV, usually painted as something of a simpleton, whilst Samuel Sharp notes the odd order of priorities followed by the nobility.

JOSEPH ADDISON

One would wonder how the Spaniards, who have but very few forces in the kingdom of Naples, should be able to keep a people from revolting, that

* 'The feast of reason and the flow of soul' (Pope, *The First Satire of the Second Book of Horace Imitated*, I. 128).

has been famous for its mutinies and seditions in former ages. But they have so well contrived it, that though the subjects are miserably harassed and oppressed, the greatest of their oppressors are those of their own body ... Insomuch, that when the king has been upon the point of selling a town to one of his barons, the inhabitants have raised the sum upon themselves, and presented it to the king, that they might keep out of so insupportable a slavery. Another way the Spaniards have taken to grind the Neapolitans, and yet to take off the odium from themselves, has been by erecting several courts of justice, with a very small pension for such as sit at the head of them, so that they are tempted to take bribes, keep causes undecided, encourage law-suits, and do all they can to fleece the people, that they may have wherewithal to support their own dignity. It is incredible how great a multitude of retainers to the law there are at Naples. It is commonly said, that when Innocent XI had desired the Marquis of Carpio to furnish him with thirty thousand head of swine, the Marquis answered him, that for his swine he could not spare them, but if his Holiness had occasion for thirty thousand lawyers, he had them at his service. These gentlemen find a continual employ for the fiery temper of the Neapolitans, and hinder them from uniting in such common friendships and alliances as might endanger the safety of the government. There are very few persons of consideration who have not a cause depending; for when a Neapolitan cavalier has nothing else to do, he gravely shuts himself up in his closet, and falls a tumbling over his papers to see if he can start a law-suit, and plague any of his neighbours.

WILLIAM BECKFORD

I was obliged to hurry to the palace in form and gala. A courtly mob had got thither upon the same errand, daubed over with lace and most notably be-periwigged. Nothing but bows and salutations were going forward on the staircase, one of the largest I ever beheld, and which a multitude of prelates and friars were ascending, in all the pomp of awkwardness. I jostled along to the presence chamber, where his Majesty was dining alone, in a circular enclosure of fine clothes and smirking faces. The moment he had finished, twenty long necks were poked forth, and it was a glorious struggle, amongst some of the most decorated, who first should kiss his hand. Doing so was the great business of the day, and everybody pressed forward to the best of their abilities. His Majesty seemed to eye nothing but the end of his nose, which is doubtless a capital object. Though people have imagined him a weak monarch, I beg leave to differ in opinion, since he has the boldness to prolong his childhood and be happy, in spite of years and

King Ferdinand IV of Naples. According to Mrs Thrale, 'his subjects ... know the worst of him is that he shoots at the birds, dances with the girls, eats macaroni, and helps himself to it with his fingers'

conviction. Give him a boar to stab, and a pigeon to shoot at, a battledore or an angling rod, and he is better contented than Solomon in all his glory, and will never discover, like that sapient sovereign, that all is vanity and vexation of spirit. His courtiers in general have rather a barbaric appearance, and differ little in the character of their physiognomies from the most savage nations. I should have taken them for Calmucks or Samoieds, had it not been for their dresses and European finery.

SAMUEL SHARP

What I said in my former letter with regard to the cheapness of servants, will account for the shewy appearance some of the Quality make here, with small fortunes; but what enables them also to support a large household, and a vast quantity of coach horses and carriages, is the circumstance of confining themselves to that one luxury. They have no expensive country-houses and gardens, no hounds, no race-horses, no parliament elections, and, in short, no great demands for the education of their children, disposing of all the girls in convents, upon very easy terms, whilst they are children, where they are left all their lives, unless they provide them husbands; for single young Ladies are not suffered to appear in the world, neither at spectacles nor visits.

The tomb of the priestess Mamia in the Street of the Tombs, Pompeii, in about 1778, by Francesco (son of Giovanni Battista) Piranesi and coloured by Jean-Louis Desprez

Another reason why the Neapolitan Gentry can figure with their equipages, is, the very small expence they admit at their tables. It is not usual here to dine or sup at each others houses, and there are some who never do, except only on Christmas-Day, or, perhaps, during the week; nay, they are, in general, so unaccustomed to entertain one another, that the greater number seldom receive their friends but upon weddings, deaths, and lyings in: They also carry their parsimony so far, as to lock up their fine furniture in the intervals of those ceremonies. Upon these occasions they are very pompous, and, what is extraordinary, the lying-in Ladies receive company in great crowds, the day after their delivery, which, however, as soon as the compliments are paid, retire immediately into the adjacent chambers, where they form themselves into card parties, or *converzationi* . . .

Some of their Princes have forty or fifty coach-horses, more than twenty different carriages, thirty, forty, or fifty domesticks and pages, besides four or five (and I once saw six) running footmen before their chariots. A running footman seems almost an indispensible necessary of life here: for a Gentleman never rides post on the road near Naples, nor takes an airing, without being preceded by one of these poor breathless fellows. It may be observed, however, that a running footman in the crowded streets of Naples is very useful, where the pavement is so smooth, and the noise of the crowd so great, that the motion of a coach is hardly heard, and many would be trampled by the horses, if they had not timely notice to get out of the way.

This love of shew seems to be more the characteristick of an Italian than even of a Frenchman, and is a striking novelty to an Englishman. In Great Britain, when a Gentleman can live comfortably within doors, and has a surplus, he thinks of a coach; but in Italy a coach and servants seem to be the first object, and when they are provided, they do as they can for the rest. The Italian turn for grandeur appears not only in this splendour of their equipages, but in the very genius of their language. What we call in England a little crash of musick, composed of two or three instruments, is pompously stiled in Italy an *Academia*. If you send your servant on a trifling halfpenny errand, he tells you, upon his return, he has executed the *ambasciata*; and so in other instances.

King Ferdinand of Naples prided himself on being a man of the people, the Lazzarone *King. Mrs Thrale reported him selling the fish he himself caught in the Bay as dear as possible and then giving the money away. The* Lazzaroni, *the poorest inhabitants of Naples, were in themselves one of its sights. Henry Swinburne describes their habits in the late 1770s, Mrs Thrale their tattoos, and Samuel Sharp the strange entertainment called the Cocagna, laid on for their benefit by the king.*

HENRY SWINBURNE

At that rainy time of the year, few are so wretched and helpless as to lie in the street, but most of the vagrants resort to the caves under Capodi Monte, where they sleep in crowds like sheep in a pinfold. As they are thus provided with a dwelling, for which no rent is exacted, they also procure food without the trouble of cooking or keeping house: the markets and principal streets are lined with sellers of macaroni, fried and boiled fish, puddings, cakes, and vegetables of all sorts; where, for a very small sum, which he may earn by a little labour, running of errands, or picking of pockets, the lazaro finds a ready meal at all hours: the flaggon hanging out at every corner invites him to quench his thirst with wine; or if he prefers water, as most of them do, there are stalls in all the thoroughfares, where lemonade and iced water are sold. The passion for iced water is so great and so general at Naples, that none but mere beggars will drink it in its natural state; and, I believe, a scarcity of bread would not be more severely felt than a failure of snow.

It is brought in boats every morning from the mountains behind Castelamare, and is farmed out at a great rent: the Jesuits, who possessed a large capital, as well as the true spirit of enterprize, had purchased the exclusive privilege of supplying the city with it.

Very little suffices to clothe the lazaro, except on holidays; and then he is indeed tawdrily decked out, with laced jacket and flame-coloured stockings: his buckles are of enormous magnitude, and seem to be the prototype of those with which our present men of mode load their insteps. The women are also very splendid on those days of shew; but their hair is then bound up in tissue caps and scarlet nets, a fashion much less becoming than their every day simple method.

MRS THRALE

I have seen Italians from other States greatly shocked at the grossness of these their unenlightened neighbours, particularly the half-Indian custom of burning figures upon their skins with gunpowder; these figures large and oddly displayed too, according to the coarse notions of the wearer. As the weather is exceedingly warm, and there is little need of clothing for comfort, our lazaroni have small care about appearances, and go with a vast deal of their persons uncovered, except by these strange ornaments. The man who rows you about this lovely bay, has perhaps the angel Raphael, or the blessed Virgin Mary, delineated on one brawny sun-burnt leg, the saint of the town upon the other. His arms represent the Glory, or the seven spirits of God, or some strange things, while a brass medal hangs from his neck, expressive of his favourite martyr, who, they confidently affirm, is so madly venerated by these poor uninstructed mortals, that when the mountain burns, or any great disaster threatens them, they beg of our Saviour to speak to St Januarius in their behalf, and intreat him not to refuse them his assistance ...

The Napolitani have no inclination to lose their old classical character for laziness ... I wonder, however, whether our people would work much, surrounded by similar circumstances; I fancy not. Englishmen, poor fellows! must either work or starve. These folks want for nothing – a house would be an inconvenience to them; they like to sleep out of doors, and it is plain they have small care for clothing, as many who possess decent habiliments enough throw almost all off till some holiday, or time of gala, and sit by the seaside playing at moro [a game] with their fingers.

A Florentine nobleman told me once, that he asked one of these fellows to carry his portmanteau for him, and offered him a carline – no small sum, certainly, to a Neapolitan, and rather more in proportion than an English shilling – he had not twenty yards to go with it:

The entrance to Pompeii in about 1778, by F. Piranesi and J.-L. Desprez

'Are you hungry, master?' cries the fellow.

'No,' replied Count Manucci; 'but what of that?'

'Why, then, no more am I,' was the answer; 'and it is too hot weather to carry burdens;' so turned about upon the other side, and lay still.

This class of people, amounting to a number that terrifies one but to think on – some say sixty thousand souls, and experience confirms no less – give the city an air of gaiety and cheerfulness, that one cannot help honestly rejoicing in. The Strada del Toledo is one continual crowd – nothing can exceed the confusion to a walker; and here are little gigs drawn by one horse, which, without any bit in his mouth, but a string tied round his nose, tears along with inconceivable rapidity a small narrow gilt chair, set between the two wheels, and no spring to it, nor anything else which can add to the weight; and this flying car is a kind of fiacre you pay so much for a drive in, I forget the sum.

SAMUEL SHARP

I shall now give you a description of the Cocagna, a strange, wild, and barbarous entertainment given to the populace here four Sundays successively in the Carnival. Opposite to the King's palace, at thirty or forty yards distance, they build a kind of booth, with deal boards, of about the size of the largest booth in Bartholomew fair, but a little different in form, being rather a scaffolding than booth, and having no top or covering; there is some kind of order or architecture in it, there being at each end two large doors, supported each by two columns: You ascend by these doors into the body of the building, which rises to a height equal to that of a moderate house in London. Upon the several parts of the scaffolding, are intermixed a variety of bushes and branches of evergreens; and behind the whole, and indeed in the midst of it, are some painted scenes, to render the object gaudy, and to deceive the eye with a view of a distant landscape. The sides of the building are studded with a prodigious number of loaves, placed in an architectural order, and likewise with a great quantity of joints of meat. Amongst the bushes are thirty or forty living sheep, some hogs, a few small beeves, and a great many living fowls. Now, the business of the day is to sacrifice these poor creatures to the hunger of the mob; to do which with some order, the soldiery, to the number of three thousand men, surround the building, to keep off the people till the king appears in the gallery, who waves his handkerchief for a sign when to begin the ceremony. Upon this the soldiers open their ranks, and all the mob rush in, and each, as he can, seizes his prey, and carries off the provision and the living animals. The whole operation is almost instantly over. You may imagine they form into little confederacies, or partnerships, for the more convenient execution of this purpose, and the carrying off a sheep or an ox. There has been in these riots much mischief done formerly, but this year I do not find that any man was either killed or hurt. The four companies of butchers, bakers, fishmongers, and poulterers, defray the charges of the four days.

An Englishman beholds with astonishment so many thousands collected together, and behaving so peaceably. In London, upon such an occasion of jollity and riot, one half of the croud would have been drunk; we should have seen one party quarrelling, another fighting, some laughing, all noisy; and, to compleat the confusion, perhaps, two or three dead cats hurled about from one to another, during the whole time of waiting.

Naples had a unique attraction in Vesuvius and its associated volcanic phenomena. We go with Fynes Moryson to the Grotto del Cane, which remained a draw into the nineteenth century, before climbing Vesuvius, after a recent eruption, with Henry Swinburne. Mrs Thrale adds further comment on 'this amazing mountain'.

FYNES MORYSON

At the foote of the inside of the Mountaine next to Naples, there is a venimous Cave, vulgarly called la grotta del' can', that is the Cave of the dogge; because they trie the poison by putting dogs into it. This Cave is some eight foote high, and sixe broad, and goeth some foure paces under the Mountaine, where a signe is set, beyond which, if any living thing passe, it presently dies ... We gave two poli to a woman (dwelling there) for a dog, to trie the poyson with it, which dog wee fastened to a long staffe, and so thrust him into the cave, holding him there, till he seemed dead, and being taken out, would not move for any blowes wee gave it; then according to the fashion, wee cast the dog into the Lake, and when he was drawne out, he began by little and little to move, and at last, being come to his senses, ranne away, as if he had been madde ...

Many have tried, that living things cast into that cave, and held there for longer time then is usuall, could never be fetched againe to life by this or any other water. They report, that a French Gentleman of Tournan trying to fetch a stone out of this cave beyond the aforesaid signe, paied for his curiosity by unrecoverable death. And that the French King Charles VIII, commanding an Asse to be thrust into this cave, the beast could never be fetched to life againe. And that don John, base sonne of the Emperour Charles V, forced a Gally-slave to goe into this cave, and he falling dead, forced another slave to fetch him out, who likewise fell dead, and that hee killed the third slave with his owne hand, because hee refused to fetch out his two dead fellowes. Many cast frogs into this cave, and except they presently leape back, this vapour kills them, which is said to rise out of Mines of Brimstone and other mettals.

HENRY SWINBURNE

A two-wheeled chaise conveyed me about eight miles from Naples, to the place where the lava ceased to run, after filling up a road, overturning some cottages, and consuming a wide tract of vineyards. The poplars, to which the vines were tied, were burnt or crushed beneath the weight of the cooler lumps that tumbled off on each side from the fiery mass. The surface of this black and now stagnant river is very uneven, full of points and protuberances, and broken into chasms. It answers the idea I have of a rocky mountain overturned into a valley, and shattered to pieces by an earthquake. In colour, the lava resembles slag, or the first clearings of an iron mine. The intense heat that still issued from it, though the flames were not visible by day-light, kept me at a distance. By night, fire may be seen through the crevices of the dusky crust. It had run close to a lava of seventeen years date, which is not yet sufficiently triturated by the action of air, to afford hold to the seeds of any plant, except a long hoary moss, commonly the first settler on these cinders, which are infinitely softer, and sooner crumbled to dust, than the *Sciarras* of Ætna.

After satisfying my curiosity with an attentive examination of these objects, I returned to Portici, hired a guide and mule, and rode up through

Vesuvius erupting, by Volaire, who specialised in painting the volcano

the vineyards to the foot of the mountain, where vegetation terminates in a long coarse grass, the only plant that can bear the vicinity of the hot ashes and sulphureous exhalations. I ascended the steep cone of cinders in a direct line, up to the ancles at every step in purple lukewarm ashes. The heat was not very powerful till we came within a few yards of the summit, and there smoke breaks out through many crannies. On the Portici side there is very little lava, except a few scattered stones that serve to rest upon. It is impossible to give a just idea of the fatigue of this climbing. Before that day I had mounted some very exalted points of the Alps, and clambered up the highest peak of the Pyrenees, without feeling such oppressive weariness and exhaustion of spirits and strength as I experienced on Vesuvius. Perhaps, the mephitic effluvium, which attacked my respiration, may also have had a debilitating effect upon my nerves and muscles. I should hardly have been able to proceed, had I not held by my guide, who went before with a handkerchief tied round his waist.

I confess I was a good deal disappointed on reaching the summit; for the descriptions I had read had raised in my imagination an expectation of every thing that could be glaring and striking in colours, pompous and tremendous in a scene of igneous phænomena; but the late eruption had,

198

for a time, laid all the mountain's fury asleep, and every thing was dull and dark. The vent, by which the lava ran out, is much below the top of the mountain, and on that side the sulphureous steams are very pungent. I was on the point of returning rather frustrated of my hopes, when a curling column of smoke and flame rose slowly out of the gloomy abyss, and brought up with it a thick white cloud, that had hitherto rendered the crater impervious to my sight. The wind quickly caught hold of this column, and whirled it round the immense caldron several times with inconceivable noise and velocity, till it forced part of the smoke to fly off horizontally from the mountain, and dashed the remainder back into its original cavern. During this conflict, on the opposite side to that where we stood, I had a peep very far into the crater. The sides seemed all lava and scoria, with very little variety in the tints, closed at bottom by an impenetrable screen of smoke. I have seen old ruined coalpits, that afford a tolerable idea of this volcanic kettle. As soon as the smoke was driven away, the roaring below grew loud, and frequent explosions were heard with a hollow sound; and at every throe, which caused a very considerable commotion in the thin arch on which we stood, a shower of red-hot stones was shot up; but not rising many feet above the mountain, they did not come within the sweep of the wind, and so fell back perpendicularly into the rumbling gulf.

MRS THRALE

Our eagerness to see sights has been repressed at Naples only by finding everything a sight; one need not stir out to look for wonders sure, while this amazing mountain continues to exhibit such various scenes of sublimity and beauty at exactly the distance one would choose to observe it from – a distance which almost admits examination, and certainly excludes immediate fear. When in the silent night, however, one listens to its groaning, while hollow sighs, as of gigantic sorrow, are often heard distinctly in my apartment, nothing can surpass one's sensations of amazement, except the consciousness that custom will abate their keenness. I have not, however, yet learned to lie quiet, when columns of flame, high as the mountain's self, shoot from its crater into the clear atmosphere with a loud and violent noise; nor shall I ever forget the scene it presented one day to my astonished eyes, while a thick cloud, charged heavily with electric matter, passing over, met the fiery explosion by mere chance, and went off in such a manner as effectually baffles all verbal description, and lasted too short a time for a painter to seize the moment and imitate its very strange effect. Monsieur de Vollaire, however, a native of France, long resident in this city, has obtained, by perpetual observation, a power of representing Vesuvius without that black shadow, which others have thought necessary to increase the contrast, but which greatly takes away all resemblance of its original.

That the situation of the crater changed in this last eruption is of little consequence; it will change and change again I suppose. The wonder is that nobody gets killed by venturing so near, while red-hot stones are flying about them so. The Bishop of Derry* did very near get his arm broke; and the Italians are always recounting the exploits of these rash Britons who look into the crater, and carry their wives and children up to the top; while we are, with equal justice, amazed at the courageous Neapolitans, who build little snug villages and dwell with as much confidence at the foot of Vesuvius, as our people do in Paddington or Hornsey. When I inquired of an inhabitant of these houses how she managed, and whether she was not frightened when the volcano raged, lest it should carry away her pretty little habitation: 'Let it go,' said she, 'we don't mind now if it goes to-morrow, so as we can make it answer by raising our vines, oranges, etc., against it for three years, our fortune is made before the fourth arrives; and then if the red river comes we can always run away, *scappar via*, ourselves, and hang the property. We only desire three years' use of the mountain as a hot wall or forcing-house, and then we are above the world, thanks be to God and St Januarius.'

Sir William Hamilton, the British Envoy at Naples, made himself the great expert on the behaviour of Vesuvius, but this was only one of his claims to fame. His second wife Emma, his nephew's discarded mistress, was admired by all who met her, including Goethe, who left a description of her 'attitudes' or impersonations in 1787. Nine years later her magic still worked for J. B. S. Morritt. In 1798 it worked with even more effect on Nelson.

J. B. S. MORRITT

Seeing her only can give you an adequate idea of what she is, as you may suppose from the reason given by her husband for marrying her, namely, 'that she only of the sex exhibited the beautiful lines he found on his Etruscan vases'.

Every man has a reason for marrying, and this is certainly a new one, though perhaps as good a reason as most others. If one may judge from effects, the case is so indeed, for no creature can be more happy or satisfied than he is in showing her off, which he does exactly as I have seen a wax figure exhibited, placing you in the most favourable lights, and pointing

* Frederick Augustus Hervey, 4th Earl of Bristol, the 'Mitred Earl', 1730–1803. This incident happened in 1766, see p. 174.

Sir William Hamilton, and the King and Queen of Naples watch a lava flow in 1771, by Fabris, from Hamilton's book on volcanoes, *Campi Phlegraei*

out in detail before her all the boasted beauties of his *chère moitié*, and, luckily for him, without any more bad effects upon her than would happen if she were a wax figure; which is wonderful considering the pains he takes and the country he takes them in.

We have met with the greatest civility from both, and if I were to say we did not admire her, the only excuse I could add must be that we were blind, for it can't happen to anybody that is not so. You may suppose her really an extraordinary woman, without education, without friends, without manners, when she came here; she has added to all the outward accomplishments of a woman of education a knowledge of Italian, French, and music, which last, with a very fine voice, she executes divinely. Add to these the most difficult of all, the *ton* of society, which she has raised herself to, and though not the *most* elegant, she is certainly on a par with most women of the circles she is in. This would be alone a proof of very superior sense, but her conduct to her husband is a stronger one. As he does nothing but admire her, and make other people admire her, from morning till night, as he would a fine painting, it is a delicate point, and yet she manages it so well that without affectation and without prudery (which would only make people recollect how times are altered) she keeps him and everybody else in order and behaves in the most exceptional manner ...

[For her attitudes] her toilet is merely a white chemise gown, some shawls, and the finest hair in the world, flowing loose over her shoulders.

Emma Hamilton in 1785, by Romney, the year before she came to Naples

These set off a tall, beautiful figure, and a face that varies for ever, and is always lovely. Thus accoutred, with the assistance of one or two Etruscan vases and an urn, she takes almost every attitude of the finest antique figures successively, and varying in a moment the folds of her shawls, the flow of her hair; and her wonderful countenance is at one instant a Sibyl, then a Fury, a Niobe, a Sophonisba drinking poison, a Bacchante drinking wine, dancing, and playing the tambourine, an Agrippina at the tomb of Germanicus, and every different attitude of almost every different passion. You will be more astonished when I tell you that the change of attitude and countenance, from one to another, sometimes totally opposite, is the work of a moment, and that this wonderful variety is always delicately elegant, and entirely studied from the antique designs of vases and the figures of Herculaneum, or the first pictures of Guido, etc., etc.

She sometimes does above two hundred, one after the other, and, acting from the impulse of the moment, scarce ever does them twice the same. In short, suppose Raphael's figures, and the ancient statues, all flesh and blood, she would, if she pleased, rival them all. What is still better is that she acts with the greatest delicacy, and represents nothing but what the most modest woman may see with pleasure. It is extraordinary, too, that, when not acting, her manners and air are noble, and the moment she pleases her whole figure is elegance itself. We passed the day very happily, as we dined there afterwards, and in the evening had music and a new piece of acting in the character of Nina. With her hair about her *ears*, or rather her *ankles*, she sang a beautiful scene of Paenillo, where she is supposed mad for the absence of her lover, and acted till she made us shudder and cry. A quarter of an hour after, in the dress of a Neapolitan *paysanne*, she danced the tarantella with castagnets, and sung vaudevilles till she convinced us all that acting was a joke to her talents, and I assure you I never saw in my life *any* actress half her equal either in elegance or variety. A painter who was of the morning party when she performed her attitudes cried with pleasure the whole time. When one does a thing well, however, we sometimes misplace it; and so she is rather apt to continue the acting in real life, where I think she approaches less to nature than when she acts professedly. Her conduct, *au reste*, is unexceptionable, and the *only* instance among the beau-monde at Naples (where morality is not at its greatest perfection, as you may have heard).

The pleasures of swimming in the Bay of Naples were demonstrated by Sir William, as described by Lord Herbert in 1779. Patrick Brydone also enjoyed swimming there in 1770 and saw it as the best antidote to the depressing effects of the Sirocco wind.

LORD HERBERT

Sir William Hamilton's Cassino is at Pausilippo and is the last house a carriage can arrive at. It is built on a small rock and consists of three rooms and a kitchen with a very diminutive garden. There are two flights of stairs to come up to it. When the weather is fine a small terrass before the building constitutes the Setting Room, with a large Venetian blind over it to guard it from the heat of the sun. Sir W. generally dines here, for at two the sun is off and while everybody is broiling at Naples he is enjoying the cool of the said Cassino. You may judge from this that the owner, not of this book, but of the Cassino is a man of sense ... Sir William called on me at eight to carry me on the water to see him, his monkey and one of his boatman's boys bathe, the said company bathe together every morning. The monkey is a very remarkable clever fellow, bearing the name of Jack. The boy though perhaps inferior to him both in sense and understanding deserves to be mentioned, his name then is pronounced Aiātan. I breakfasted with Sir William, came home, dressed and at twelve went sailing with Lord Maynard* ... In the evening we went a second time a-sailing after which I returned home to read my letters more at ease than I had done before.

* Charles, 2nd Viscount Maynard (1752–1824). He married, in 1776, Nancy Parsons the actress, who had been the mistress of the Dukes of Grafton and Dorset.

A music party in Naples at Lord Fortrose's house, 1771, by Fabris. The young Mozart is thought to be the seated figure in brown

PATRICK BRYDONE

The most disagreeable part of the Neapolitan climate is the sirocc or south-east wind, which is very common at this season. It is infinitely more relaxing, and gives the vapours in a much higher degree, than the worst of our rainy Novembers. It has now blown for these seven days without intermission; and has indeed blown away all our gaiety and spirits; and if it continues much longer, I do not know what may be the consequence. It gives a degree of lassitude, both to the body and mind, that renders them absolutely incapable of performing their usual functions. It is not perhaps surprising, that it should produce these effects on a phlegmatic English constitution; but we have just now an instance, that all the mercury of France must sink under the load of this horrid, leaden atmosphere. A smart Parisian marquis came here about ten days ago: he was so full of animal spirits that the people thought him mad. He never remained a moment in the same place; but, at their grave conversations, used to skip from room to room with such amazing elasticity, that the Italians swore he had got springs in his shoes. I met him this morning, walking with the step of a philosopher; a smelling bottle in his hand, and all his vivacity extinguished. I asked what was the matter? '*Ah! mon ami,*' said he, '*je m'ennui à la mort; – moi, qui n'ai jamais sçu l'ennui. Mais cet execrable vent m'accable; et deux jours de plus, et je me pend.*' [Ah! my friend, I am depressed to death – I, who have never known depression. But this frightful wind gets me down. Two more days of it and I will hang myself.]

The natives themselves do not suffer less than strangers; and all nature seems to languish during this abominable wind. A Neapolitan lover avoids his mistress with the utmost care in the time of the sirocc, and the indolence it inspires, is almost sufficient to extinguish every passion. All works of genius are laid aside, during its continuance; and when any thing very flat or insipid is produced, the strongest phrase of disapprobation they can bestow is, '*Era scritto in tempo del sirocco;*' that it was writ in the time of the sirocc ...

Sea-bathing we have found to be the best antidote against the effects of the sirocc; and this we certainly enjoy in great perfection. Lord Fortrose, who is the soul of our colony here, has provided a large commodious boat for this purpose. We meet every morning at eight o'clock, and row about half a mile out to sea, where we strip and plunge into the water: Were it not for this, we should all of us have been as bad as the French marquis. My lord has ten watermen, who are in reality a sort of amphibious animal, as they live one half the summer in the sea. Three or four of these generally go in with us, to pick up stragglers, and secure us from all accidents. They dive with ease to the depth of forty, and sometimes of fifty feet, and bring up quantities of excellent shellfish during the summer months; but so great is their devotion, that every time they go down they make the sign of the cross, and mutter an Ave Maria, without which they think they should certainly be drowned; and were not a little scandalized at us for omitting this ceremony. To accustom us to swimming in all circumstances, my lord has provided a suit of clothes, which we wear by turns; and from a very short practice, we have found it almost as commodious to swim with as without them; we have likewise learned to strip in the water, and find it no very difficult matter: And I am fully persuaded, from being accustomed to this kind of exercise, that in case of shipwreck we should have greatly the advantage over those who had never practiced it; for it is by the embarrassment from the clothes, and the agitation that people are thrown into, from finding themselves in a situation they had never experienced before, that so many lives are lost in the water.

After bathing, we have an English breakfast at his lordship's; and after breakfast, a delightful little concert, which lasts for an hour and a half.

Moving antiquities from Herculaneum to Naples in 1779, by F. Piranesi
and J.-L. Desprez

Barbella, the sweetest fiddle in Italy, leads our little band. This party, I
think, constitutes one principal part of the pleasure we enjoy at Naples.

*In 1755 Robert Adam visited Herculaneum, a moment of the greatest significance
for the future of English taste. In the late 1770s Henry Swinburne was present at
the opening of some rooms at the smaller site of Stabia and described the highly
unscientific approach in those early days of archaeology.*

ROBERT ADAM

With great pleasure and much astonishment we viewed the many curious
things that have been dug out of it, consisting of statues, busts, fresco
paintings, books, bread, fruits, all sorts of instruments from a mattock to
the most curious Chirurgical probe. We traversed an amphitheatre with
the light of torches and pursued the tracks of palaces, their porticoes and
different doors, division walls and mosaic pavements. We saw earthen vases
and marble pavements just discovered while we were on the spot and were
shown some feet of tables in marble which were dug out the day before we
were there. Upon the whole this subterranean town, once filled with
temples, columns, palaces and other ornaments of good taste is now exactly
like a coal-mine worked by galley-slaves who fill up the waste rooms
they leave behind them according as they are obliged to go a-dipping or
strikeways. I soon perceived that the vulgar notion of its being swallowed

up by an earthquake was false, but it was still worse. It was quite overcome with a flood of liquid stone from Mount Vesuvius which runs out upon an eruption, is called lava and when cool is as hard as our whinstone: of this you find a solid body of 50 or 60 feet high many places, which had come down with such force from the hill as to overturn all houses and everything else it met with. And it penetrated houses by doors and windows as may be seen by the above mentioned amphitheatre of [which] most of the entrances are filled up as if they had been built up artificially with solid rock.

I am afraid they will never be able to make anything of the books they have found. They are so black and rotten that they are no sooner touched than they fall to ashes. A priest has invented a machine by which he separates the leaves by degrees and has made out a few pages of a treatise wrote in Greek by one Bion in defence of the Epicurean Philosophy and another treatise against music, the author not known. The other Rolls of Books they have not yet been able to unfold and I'm afraid never will.

HENRY SWINBURNE

Having received an invitation to be present at the opening of some lately discovered rooms at Stabia, I went thither with a party ... Stabia was a long string of country houses, rather than a town ... In the catastrophe of seventy-nine [AD], the wind blowing furiously from the north, brought the ashes of Vesuvius upon it; all the country was covered with cinders and rapilli, or small pumice-stones, many yards deep. Towns, houses, and trees, were buried, and their situations remained marked in the plain by hillocks like barrows. Stabia, though six miles from the mountain, was overwhelmed and lost, till it was casually discovered about twenty-eight years ago. The earthquake had so damaged the buildings, that none of them can be preserved, and therefore as soon as every thing curious is taken out, the pits are filled up again. The ashes penetrated into all parts, and consumed every thing that was combustible.

On our arrival, the workmen began to break into the subterraneous rooms, and, as the soil is all a crumbling cinder, very little labour was requisite to clear them. When opened, the apartments presented us with the shattered walls, daubed rather than painted with gaudy colours in compartments, and some birds and animals in the cornices, but in a coarse style, as indeed are all the paintings of Stabia. In a corner, we found the brass hinges and lock of a trunk; near them, part of the contents, viz. ivory flutes in pieces, some coins, brass rings, scales, steel-yards, and a very elegant silver statue of Bacchus, about two inches high, represented with a crown of vine leaves, buskins, and the horn of plenty.

The first discovery of the Temple of Isis at Pompeii in 1765, by Fabris, from Hamilton's book *Campi Phlegraei*

Henry Swinburne tells some amusing anecdotes about the lighting and funeral arrangements in Naples, then Mrs Thrale comments on a street pageant. Lastly Dr Burney investigates recruitment of male castrati singers and Samuel Sharp is less than wholeheartedly enthusiastic about the great San Carlo opera house, built in 1737.

HENRY SWINBURNE

Naples has neither watchmen nor lamps; but of late years darkness has been dispelled in many streets by the piety of Father Rocco, a Dominican friar, who rules the mob with absolute controul; he persuades them to subscribe oil for lamps to burn before images, which he fixes up in the most convenient places, and thus turns their devotion to public account; this extraordinary man, whose manners are clownish, and address adapted to the people he governs, carries all before him with rude energy, beats the quarrelsome into peace, strips the shops and distributes their victuals among the poor; decides petty law-suits, and suffers no appeal to lie from his sentence. The court understands his importance, and has often experienced the good effects of his mediation; though of late years an attention to the plentiful supply of cheap provisions, and a strong garrison, have kept the populace quiet, to a degree unknown in former times, yet particular circumstances may yet render a Neapolitan mob formidable to government. During a late eruption of Vesuvius, the people took offence at the new theatre being more frequented than the churches, and assembled in great numbers to drive the

The discovery of a skeleton at Pompeii, by Fragonard

nobility from the opera; they snatched the flambeaux from the footmen, and were proceeding tumultuously to the cathedral to fetch the head of San Gennaro [St Januarius], and oppose its miraculous influence to the threats of the blazing volcano: this would undoubtedly have ended in a very serious sedition, if father Rocco had not stept forth, and after reproaching them bitterly with the affront they were about to put upon the saint by attending his relicks with torches taken from mercenary hands, ordered all to go home and provide themselves with wax tapers; the crowd dispersed, and proper measures were taken to prevent its gathering again.

The reader must not be surprized to hear that torches should be esteemed so necessary an appendage to piety, for at Naples nothing is done in religious matters without lights of some sort ... In funeral ceremonies, it is usual to hire clergymen called Fratanzari, who having no patrimony, earn as much by their fees on these occasions as pays for their ordination; but it is very common for them to dress up the vagabonds of the streets in their cloaths, and send them to sing and pray in their stead; these fellows are always attended by a friend who holds a paper bag into which they make the taper sweal and waste as much as possible. At the burial of an archbishop of Naples, four hundred friars attended with wax-lights, but some thieves let loose a mad ox among them, and in the confusion ran away with the candles. At another great funeral, a gang of rogues disguised themselves like clerks and sacristans, and demanded from each assistant his taper, which they extinguished, and carried off with the utmost hypocritical composure ...

I was one day witness of the funeral of an old fisherman. The actions of his widow were so overstrained as to be truly ridiculous: she tore off her hair and clothes, and yelled in the most hideous manner, till her step-sons appeared to take possession of the goods: she then turned her fury upon them, and beat them out of the house. The priests now came for the body; and she opposed their entry for a decent length of time; but at last, suffering herself to be overpowered by numbers, flew to the window with her daughters and her mother (who, from having outlived many relations, had scarce a hair left on her head) and there beat her breast, scratched her cheeks, and threw whole handfuls of hair towards the bier with the frantic gestures of a demoniac. The procession was no sooner out of sight, than all was quiet; and in five minutes I heard them laughing and dancing about the room, as if rejoicing to be rid of the old churl.

MRS THRALE

But I am called from my observations and reflections, to see what the Neapolitans call '*Il trionfo di Policinello*' [Punch], a person for whom they profess peculiar value ...*

The triumph was a pageant of prodigious size, set on four broad wheels like our waggons, but larger; it consisted of a pyramid of men, twenty-eight in number, placed with wonderful ingenuity all of one size, dressed in one uniform, viz., the white habit and puce-coloured mask of caro Policinello; disposed too with that skill which tumblers alone can either display or describe; a single figure, still in the same dress, crowning the whole, and forming a point at the top, by standing fixed on the shoulders of his companions, and playing merrily on the fiddle; while twelve oxen of a beautiful white colour, and trapped with many shining ornaments, drew the whole slowly over the city, amidst the acclamations of innumerable spectators, that followed and applauded the performance with shouts.

What I have learned from this show, and many others of the same kind, is of no greater value than the derivation of his name who is so much the favourite of Naples: but from the mask he appears in, cut and coloured so as exactly to resemble a flea, with hook nose and wrinkles, like the body of that animal; his employment, too, being ever ready to hop, and skip, and jump about, with affectation of uncommon elasticity, giving his neighbours a sly pinch from time to time: all these circumstances, added to the very

* 'Punchinello is to the Neapolitan stage what Harlequin is to other Italian ones ... Punchinello is the wit, the droll ... has the exclusive privilege of saying good things and *double entendres*,' Henry Swinburne.

intimate acquaintance and connection all the Neapolitans have with this, the least offensive of all the innumerable insects that infest them; and, last of all, his name, which, corrupt it how we please, was originally Pulicinello; leaves me persuaded that the appellation is merely 'little flea'.

CHARLES BURNEY

I enquired throughout Italy at what place boys were chiefly qualified for singing by castration, but could get no certain intelligence ... However, with respect to the Conservatorios at Naples, Mr Gemineau, the British consul, assured me that the young *Castrati* came from Lecce in Apulia; but, before the operation is performed, they are brought to a Conservatorio to be tried as to the probability of voice, and then are taken home by their parents for this barbarous purpose. It is, however, death by the laws to all those who perform the operation, and excommunication to everyone concerned in it, unless it be done, as is often pretended, upon account of some disorders which may be supposed to require it, and with the consent of the boy. And there are instances of its being done even at the request of

'Thou tuneful scare-crow': a caricature of Farinelli (centre) made when he was in England in 1735, by J. Goupy and Dorothy Boyle, Countess of Burlington. He was the most famous of all castrati

the boy himself, as was the case of the Grassetto at Rome. But as to these previous trials of the voice, it is my opinion that the cruel operation is but too frequently performed without trial, or at least without sufficient proofs of an improvable voice; otherwise such numbers could never be found in every great town throughout Italy, without any voice at all, at least without one sufficient to compensate such a loss.*

SAMUEL SHARP

The amazing extent of the stage, with the prodigious circumference of the boxes, and height of the cieling, produce a marvellous effect on the mind, for a few moments; but the instant the Opera opens, a spectator laments this striking sight. He immediately perceives this structure does not gratify the ear, how much soever it may the eye. The voices are drowned in this immensity of space, and even the orchestra itself, though a numerous band, lies under a disadvantage ... It is so much the fashion at Naples, and, indeed, through all Italy, to consider the Opera as a place of rendezvous and visiting, that they do not seem in the least to attend to the musick, but laugh and talk through the whole performance, without any restraint ... I had been informed that ... when a favourite song was singing, or the King was present, they observed a deep silence: I must, however, deny the fact in both cases ...

An Englishman wonders at this behaviour of the Italians; he comes with a notion that they are all enthusiastically fond of musick; that there is something in the climate which gives them this propensity, and that their natural genius is nursed and improved by a musical education: Upon enquiry, he finds his opinion almost groundless; very few Gentlemen here practice the fiddle, or any other instrument, and all the young Ladies are placed in convents, where they remain until they marry, or take the veil, and where musick is seldom a part of their education; nor can it be supposed that any woman, after marriage, undertakes so laborious a task as that of making a proficiency on the harpsichord ... I found it impossible, at Venice and here, to hire a harpsichord fit to play on; so small is the demand, I presume, for that instrument ...

The Pit here, as I have already hinted, is very ample; it contains betwixt five and six hundred seats, with arms resembling a large elbow chair, besides an interval all through the middle, and a circuit all round it, under the boxes, both of which I judge, in a crowded house, will hold betwixt one and

* When touring Germany in 1772, Burney reported that there were fifteen castrati at the Duke of Würtemberg's music conservatory at Ludwigsburg, 'the court having in its service two Bologna surgeons expert in this vocal manufacture'.

A Neapolitan coastal scene, by Claude Joseph Vernet, who often invented large parts of his coastal compositions

two hundred people standing. The seat of each chair lifts up like the lid of a box, and has a lock to fasten it. There are, in Naples, Gentlemen enough to hire by the year the first four rows next to the orchestra; who take the key of the chair home with them, when the Opera is finished, lifting up the seat, and leaving it locked. By this contrivance, they are always sure of the same place, at whatever hour they please to go to the Opera; nor do they disturb the audience, though it be in the middle of a scene, as the intervals betwixt the rows are wide enough to admit a lusty man to walk to his chair, without obliging any body to rise ...

The grand Opera being the only object of the Neapolitans, the others are forbidden, by authority, to bring any dancers on their stage, without a special licence, lest they should divert the attention of the public from the King's Theatre. I must not omit a foolish singularity, in relation to the women dancers at Naples, that, in consequence of an order from court, in the late King's time, they all wear black drawers. I presume it was from some conceit on the subject of modesty, but it appears very odd and ridiculous.

One of the temples at Paestum, by Piranesi, who would not admit they were Greek.
The figures are by his son Francesco

Southern Italy

The temples built at Paestum on the coast about seventy miles south of Naples by the ancient Greek colonists were only 'discovered' in the early eighteenth century by Count Gazola, commander of the Neapolitan artillery, and Bishop Berkeley. When James Adam, the over-fastidious brother of Robert, went there in 1761 he was still pioneering. He did not think the 'early, inelegant unenriched Doric' style worth the lack of milk and butter or the superabundance of fleas there. Henry Swinburne puts him in his place.

The majesty of this ruin must excite admiration, even in those whose taste inclines them to relish only that luxuriant and ornamental species of architecture in which the ancient Romans delighted, and in which their successors, the modern Romans, have suffered their genius and imagination to wanton almost without bounds; an eye that brightens only with the view of nice Corinthian foliage, and the minute members of the composite order, will perhaps receive no delectable impression from the sight of such massive proportions, such simple and solid parts as these. An observer must have reflected seriously on the art, and weighed the purposes of each building, with the intention of the architect, before he can bring himself to allow these noble remains of antiquity the praise they so richly deserve.

Puglia, Italy's heel, was an area far off the ordinary Grand Tourist's beaten track, but some of Henry Swinburne's lively descriptions are worth rescuing from obscurity. We join him first near Manfredonia, then musing over the ancient battlefield of Cannae where Hannibal defeated the Romans, followed by an uncomfortable picnic near Monopoli, and a farcical tragedy at Francavilla.

Our next stage was to Manfredonia, twenty miles through a flat pasture covered with asphodels, thistles, wild artichokes, and fennel-giant; of the last are made bee-hives and chair-bottoms; the leaves are given to asses, by way of a strengthener, and the tender buds are boiled and eaten as a delicacy by the peasants. This plant covers half the plain, and rises to such a height, that there is an instance, in one of the wars between France and Spain, of the Spaniards having marched through it undiscovered ... All sorts of vegetables abound here, for flavour and succulency infinitely superior to those raised by continual waterings in the cineritious soil of Naples; lettuce in particular is delicious, fish plentiful and cheap; the rocky shore covered with shell-fish, alga, and balls called *pila marina*, which are nothing more than a conglomeration of the finer fibres of submarine roots detached from their plants, and rolled up by the undulating motion of the water; of these fibres a delicate paper has been obtained by an experimental philosopher, whose studies in natural history are always directed by patriotic views, and the hope of strikeing out discoveries of public utility.

The traces of the town of Cannæ are very faint, consisting of fragments of altars, cornices, gates, walls, vaults, and underground granaries ... At the foot of the hill is a large arch over a marble trough, which receives the waters of a copious spring. Here we found a camp of Abruzzese shepherds on the point of departing for the mountains. Rough in aspect, dialect, and dress, but civil and hospitable, they offered us milk, cheese, and cold meat. The chief of them gave us some brass coins of Zeno and Leo, found among the ruins; and seemed astonished at our offering to pay him for such baubles.

   The hill above the well being rather higher than the rest, served as a reconnoitring post, where I inspected my notes, and took drawings of the country, before I entered the field of battle. My eyes now ranged at large over the vast expanse of unvariegated plains. All was silent; not a man, not an animal, appeared to enliven the scene. We stood on ruins, and over vaults; the banks of the river were desert and wild. My thoughts naturally assumed the tint of the dreary prospect, as I reflected on the fate of Rome and Carthage. Rome recovered from the blow she received in these fields; but her liberty, fame, and trophies have long been levelled in the dust. Carthage lies in ruins less discernible than these of the paltry walls of Cannæ: the very traces of them have almost vanished from the face of the earth. The daring projects, marches, and exploits of her hero, even the victory obtained on this spot, would, like thousands of other human achievements, have been long ago buried in oblivion, had not his very enemies consigned him to immortality; for the annals of Carthage exist no more: one common ruin has swallowed all.

Next morning I was on horseback [and had left Monopoli] before sun-rise, intending to make a very long day's journey; and being apprehensive, from

Henry Swinburne,
by Batoni

the heavy feel of the air, that I should suffer from intense heat in the noon-tide hours. My prognostics were but too just; for a hotter sun, and a more stifling sultriness, could not be felt in the dog-days ... The cystus, which grows in great abundance on these waste lands, exhaled so powerful an effluvium, when the sun had been risen some time, that I was overcome with it. One of the servants, already half dead with heat and fatigue, had the additional ill-fortune of being frightened almost out of his wits. As we were trotting along the burning sands, he on a sudden gave a loud shriek, and threw himself from his horse, crying out that he was a dead man, for either a scorpion, a tarantula, or a serpent had stung him on the instep. On pulling off his boot, I found that his terrors and pains were caused by the rays of the sun, which had penetrated through a hole in the upper leather, and raised a blister on the skin. The preposterous gestures and expressions of this lazzarone supported my spirits till we arrived at a small single house, consisting of a kitchen, loft, and stable, lately erected for the convenience of travellers, by the agents of the Order of Malta, to which the land belongs. The kitchen was too hot for me to breathe in, and the other two apartments as full of fleas as Shakespeare's inn at Rochester; so that my only refuge was the narrow shade of the house, which was contracted every minute more and more, as the sun advanced towards the meridian. Behind the house then I sat down, to dine upon the fare we had brought in our wallet. Unluckily I had not thought of wine or water, neither of which were now to be had tolerably drinkable; so that I was obliged to content myself with the water of a cistern full of tadpoles, and qualify it with a large quantity of wine, that resembled treacle much more than the juice of the grape. While

217

I held the pitcher to my lips, I formed a dam with a knife, to prevent the little frogs from slipping down my throat. Till that day I had had but an imperfect idea of thirst.

And now the Rector of the College [at Francavilla], the Father Guardian of the Capuchins, and the Magistrates, entered in great form. The first addressed me in a short, polite speech, which he uttered with some embarrassment. My introducer of Ambassadors whispered in my ear, that the Rector had composed a very eloquent harangue for *two* illustrious travellers; but on finding only one, had been obliged to lay it aside, as he could not at a minute's warning adapt to the singular all the figures of rhetoric which were addressed to the dual number. What I lost in his discourse, was made up to me by the friar, who, with a nasal tone and many bows, bestowed upon me every possible virtue, and struck out such wild metaphors, as quite enchanted his auditors, and almost threw me off my guard. He acquainted the company, that I travelled into foreign parts to collect oil for the lamps of science in my own country; that my mother wit was the wick, and my eloquence the flame ...

The principal parish-church is new, gay, and well lighted; but so stuccoed, festooned, and flowery, that the whole decoration is a mere chaos. The plan was drawn at Rome, but executed by a Puglian architect, who from caprice or blunder reversed the disposition of the parts, and opened the chief door at the head of the Latin cross, a place usually allotted to the altar and choir. This alteration is no improvement in the art, but, on the contrary, an experiment productive of very aukward effects. In a side chapel is a dark portrait of the Madonna, which was the cause of the foundation of the town ...

After a long and tiresome meal, I was left to take my afternoon nap, and in the evening entertained with the tragedy of Judith and Holofernes, acted by the young people of the town, in a theatre belonging to the castle. Their rude accent, forced gestures, and strange blunders in language, rendered their dismal drama a complete farce. When the heroine murdered the general, the whole house shook with thundering bursts of applause; the upper part of his body was hidden by the side scenes; the lower parts lay on a couch upon the stage, and in the agonies of death were thrown into such convulsions, kickings, and writhings, as melted the hearts and ravished the souls of the attentive audience. Judith then came forward, and repeated a long monologue, with her sword in one hand, and a barber's block [crude wooden head], dripping with blood, in the other. Never was tragedy-queen sent off the stage with louder or more sincere acclamations.

Sicily

Patrick Brydone's first target in Sicily was the ascent of the volcano Etna, at nearly 11,000 feet a much more daunting proposition than Vesuvius (under 4,000 feet). But first we hear him on the erotic potential of nuns at Messina, what must be the original of every subsequent Mafia protection racket, and a cleric in Catania persecuted for his scientific observations.

After dinner our depute-consul (a Sicilian) carried us to several convents, where we were received by the nuns with great politeness and affability. We conversed with them for some hours through the grate, and found some of them by no means deficient, either in point of knowledge or sprightliness; but none of them had sincerity enough (which we met with in Portugal more than once) to acknowledge the unhappiness of their situation. All pretended to be happy and contented, and declared they would not change their prison for the most brilliant situation in life. However, some of them had a soft melancholy in their countenances, that gave the lie to their words; and I am persuaded, in a tete-a-tete, and on a more intimate acquaintance, they would have told a very different story. Several of them are extremely handsome; but, indeed, I think they always appear so; and am very certain, from frequent experience, that there is no artificial ornament, or studied embellishment whatever, that can produce half so strong an effect, as the modest and simple attire of a pretty young nun, placed behind a double iron grate.

Now, who do you think these trusty guards are composed of? Why of the most daring, the most hardened villains, perhaps, that are to be met with upon earth, who, in any other country, would have been broken upon the wheel, or hung in chains; but are here publickly protected, and universally feared and respected ... In this east part of the island, called Val Demoni, (from the devils that are supposed to inhabit mount Ætna) it has ever been found impracticable to extirpate the banditti; there being numberless

A cave on Mount Etna, by J. R. Cozens

caverns and subterraneous passages in that mountain, where no troops could possibly pursue them: That besides, as they are known to be perfectly determined and resolute, never failing to take a dreadful revenge on all who have offended them, the prince of Villa Franca has embraced it, not only as the safest, but likewise as the wisest, and most political scheme, to become their declared patron and protector ...

In some circumstances these banditti are the most respectable people of the island; and have by much the highest and most romantic notions of what they call their point of honour. That, however criminal they may be with regard to society in general; yet, with respect to one another, and to every person to whom they have once professed it, they have ever maintained the most unshaken fidelity. The magistrates have often been obliged to protect them, and even pay them court, as they are known to be perfectly determined and desperate; and so extremely vindictive, that they will certainly put any person to death, who has ever given them just cause of provocation. On the other hand, it never was known that any person who had put himself under their protection, and shewed that he had confidence in them, had cause to repent of it, or was injured by any of them, in the most minute trifle; but on the contrary, they will protect him from impositions of every kind, and scorn to go halves with the landlord, like most other conductors and travelling servants; and will defend him with their lives, if there is occasion.

Canonico Recupero, who obligingly engages to be our Cicerone, has shewn us some curious remains of antiquity; but they have been all so shaken and shattered by the mountain, that hardly any thing is to be found entire. Near to a vault, which is now thirty feet below ground, and has probably been a burial place, there is a draw-well, where there are several strata of lavas, with earth to a considerable thickness over the surface of each stratum. Recupero has made use of this as an argument to prove the great antiquity of the eruptions of his mountain. For if it requires two thousand years or upwards to form but a scanty soil on the surface of a lava, there must have been more than that space of time betwixt each of the eruptions which have formed these strata. But what shall we say of a pit they sunk near to Jaci, of a great depth? They pierced through seven distinct lavas one under the other, the surfaces of which were parallel, and most of them covered with a thick bed of rich earth. Now, says he, the eruption which formed the lowest of these lavas, if we may be allowed to reason from analogy, must have flowed from the mountain at least 14,000 years ago.

Recupero tells me he is exceedingly embarrassed by these discoveries in writing the history of the mountain. That Moses hangs like a dead weight upon him, and blunts all his zeal for inquiry; for that really he has not the conscience to make his mountain so young as that prophet makes the world. What do you think of these sentiments from a Roman Catholic divine? The bishop, who is strenuously orthodox – for it is an excellent see – has already warned him to be upon his guard, and not to pretend to be a better natural historian than Moses; nor to presume to urge any thing that may in the smallest degree be deemed contradictory to his sacred authority.

After getting a comfortable nap on our bed of leaves in the Spelonca [cave] del Capriole, we awoke about eleven o'clock; and melting down a sufficient quantity of snow, we boiled our tea-kettle, and made a hearty meal, to prepare us for the remaining part of our expedition. We were nine in number; for we had our three servants, the Cyclops (our conductor) and two men to take care of our mules. The Cyclops now began to display his great knowledge of the mountain, and we followed him with implicit confidence. He conducted us over 'Antres vast, and Deserts wild',* where scarce human foot had ever trod. Sometimes through gloomy forests, which by day-light were delightful; but now, from the universal darkness, the rustling of the trees; the heavy, dull, bellowing of the mountain; the vast expanse of ocean stretched at an immense distance below us; inspired a kind of awful horror. Sometimes we found ourselves ascending great rocks of lava, where, if our mules should make but a false step, we might be thrown headlong over the precipice. However, by the assistance of the Cyclops, we overcame all these difficulties; and he managed matters so well, that in the space of two hours we found we had got above the regions of vegetation; and had left the forests of Ætna far behind. These appeared now like a dark and gloomy gulph below us, that surrounded the mountain.

The prospect before us was of a very different nature; we beheld an expanse of snow and ice that alarmed us exceedingly, and almost staggered our resolution. In the center of this, but still at a great distance, we descried the high summit of the mountain, rearing its tremendous head, and vomiting out torrents of smoke. It indeed appeared altogether inaccessible, from the vast extent of the fields of snow and ice that surrounded it. Our diffidence was still increased by the sentiments of the Cyclops. He told us, it often happened, that the furnace of the mountain being hot below, melted the snow in particular spots, and formed pools of water, where it was impossible to foresee our danger; that it likewise happened, that the surface of the water, as well as the snow, was sometimes covered with black ashes, that rendered it exceedingly deceitful; that however, if we thought proper, he would lead us on with as much caution as possible. Accordingly, after holding a council of war, which you know people generally do when they are very much afraid, we detached our cavalry to the forest below, and prepared to climb the snows. The Cyclops, after taking a great draught of brandy, desired us to be of good cheer; that we had plenty of time, and might take as many rests as we pleased. That the snow could be little more than seven miles, and that we certainly should be able to pass it before sunrise. Accordingly, taking each of us a dram of liqueur, which soon removed every objection, we began our march.

The ascent for some time was not steep; and as the surface of the snow sunk a little, we had tolerable good footing; but as it soon began to grow steeper, we found our labour greatly increase: however, we determined to persevere, calling to mind in the midst of our labour, that the emperor

* 'Antres vast and desarts idle', Shakespeare, *Othello*, Act 1, Scene iii. An antre is a cave.

Adrian and the philosopher Plato had undergone the same; and from the same motive too, to see the rising sun from the top of Ætna. After incredible labour and fatigue, but at the same time mixed with a great deal of pleasure, we arrived before dawn at the ruins of an ancient structure, called *Il Torre del Filosofo*, supposed to have been built by the philosopher Empedocles ...

The sky was clear, and the immense vault of the heavens appeared in awful majesty and splendour. We found ourselves more struck with veneration than below, and at first were at a loss to know the cause; till we observed with astonishment, that the number of stars seemed to be infinitely increased; and the light of each of them appeared brighter than usual. The whiteness of the milky way was like a pure flame that shot across the heavens; and with the naked eye we could observe clusters of stars that were invisible in the regions below ...

After contemplating these objects for some time, we set off, and soon after arrived at the foot of the great crater of the mountain. This is of an exact conical figure, and rises equally on all sides ... We found this mountain excessively steep; and although it had appeared black, yet it was likewise covered with snow, but the surface (luckily for us) was spread over with a pretty thick layer of ashes, thrown out from the crater. Had it not been for this, we never should have been able to get to the top; as the snow was every where frozen hard and solid, from the piercing cold of the air.

In about an hour's climbing, we arrived at a place where there was no snow; and where a warm and comfortable vapour issued from the mountain, which induced us to make another halt ... From this spot it was only about 300 yards to the highest summit of the mountain, where we arrived in full time, to see the most wonderful and most sublime sight in nature.

The whole atmosphere by degrees kindled up, and shewed dimly and faintly the boundless prospect around. Both sea and land looked dark and confused, as if only emerging from their original chaos; and light and darkness seemed still undivided; till the morning by degrees advancing, completed the separation. The stars are extinguished, and the shades disappear. The forests, which but now seemed black and bottomless gulphs, from whence no ray was reflected to shew their form or colours, appear a new creation rising to the sight; catching life and beauty from every increasing beam. The scene still enlarges, and the horizon seems to widen and expand itself on all sides; till the Sun, like the great Creator, appears in the east, and with his plastic ray completes the mighty scene. All appears enchantment; and it is with difficulty we can believe we are still on earth. The senses, unaccustomed to the sublimity of such a scene, are bewildered and confounded; and it is not till after some time, that they are capable of

separating and judging of the objects that compose it. The body of the
Sun is seen rising from the ocean, immense tracks both of sea and land
intervening; the islands of Lipari, Panari, Alicudi, Strombolo, and Volcano,
with their smoking summits, appear under your feet; and you look down
on the whole of Sicily as on a map; and can trace every river through all its
windings, from its source to its mouth. The view is absolutely boundless
on every side; nor is there any one object, within the circle of vision, to
interrupt it; so that the sight is every where lost in the immensity: and I am
persuaded it is only from the imperfection of our organs, that the coasts of
Africa, and even of Greece, are not discovered, as they are certainly above
the horizon. The circumference of the visible horizon on the top of Ætna
cannot be less than 2,000 miles: At Malta, which is near 200 miles distant,
they perceive all the eruptions from the second region; and that island is
often discovered from about one half the elevation of the mountain; so that
at the whole elevation, the horizon must extend to near double that distance,
or 400 miles, which makes 800 for the diameter of the circle, and 2,400 for
the circumference.

*Patrick Brydone sprained his ankle on the descent which swiftly dissipated the
sublimities of the summit. When travelling to the south-west of Etna Henry
Swinburne stumbled on the archetypal Sicilian story, in his words a tale of 'love,
murder, banditti, marriage, the archpriest, and the devil'.*

Wrapt up in the contemplation of Etna and its grand circumference, I
suffered my mule to proceed at its own rate ... A runner of water drew my
beast out of the path to a well, where an old woman was lying on the ground
beating her breast and tearing her hair; she was at the same time, with
astonishing volubility of tongue, scolding a very pretty girl, who stood near
her with a sullen contemptuous countenance and steady attitude. My mule
seemed as much surprized as I was with her noise and gestures, and both
of us hesitated some moments whether to approach or pass at a distance.
However, as the sight of me had checked the matron's violence, I ventured
to draw near and ask the cause of it. That instant both the females sprang
forwards and addressed me together ...

    This girl had been promised in marriage by her mother, the old woman,
to a young man of their town, but a few days before the time, on which the
wedding was to take place, he was drawn into a scuffle in which he killed
his antagonist. Upon this, he fled to the mountains and joined the company
of a famous captain of out-laws, who for twenty years had defied the
whole tribe of thief-takers ... However, the lover was scarce entered as an

associate, before the captain and all his followers were surprized and carried in chains to Catania. This account having reached the native town of the bridegroom, a meeting of his friends had been held, wherein the archpriest and a lawyer had proposed that a sum of money should be raised, which they would carry to Catania to buy him off; but unluckily the meeting was poor, and the only resource they had was in a legacy left to the bride by an uncle: This money she steadily refused to part with for a highwayman, a fellow she would never marry though he were to come back. Here the mother slipped in a few words to inform me, that the cause of this refusal did not lie in her daughter's delicacy, but in her inconstancy; for she had fallen in love with another man, who had seduced her affections by secrets of the black art that he had learnt at Malta.

The storm now began to rage again, and with much difficulty I obtained a hearing. I told them I suspected the lawyer meant to trick them out of their money, as it was impossible it could be of any avail in the case. I had been informed that the out-laws, whom the magistrates were determined to make an example of, would be hanged before he could reach Catania; and I, therefore, advised the two females to shake hands and be friends. They did so with the same vehemence that they had displayed in the course of the quarrel, and walked merrily along with me towards the town.

Apart from Etna, Sicily's other great attractions were the sites of the ancient Greek cities at Agrigento (Girgenti), Selinunte (Selinus), and Segesta. Patrick Brydone gets into convivial company at Agrigento, while Henry Swinburne describes the scene of massive primeval devastation at Selinunte.

PATRICK BRYDONE

The Sicilians eat of every thing, and attempted to make us do the same. The company was remarkably merry, and ... begged us to make a bowl of punch, a liquor they had often heard of, but had never seen. The materials were immediately found, and we succeeded so well, that they preferred it to all the wines on the table, of which they had a great variety. We were obliged to replenish the bowl so often, that I really expected to see most of them under the table. They called it Pontio, and spoke loudly in its praise; declaring that Pontio (alluding to Pontius Pilate) was a much better fellow than they had ever taken him for. However, after dinner, one of them, a reverend canon, grew excessively sick, and while he was throwing up, he turned to me with a rueful countenance, and shaking his head, he groaned out, '*Ah, Signor Capitano, sapeva sempre che Pontio era un grande traditore*' – 'I always knew that Pontius was a great traitor.' Another of them overhearing him, exclaimed – *'Aspettatevi Signor Canonico,'* – 'Not so fast (said he) my good Canon.' *'Niente al pregiudizio di Signor Pontio, vi prego. Recordate, che Pontio v'ha fatto un canonico; – et Pontio ha fatto sua eccellenza uno Vescovo – Non scordatevi mai di vostri amici'* – 'Please say nothing against Pontius. Remember he made you a canon, and your excellency a Bishop. Do not speak ill of your friends.'

I should have told you, that it was an annual feast given by the nobility of Agrigentum to the bishop. It was served in an immense granary, half full of wheat, on the sea shore, chosen on purpose to avoid the heat. The whole was on plate: and what appeared singular to us, but I believe is a much better method than ours; great part of the fruit was served up with the second course, the first dish of which that went round was strawberries. The Sicilians were a good deal surprised to see us eat them with cream and sugar, yet upon trial they did not at all dislike the composition.

HENRY SWINBURNE

I rode seven miles into the south vale, a rich inclosed district like the country round Naples; it is watered by the Madiuni, a clear romantic stream; the rising grounds are planted with vines and olive trees, while orange groves shade the low land; among these are some mulberry stocks, on which the orange is grafted, and produces fruit with a blood-coloured pulp. As I approached the sea, the face of the country altered to smooth green swells with tufts of lentiscus [the mastic plant], but no trees. The river passes through a long line of hills, which exhibit the most extraordinary assemblage of ruins in Europe: the remains of Selinus; they lie in several stupendous heaps with many columns still erect, and at a distance resemble a large town with a crowd of steeples; my servants took them for such, and were quite rejoiced at the thoughts of the very grand city they were coming to; nothing could exceed their disappointment when they reached the top of the hill, and found silence and desolation, where they expected busy crowds and the noisy hum of a populous place ...

The second temple is ruined with more order, and is easily described; it had six columns in the fronts and eleven on each side, in all thirty-four; their diameter is five feet; they were all fluted, and most of them now remain standing as high as the second course of stones. The pillars of the third temple were also fluted, and have fallen down so very entire, that the five pieces which composed them lie almost close to each other, in the order they were placed in when upright; the cella does not exceed the vestibule in extent. All these temples are of the old Doric order, without a base, and of a much more massive proportion than the Segestan edifice.

The ruins at Selinus, by Thomas Hearne. This bears out Henry Swinburne's description of 'several stupendous heaps'

It is said that the city was destroyed by the Carthaginians and that these proud fanes were levelled to the ground by the hand of man; but it is at least as probable that they were shaken and overthrown by an earthquake; their prodigious volume must have rendered it a difficult task to overset them, and the regularity with which the column of the smaller temples are thrown down argues the effect of some uniform general concussion. It is hard to attribute such devastation solely to human malice; and whoever beholds these enormous masses, scattered in heaps upon the plain, must of course accuse nature of having had some share in this victory over the pride of art.

Selinus was a flourishing state during the period of four centuries, till it was taken and destroyed by Hannibal, a Carthaginian general,* in the 359th year of Rome. This city did not recover from its calamities under Roman government, for Strabo speaks of it as uninhabited. Selinus must, however, have risen out of its ashes during the lower [Byzantine] empire, for it is mentioned as one of the first considerable places taken by the Saracens, and one of the last they abandoned. It was razed to the ground by the Normans.

I had laid a plan of passing the night near these venerable relics of remote antiquity that I might have more leisure to examine them, and also enjoy

* No relation of the famous Carthaginian.

the pleasure of viewing them in all the tints and shades cast upon them by the rays of departing day, the beams of the moon, and the first dawn of the ensuing morning, but the holiday diversions and ceremonies had carried away every inhabitant of the farm houses – I was therefore necessitated to return to Castelvetrano.

In Palermo Patrick Brydone visited the catacombs of the Capuchin convent, while at Bagheria, some miles to the east, the bizarre palace of the Prince of Palagonia was visited by both Brydone and Swinburne (and later by Goethe). Swinburne describes the approach to it and Brydone the interior.

PATRICK BRYDONE

It is a vast subterraneous apartment, divided into large commodious galleries, the walls on each side of which are hollowed into a variety of niches, as if intended for a great collection of statues; these niches, instead of statues, are all filled with dead bodies, set upright upon their legs, and fixed by the back to the inside of the nich: their number is about three hundred: they are all dressed in the clothes they usually wore, and form a most respectable and venerable assembly. The skin and muscles, by a certain preparation, become as dry and hard as a piece of stock-fish [dried cod]; and although many of them have been here upwards of two hundred and fifty years, yet none are reduced to skeletons; the muscles, indeed, in some appear to be a good deal more shrunk than in others; probably because these persons had been more extenuated at the time of their death.

Here the people of Palermo pay daily visits to their deceased friends, and recall with pleasure and regret the scenes of their past life: here they familiarise themselves with their future state, and chuse the company they would wish to keep in the other world. It is a common thing to make choice of their nich, and to try if their body fits it, that no alterations may be necessary after they are dead; and sometimes, by way of a voluntary penance, they accustom themselves to stand for hours in these niches.

HENRY SWINBURNE

To this extraordinary place the traveller is admitted through a huge gate, on the plinth of which are fixed six collossal white-washed statues of hussards or halberdiers, to dispute the entrance of an avenue three hundred yards long, not of cypresses, elms, or orange trees, but of monsters.

On each hand is a parapet wall loaded with more horrible figures than were ever raised by Armida and all the enchanters of Ariosto. Busts of Punchinellos and Harlequins, with snakes twisted round them; the heads of dwarfs with huge perriwigs, of asses and horses with laced cravats and ruffs, compose the lower range of this gallery, and at intervals of ten yards are clustered pillars, supporting curious groups of figures; some are musicians, others pigmies, opera heroes, old women grinning, lions and other beasts, seated at tables with napkins under their chins, eating oysters; princesses with feathers and furbelows, ostriches in hoops, and cats in boots. In short, more unaccountable mixtures of company, and unnatural representations of creatures than I had patience to note, or memory to record. They are luckily all made of so soft and perishable a stone, that we need be under no apprehensions of this collection passing to posterity as a monument of the taste of the eighteenth century. Many enormous noses and preposterous limbs have already crumbled to dust.

PATRICK BRYDONE

Some of the apartments are spacious and magnificent, with high arched roofs; which instead of plaister or stucco, are composed entirely of large mirrors, nicely joined together. The effect that these produce (as each of them make a small angle with the other) is exactly that of a multiplying glass; so that when three or four people are walking below, there is always the appearance of three or four hundred walking above ... All the chimney-pieces, windows, and side-boards are crowded with pyramids and pillars of tea-pots, caudle-cups, bowls, cups, saucers, etc. strongly cemented together; some of these columns are not without their beauty: one of them has a large china chamber-pot for its base, and a circle of pretty little flower-pots for its capital; the shaft of the column, upwards of four feet long, is composed entirely of tea-pots of different sizes, diminished gradually from the base to the capital ...

Most of the rooms are paved with fine marble tables of different colours, that look like so many tomb-stones. Some of these are richly wrought with lapis lazuli, porphyry, and other valuable stones; their fine polish is now gone, and they only appear like common marble; the place of these beautiful tables he has supplied by a new set of his own invention, some of which are not without their merit. These are made of the finest tortoise-shell mixed with mother of pearl, ivory, and a variety of metals; and are mounted on fine stands of solid brass.

The windows of this inchanted castle are composed of a variety of glass of every different colour, mixed without any sort of order or regularity. Blue, red, green, yellow, purple, violet. – So that at each window, you may have the heavens and earth of whatever colour you chuse, only by looking through the pane that pleases you.

The house-clock is cased in the body of a statue; the eyes of the figure move with the pendulum, turning up their white and black alternately, and make a hideous appearance.

His bed-chamber and dressing-room are like two apartments in Noah's ark; there is scarce a beast, however vile, that he has not placed there; toads, frogs, serpents, lizards, scorpions, all cut out in marble, of their respective colours. There are a good many busts too, that are not less singularly imagined. – Some of these make a very handsome profile on one side; turn to the other, and you have a skeleton; here you see a nurse with a child in her arms; its back is exactly that of an infant; its face is that of a wrinkled old woman of ninety ...

The family statues are charming; they have been done from some old pictures, and make a most venerable appearance; he has dressed them out from head to foot, in new and elegant suits of marble; and indeed the effect it produces is more ridiculous than any thing you can conceive. Their shoes are all of black marble, their stockings generally of red; their clothes are of different colours, blue, green, and variegated, with a rich lace of *giall' antique*. The periwigs of the men and head-dresses of the ladies are of fine white; so are their shirts, with long flowing ruffles of alabaster.

A caricature, by Giovanni Battista Tiepolo – the supreme eighteenth-century Venetian painter

Switzerland

Once their time in Italy was completed, Tourists often headed home through Switzerland. Evelyn describes adventures going via the Simplon Pass and Addison singles out some still very recognisable national characteristics (as well as being fascinated at Fribourg by another example of Capuchin enterprise to match the catacombs in Palermo: an 'escargatoire' or snail farm to provide a type of meat acceptable during Lent). Fynes Moryson's slightly prurient interest was excited by the hot sulphur baths at Baden, north of Zurich.

JOHN EVELYN

Some of these vast mountains were but one entire stone, 'twixt whose clefts now and then precipitated great cataracts of melted snow and other waters, which made a terrible roaring, echoing from the rocks and cavities; and these waters in some places breaking in the fall wett us as if we had pass'd through a mist, so as we could neither see nor heare one another, but trusting to our honest mules we jogged on our way. The narrow bridges in some places made onely by felling huge fir trees and laying them athwart from mountaine to mountaine over cataracts of stupendious depth, are very dangerous, and so are the passages and edges made by cutting away the maine rock; others in steps; and in some places we passe betweene mountains that have ben broken and fallen on one another, which is very terrible, and one had neede of a sure foote and steady head to climb some of these precipices, besides that they are harbours for beares and wolves who have sometimes assaulted travellers. In these straights we frequently alighted, now freezing in the snow, and anon frying by the reverberation of the sun against the cliffs as we descend lower, when we meete now and then a few miserable cottages so built upon the declining of the rocks as one would expect their sliding down. Amongst these inhabite a goodly sort of people having monstrous gullets or wenns of fleshe growing to their throats, some of which I have seene as big as an hundred pound bag of silver hanging under their chinns, among the women especialy, and that so ponderous as that to ease them many wear linen cloth bound about their head and coming under the chin to support it ... Their drinking so much snow-water is thought to be the cause of it [goitre]; the men using more wine are not so strumous as the women ...

Approaching [Mount Simplon], Captaine Wray's water-spaniel (a huge filthy cur that had follow'd him out of England) hunted an heard of goates downe the rocks into a river made by the melting of the snow. Ariv'd at our cold harbour (tho' the house had a stove in every roome) and supping on cheese and milk with wretched wine, we went to bed in cupboards so high from the floore that we climb'd them by a ladder; we were covered with feathers, that is we lay between two ticks stuff'd with them, and all little enough to keepe one warme. The cieling of the rooms are strangely low for those tall people. The house was now, in September, halfe cover'd with snow, nor is there a tree or bush growing within many miles.

From this uncomfortable place we prepared to hasten away the next morning, but as we were getting on our mules, comes a huge young fellow demanding mony for a goat which he affirm'd that Capt. Wray's dog had kill'd; expostulating the matter and impatient of staying in the cold, we set spurrs and endeavour'd to ride away, when a multitude of people being by this time gotten together about us (for it being Sonday morning and attending for the priest to say masse) they stopp'd our mules, beate us off our saddles, and disarming us of our carbines, drew us into one of the roomes of our lodging, and set a guard upon us. Thus we continu'd prisoners till masse was ended, and then came halfe a score grim Swisse, who taking on them to be magistrates sate downe on the table, and condemn'd us to pay a pistole for the goate and ten more for attempting to ride away.

Beginning now to descend a little, Capt. Wray's horse (that was our sumpter and carried all our baggage) plunging thro' a bank of loose snow slid downe a frightfull precipice, which so incens'd the choleriq cavalier his master that he was sending a brace of bullets into the poore beast, least our guide should recover him and run away with his burthen; but just as he was lifting up his carbine we gave such a shout, and so pelted the horse with snow-balls, as with all his might plunging through the snow he fell from another steepe place into another bottome neere a path we were to passe. It was yet a good while ere we got to him, but at last we recovered the place, and easing him of his charge hal'd him out of the snow, where he had ben certainly frozen in if we had not prevented it before night ...

Late at night we got to a towne called Briga at the foote of the Alpes, in the Valtoline. Almost every doore had nail'd on the outside and next the streete a beare's, wolfe's, or foxe's head, and divers of them all three; a savage kind of sight, but as the Alpes are full of these beasts the people often kill them. The next morning we return'd our guide, and tooke fresh mules and another to conduct us to the Lake of Geneva, passing thro' as pleasant a country as that we had just travel'd was melancholy and troublesome.

JOSEPH ADDISON

I have often considered, with a great deal of pleasure, the profound peace and tranquillity that reigns in Switzerland and its alliances ... As the inhabitants of these countries are naturally of a heavy, phlegmatic temper, if any of their leading members have more fire and spirit than comes to their share, it is quickly tempered by the coldness and moderation of the rest who sit at the helm with them ... It is the great endeavour of the several cantons of Switzerland, to banish from among them everything that looks like pomp or superfluity. To this end the ministers are always preaching, and the governors putting out edicts against dancing, gaming, entertainments, and fine clothes ... Should dressing, feasting, and balls, once get among the cantons, their military roughness would be quickly lost, their tempers would grow too soft for their climate, and their expenses out-run their incomes ... It is the custom to divide their estates equally among all their children, by which means every one lives at his ease without growing dangerous to the republic ... This is absolutely necessary in these little republics, where the rich merchants live very much within their estates, and by heaping up vast sums from year to year, might become formidable to the rest of their fellow-citizens, and break the equality.

FYNES MORYSON

These waters [of the Baths of Baden] are so strong of brimstone, as the very smoake warmeth them that come neere, and the waters burne those that touch them. Of these one is called the Marques Bath, and is so hot, as it will scald off the haire of a Hogge: many having no disease but that of love, howsoever they faine sickenesse of body, come hither for remedy, and many times find it. Weomen come hither as richly attired as if they came to a marriage: for Men, Weomen, Monkes, and Nunnes, sit all together in the same water, parted with boords, but so as they may mutually speake and touch, and it is a rule here to shun all sadnes, neither is any jealousie admitted for a naked touch. The waters are so cleere as a penny may be seene in the bottome, and because melancholy must be avoided, they recreate themselves with many sports, while they sit in the water; namely at cards, and with casting up and catching little stones, to which purpose they have a little table swimming upon the water, upon which sometimes

A view of Baden in Switzerland in 1642

they doe likewise eate. These Bathes are very good for Weomen that are barren. They are also good for a cold braine, and a stomacke charged with rhume; but are hurtfull for hot and dry complexions, and in that respect they are held better for Weomen then Men.

So far we have encountered Boswell largely in his lecherous mode, but when staying in Geneva in December 1764 we see him put into play his capacity for fruitful discipleship, of which his Life of Johnson *is the great example. As he said of himself, 'I can tune myself so to the tone of any bearable man I am with that he is as much at freedom as with another self and, till I am gone, cannot imagine me a stranger.' He visited first Rousseau and then Voltaire. A year before, Gibbon had gone to a performance in Voltaire's private theatre at Ferney, which he described in one of his letters. There was a limit to how far Voltaire would allow himself to be a tourist attraction. Twelve years after Boswell's visit, Lord Herbert and his bear leader, the Rev. William Coxe, tried to get permission to meet Voltaire, whose reply was recorded: 'Here is Milord Pembroke sending me his 17-year-old son, when I am 82. We have nothing in common, and I am in wretched health; I cannot see him.'*

JAMES BOSWELL

I told [Rousseau] Mr Johnson's *bon mot* upon the innovators: that truth is a cow which will yield them no more milk, and so they are gone to milk the bull. He said, 'He would detest me. He would say, "Here is a corrupter: a man who comes here to milk the bull."'

I had diverted myself by pretending to help Mademoiselle Le Vasseur* to make the soup. We dined in the kitchen, which was neat and cheerful. There was something singularly agreeable in this scene. Here was Rousseau in all his simplicity, with his Armenian dress, which I have surely mentioned before now. His long coat and nightcap made him look easy and well.

Our dinner was as follows: 1. A dish of excellent soup. 2. A *bouilli* of beef and veal. 3. Cabbage, turnip, and carrot. 4. Cold pork. 5. Pickled trout, which he jestingly called tongue. 6. Some little dish which I forget. The dessert consisted of stoned pears and of chestnuts. We had red and white wines. It was a simple, good repast. We were quite at our ease. I sometimes forgot myself and became ceremonious. 'May I help you to some of this dish?' ROUSSEAU. 'No, Sir. I can help myself to it.' Or, 'May I help myself to some more of that?' ROUSSEAU. 'Is your arm long enough? A man does the honours of his house from a motive of vanity. He does not want it forgotten who is the master. I should like every one to be his own master, and no one to play the part of host. Let each one ask for what he wants; if it is there to give, let him be given it; otherwise, he must be satisfied without. Here you see true hospitality.' BOSWELL. 'In England, it is quite another matter. They do not want to be at ease; they are stiff and silent, in order to win respect.' ROUSSEAU. 'In France, you find no such gloom among people of distinction. There is even an affectation of the utmost liberty, as though they would have you understand, "We stand in no fear of losing our dignity." That is a more refined form of self-esteem.'

BOSWELL. 'Well, and do you not share that yourself?' ROUSSEAU. 'Yes, I confess that I like to be respected; but only in matters of importance.' BOSWELL. 'You are so simple. I expected to find you quite different from this: the Great Rousseau. But you do not see yourself in the same light as others do. I expected to find you enthroned and talking with a grave authority.' ROUSSEAU. 'Uttering oracles? Ha! Ha! Ha!' BOSWELL. 'Yes, and that I should be much in awe of you. And really your simplicity might lay you open to criticism; it might be said, "Monsieur Rousseau does not make himself sufficiently respected." In Scotland, I assure you, a very different tone must be taken to escape from the shocking familiarity which is prevalent in that country. Upon my word, I cannot put up with it. Should I not be justified in forestalling it by fighting a duel with the first man who should treat me so, and thus live at peace for the rest of my life?' ROUSSEAU.

* See biographical note on Boswell on p. 261.

Jean Jacques
Rousseau, painted
by Allan Ramsay in
1766

'No. That is not allowable. It is not right to stake one's life on such follies.
Life is given us for objects of importance. Pay no heed to what such men
say. They will get tired of talking to a man who does not answer them.'
BOSWELL. 'If you were in Scotland, they would begin at the very start by
calling you Rousseau; they would say, "Jean Jacques, how goes it?" with the
utmost familiarity.' ROUSSEAU. 'That is perhaps a good thing.' BOSWELL.
'But they would say, "Poh! Jean Jacques, why do you allow yourself all these
fantasies? You're a pretty man to put forward such claims. Come, come,
settle down in society like other men." And they would say it to you with a
sourness which I am unable to imitate for you.' ROUSSEAU. 'Ah, that's bad.'

There he felt the thistle, when it was applied to himself on the tender
part. It was just as if I had said, 'Hoot, Johnnie Rousseau man, what for hae
ye sae mony figmagairies [whims]? Ye're a bonny man indeed to mauk
siccan a wark; set ye up. Canna ye just live like ither fowk?' It was the best
idea could be given in the polite French language of the rude Scots sar-
castical vivacity . . .

ROUSSEAU. 'Do you like cats?' BOSWELL. 'No.' ROUSSEAU. 'I was sure
of that. It is my test of character. There you have the despotic instinct of
men. They do not like cats because the cat is free and will never consent to
become a slave. He will do nothing to your order, as the other animals do.'
BOSWELL. 'Nor a hen, either.' ROUSSEAU. 'A hen would obey your orders
if you could make her understand them. But a cat will understand you
perfectly and not obey them.' BOSWELL. 'But a cat is ungrateful and
treacherous.' ROUSSEAU. 'No. That's all untrue. A cat is an animal that can
be very much attached to you; he will do anything you please out of
friendship. I have a cat here. He has been brought up with my dog; they
play together. The cat will give the dog a blow with his tail, and the dog

236

will offer him his paw.' (He described the playing of his dog and cat with exquisite eloquence, as a fine painter draws a small piece.) He put some victuals on a trencher, and made his dog dance round it. He sung to him a lively air with a sweet voice and great taste. 'You see the ballet. It is not a gala performance, but a pretty one all the same.' I think the dog's name was Sultan. He stroked him and fed him, and with an arch air said, 'He is not much *respected*, but he gets well looked after.'

BOSWELL. 'The Anglican Church is my choice.' ROUSSEAU. 'Yes. It is no doubt an excellent religion, but it is not the Gospel, which is all simplicity. It is another kind of religion.' BOSWELL. 'The Gospel, at the outset, was simple but rigorous too, as when Paul says it is better not to marry than to marry.' ROUSSEAU. 'Paul? But that is not the Gospel.' BOSWELL. 'Then you have no liking for Paul?' ROUSSEAU. 'I respect him, but I think he is partly responsible for muddling your head. He would have been an Anglican clergyman.'

BOSWELL. 'Mr Johnson is a Jacobite, but he has a pension of £300 sterling from the King.' ROUSSEAU. 'He ought not to have accepted a pension.' BOSWELL. 'He says that he does not drink the health of King James with the wine given him by King George.' ROUSSEAU. 'But you should not employ the substance given you by this wine in attacking King George' ...

ROUSSEAU. 'The roads are bad. You will be late.' BOSWELL. 'I take the bad parts on foot; the last league of the way is good. Do you think that I shall make a good barrister before a court of justice?' ROUSSEAU. 'Yes. But I regret that you have the talents necessary for defending a bad case' ...

MADEMOISELLE. 'Sir, your man is calling for you to start.' Monsieur Rousseau embraced me. He was quite the tender Saint-Preux.* He kissed me several times, and held me in his arms with elegant cordiality. Oh, I shall never forget that I have been thus. ROUSSEAU. 'Good-bye. You are a fine fellow.' BOSWELL. 'You have shown me great goodness. But I deserved it.' ROUSSEAU. 'Yes. You are malicious; but 'tis a pleasant malice, a malice I don't dislike. Write and tell me how you are.' BOSWELL. 'And you will write to me?' ROUSSEAU. 'I know not how to reach you.' BOSWELL. 'Yes, you shall write to me in Scotland.' ROUSSEAU. 'Certainly; and even at Paris.' BOSWELL. 'Bravo! If I live twenty years, you will write to me for twenty years?' ROUSSEAU. 'Yes.' BOSWELL. 'Good-bye. If you live for seven years, I shall return to Switzerland from Scotland to see you.' ROUSSEAU. 'Do so. We shall be old acquaintances.' BOSWELL. 'One word more. Can I

---

* A character in Rousseau's novel *Julie ou la Nouvelle Héloïse*.

237

feel sure that I am held to you by a thread, even if of the finest? By a hair?'
(Seizing a hair of my head.) ROUSSEAU. 'Yes. Remember always that there
are points at which our souls are bound.' BOSWELL. 'It is enough. I, with
my melancholy, I, who often look on myself as a despicable being, as a
good-for-nothing creature who should make his exit from life – I shall be
upheld for ever by the thought that I am bound to Monsieur Rousseau.
Good-bye. Bravo! I shall live to the end of my days.' ROUSSEAU. 'That is
undoubtedly a thing one must do.* Good-bye.'

I took a coach for Ferney, the seat of the illustrious Monsieur de Voltaire.
I was in true spirits; the earth was covered with snow; I surveyed wild nature
with a noble eye. I called up all the grand ideas which I have ever entertained
of Voltaire. The first object that struck me was his church with his inscrip-
tion: 'Deo erexit Voltaire MDCCLXI'.† His château was handsome. I was
received by two or three footmen, who showed me into a very elegant
room. I sent by one of them a letter to Monsieur de Voltaire which I had
from Colonel Constant at The Hague. He returned and told me, 'Monsieur
de Voltaire is very much annoyed at being disturbed. He is abed.' I was
afraid that I should not see him. Some ladies and gentlemen entered, and I
was entertained for some time. At last Monsieur de Voltaire opened the door
of his apartment, and stepped forth. I surveyed him with eager attention, and
found him just as his print had made me conceive him. He received me
with dignity, and that air of the world which a Frenchman acquires in such
perfection. He had a slate-blue, fine frieze greatcoat night-gown, and a
three-knotted wig. He sat erect upon his chair, and simpered when he
spoke. He was not in spirits, nor I neither. All I presented was the 'foolish
face of wondering praise'.

I told him that Mr Johnson and I intended to make a tour through the
Hebrides, the Northern Isles of Scotland. He smiled, and cried, 'Very well;
but I shall remain here. You will allow me to stay here?' 'Certainly.' 'Well
then, go. I have no objections at all.'

I asked him if he still spoke English. He replied, 'No. To speak English
one must place the tongue between the teeth, and I have lost my teeth' . . .

[A few days later Boswell went back to Voltaire's house again, this time
to spend the night.] I was received with complacency and complimented

* Boswell was quoting from Rousseau's novel *Émile*, which Rousseau chose not to
recognise.
† 'Erected by Voltaire to God in 1761'. Voltaire said it was high time to dedicate one
church to God, after so many had been dedicated to saints.

Voltaire getting dressed, by Huber

on my letter ... Monsieur de Voltaire came out to us a little while, but did not dine with us. After dinner we returned to the drawing-room, where (if I may revive an old phrase) *every man soaped his own beard*. Some sat snug by the fire, some chatted, some sung, some played the guitar, some played at shuttlecock. All was full. The canvas was covered. My hypochondria began to muse. I was dull to find how much this resembled any other house in the country, and I had heavy ennui ...

Between seven and eight we had a message that Voltaire was in the drawing-room. He always appears about this time anight, pulls his bell and cries, 'Fetch Père Adam.' The good Father is ready immediately, and they play at chess together. I stood by Monsieur de Voltaire and put him in tune. He spoke sometimes English and sometimes French. He gave me a sharp reproof for speaking fast. 'How fast you foreigners speak!' 'We think that the French do the same.' 'Well, at any rate, *I* don't. I speak slowly, that's what I do'; and this he said with a most keen tone. He got into great spirits. I would not go to supper, and so I had this great man for about an hour and a half at a most interesting tête-à-tête.

BOSWELL. 'When I came to see you, I thought to see a very great, but a very bad man.' VOLTAIRE. 'You are very sincere.' BOSWELL. 'Yes, but the same [sincerity] makes me own that I find the contrary. Only, your *Dictionnaire philosophique* [troubles me]. For instance, *Ame*, the Soul – ' VOLTAIRE. 'That is a good article.' BOSWELL. 'No. Excuse me. Is it –

[immortality] not a pleasant imagination? Is it not more noble?' VOLTAIRE. 'Yes. You have a noble desire to be King of Europe. [You say,] "I wish it, and I ask your protection [in continuing to wish it]." But it is not probable.' BOSWELL. 'No, but all cannot be the one [King], and may be the other [immortal]. [Like Cato, we all say] "It must be so," till [we possess] immortality [itself].' VOLTAIRE. 'But before we say that this soul will exist, let us know what it is. I know not the cause. I cannot judge. I cannot be a juryman. Cicero says, *potius optandum quam probandum* [matter of faith rather than of demonstration]. We are ignorant beings. We are the puppets of Providence. I am a poor Punch.' BOSWELL. 'Would you have no public worship?' VOLTAIRE. 'Yes, with all my heart. Let us meet four times a year in a grand temple with music, and thank God for all his gifts. There is one sun. There is one God. Let us have one religion. Then all mankind will be brethren.' BOSWELL. 'May I write in English, and you'll answer?' VOLTAIRE. 'Yes. Farewell.'

When the company returned, Monsieur de Voltaire retired. They looked at me with complacency and without envy. Madame Denis insisted that I should sup; I agreed to this, and a genteel table was served for me in the drawing-room, where I eat and drank cheerfully with the gay company around me. I was very lively and said, 'I am magnificence itself. I eat alone, like the King of England.' In short this was a rich evening.

EDWARD GIBBON

The play they acted was my favourite Orphan of China. Voltaire himself acted *Gengis* and Madame Denys *Idamè*; but I do not know how it happened: either my taste is improved or Voltaire's talents are impaired since I last saw him. He appeared to me now a very ranting unnatural performer. Perhaps indeed as I come from Paris, I rather judged him by an unfair comparison, than by his own independent value. Perhaps too I was too much struck with the ridiculous figure of Voltaire at seventy acting a Tartar Conqueror with a hollow broken voice, and making love to a very ugly niece of about fifty. The play began at eight in the evening and ended (entertainment and all) about half an hour after eleven. The whole company was asked to stay and set down about twelve to a very elegant supper of a hundred covers. The supper ended about two, the company danced till four, when we broke up, got into our coaches and came back to Geneva, just as the gates were opened. Shew me in history or fable, a famous poet at seventy who has acted in his own plays, and has closed the scene with a supper and ball for a hundred people. I think the last is the more extraordinary of the two.

Germany, The Empire and Holland

The alternative to going over the Simplon or one of the other passes into Switzerland was to follow the River Adige up from Verona, go over the Brenner Pass, then down the valley of the Inn through the Tyrol to Bavaria. There, Beckford adopts a supercilious tone about the gardens of the ruler's palace outside Munich, before Dr Burney embarks on a raft for a horrific journey to Vienna. Lady Mary Wortley Montagu, writing to her sister in 1716, is struck there by the Imperial nobility being flat-dwellers and, writing to Lady Rich at the same time, by the appeal of 'the older woman' as well as the necessity for a lover and a husband. Lastly J. B. S. Morritt is as disconcerted as Beckford by waltzing.

WILLIAM BECKFORD

We were driven in the evening to Nymphenburg, the Elector's country palace, the bosquets, jets-d'eaux, and parterres of which are the pride of the Bavarians. The principal platform is all of a glitter with gilded Cupids and shining serpents spouting at every pore. Beds of poppies, hollyhocks, scarlet lychnis, and other flame-coloured flowers, border the edge of the walks, which extend till the perspective appears to meet and swarm with ladies and gentlemen in party-coloured raiment. The queen of Golconda's gardens in a French opera are scarcely more gaudy and artificial. Unluckily too, the evening was fine, and the sun so powerful that we were half roasted before we could cross the great avenue and enter the thickets which barely conceal a very splendid hermitage ... Then, having viewed Pagotenburg, which is, as they told me, all Chinese, and Marienburg, which is most assuredly all tinsel, we paraded by a variety of fountains in full squirt, and though they certainly did their best (for many were set agoing on purpose) I cannot say I greatly admired them. The ladies were very gaily attired, and the gentlemen, as smart as swords, bags [wigs], and pretty clothes could make them, looked exactly like the fine people one sees represented in a coloured print. Thus we kept walking genteelly about the orangery, till the carriage drew up and conveyed us to Mr T's. Immediately after supper, we

A view of Munich, by Bernardo Bellotto, the nephew of Canaletto

drove once more out of town, to a garden and tea-room, where all degrees
and ages dance jovially together till morning. Whilst one party wheel
briskly away in the valz, another amuse themselves in a corner with cold
meat and rhenish. That despatched, out they whisk amongst the dancers,
with an impetuosity and liveliness I little expected to have found in Bavaria.
After turning round and round, with a rapidity that is quite astonishing to
an English dancer, the music changes to a slower movement, and then
follows a succession of zig-zag minuets, performed by old and young,
straight and crooked, noble and plebeian, all at once, from one end of the
room to the other.

CHARLES BURNEY

The Isar, upon which the city of Munich is situated, and which empties
itself into the Danube, about a hundred miles below, though very rapid, is
too much spread and scattered into different channels, to be sufficiently
deep for a bark or any kind of passage-boat, that has a bottom to float upon
it. The current of this river is even too rapid for anything to be brought back
against it; but Bavaria being a country abounding with wood, particularly fir,
rafts, or floats made of those trees, lashed together, are carried down the
stream, at the rate of seventy or eighty miles a day. Upon these rafts, a
booth is built for passengers in common; but if anyone chooses to have a
cabin to himself, he may have it built for about four florins. I preferred this,

242

not only to avoid bad company and heat, but to get an opportunity of writing and digesting my thoughts and memorandums, being at this time very much in arrears with my musical journal.

I quitted Munich at two o'clock in the afternoon. The weather was intensely hot, and I was furnished with no means of tempering it; a clear sky and burning sun, reflected from the water, having rendered my fir cabin as insupportable as the open air. It was constructed of green boards, which exuded as much turpentine as would have vanquished all the aromatics of Arabia.

As I was utterly ignorant of the country, through which I was to pass, and the accommodations it would afford, all that my foresight had suggested to me, in the way of furniture and provisions, were a mattress, blanket, and sheets; some cold meat, with bread, and a bottle of wine; there was water in plenty always at hand.

There had been no rain in these parts of Germany for six weeks; but, when we arrived at Freising [fifteen miles from Munich], I saw a little black cloud to the westward, which, in less than half an hour, produced the most violent storm of thunder, lightning, rain, and wind, that I ever remember to have seen. I really expected every moment, that the lightning would have set fire to my cabin; it continued all night with prodigious fury, so that my man could not get back, and I was left on the water, sole inhabitant of the float, which was secured by a hawser to a wooden bridge.

Two square holes were cut in the boards of my cabin, one on each side, by way of window; the pieces were to serve as casements, one of these was lost, so that I was forced to fasten with pins, a handkerchief against the hole, to keep out wind and rain; but it answered the purpose very ill, and moreover, it rained in, at a hundred different places; drop, drip, drop, throughout my little habitation, sometimes on my face, sometimes on my legs, and always somewhere or other. This, with the violent flashes of lightning and bursts of thunder, kept off drowsiness; luckily, perhaps, for I might have caught cold, sleeping in the wet ... I lay on the mattress, as far as I could from my sword, pistols, watch-chain, and everything that might serve as a conductor ... [Two more miserable days and nights followed.] At half an hour past nine we set off for Passau, in very fine weather, which revived my spirits, and enabled me to hold my pen. The Danube abounds in rocks, some above water, and some below, which occasion a great noise by the rapidity of the current, running over, or against them.

We met this morning a gang of boats, laden with salt, from Salzburg and Passau, dragged up the river by more than forty horses, a man on each, which expense is so great, as to enhance the price of that commodity above four hundred per cent. We did not seem to move so fast now as upon the Isar, which had frequent cascades; and sometimes the float dipped so deep, as to have three or four feet of water rush suddenly into my cabin ...

[Now in Austria, we] stopped for the night, at a wretched place, which afforded no kind of refreshment; though I had indulged the hope of supplying myself here for two days to come, which being Friday and Saturday, among Austrian Catholics, I knew would be kept strictly *maigre*.*

I had now filled up the chinks of my cabin with splinters, and with hay; got a new button to the door, reconciled myself to my filthy blanket, and made a pair of snuffers out of a chip of deal; but alas! the essential failed: this was all external, and I wanted internal comfort! the last bit of my cold meat was fly-blown, to such a degree, that, ravenous as I was, I threw it into the Danube; bread too, that staff was broken! and nothing but *Pumpernickel* [rye bread] was to be had here; which is so black and sour, as to disgust two senses at a time.

This river continues running through the same woody, wild, and romantic country; which, to pass through, is pleasant and entertaining, to a stranger, but produces nothing, except firing, to the poor inhabitants. For fifty miles not a corn field or pasture is to be seen. Sheep, oxen, calves, and pigs, are all utter strangers in this land. I asked what was behind these mountains, and was answered, huge forests. At Ashach the country opens a little ...

There is such an appearance of piety here, as I never saw before in the most bigoted Catholic countries. All along the Danube, near any town, there are little chapels [wayside shrines] erected, at only twenty or thirty yards distance from each other, sometimes on the sides of these mountains, and in places too narrow for a footpath; and I saw not a house in Linz that had not a Virgin or a saint, painted or carved, upon it.

I walked about the town for near two hours. It was market day, though but for poor stuff; as nothing eatable appeared, perhaps, because it was Friday, but 'Brod', vile cheese, bad apples, pears, and plums; and of other wares, only tape, toys, ordinary missals, and wretched prints of virgins and saints. I saw not a good shop in the town, though there are many showy and fine houses. Gable ends and pear-topped steeples, in the Bavarian style, are still in fashion here ...

The raft stopped at a hovel, on the left bank of the river, where the passengers landed, and spent the night. I remained in my cabin, where, I believe, I was much better off, as to bed, than any of them; but, for

* See footnote on p.136.

provisions, we were all on a footing. Pierre, with great difficulty, clambered up the rocks, to a village, and procured me half a dozen eggs, with which he returned in triumph. But, alas! two of them were addled, and a third had a chicken in it; which, being fast day, I could not in conscience eat.

[After traversing the notorious waterfall and whirlpool at Struden – 'the shooting of London Bridge is worse' – seeing the magnificent Benedictine abbey at Melk and the Jesuit college at Krems – 'it has more the appearance of a royal palace, than anything we can boast of in England' – Burney reached Vienna.]

LADY MARY WORTLEY MONTAGU

The streets are very close and so narrow one cannot observe the fine fronts of the palaces, though many of them very well deserve observation, being truly magnificent, all built of fine white stone and excessive high. The town being so much too little for the number of the people that desire to live in it, the builders seem to have projected to repair that misfortune by clapping one town on the top of another, most of the houses being of five and some of them six stories. You may easily imagine that the streets being so narrow, the upper rooms are extreme dark, and what is an inconveniency much more intolerable in my opinion, there is no house that has so few as five or six families in it. The apartments of the greatest ladies and even of the ministers of state are divided but by a partition from that of a tailor or a shoe-maker, and I know nobody that has above two floors in any house, one for their own use and one higher for their servants. Those that have houses of their own let out the rest of them to whoever will take 'em; thus the great stairs (which are all of stone) are as common and as dirty as the street. 'Tis true when you have once travelled through them, nothing can be more surprisingly magnificent than the apartments. They are commonly a suite of eight or ten large rooms, all inlaid, the doors and windows richly carved and gilt, and the furniture such as is seldom seen in the palaces of sovereign princes in other countries: the hangings the finest tapestry of Brussels, prodigious large looking glasses in silver frames, fine Japan tables, the beds, chairs, canopies and window curtains of the richest Genoa damask or velvet, almost covered with gold lace or embroidery – the whole made gay by pictures and vast jars of Japan china, and almost in every room large lustres of rock crystal.

I can assure you that wrinkles or a small stoop in the shoulders, nay, grey hair itself, is no objection to the making new conquests ... A woman till five and thirty is only looked upon as a raw girl and can possibly make no noise in the world till about forty. I don't know what your Ladyship may think of this matter, but 'tis a considerable comfort to me to know there is upon earth such a paradise for old women, and I am content to be insignificant at present in the design of returning when I am fit to appear nowhere else.

I cannot help lamenting upon this occasion the pitiful case of so many good English ladies long since retired to prudery and ratafia [an almond-flavoured liqueur], whom, if their stars had luckily conducted them hither, would still shine in the first rank of beauties; and then that perplexing word reputation has quite another meaning here than what you give it at London, and getting a lover is so far from losing, that 'tis properly getting reputation, ladies being much more respected in regard to the rank of their lovers than that of their husbands. But what you'll think very odd, the two sects that divide our whole nation of petticoats are utterly unknown. Here are neither coquettes nor prudes. No woman dares appear coquette enough to encourage two lovers at a time, and I have not seen any such prudes as to pretend fidelity to their husbands, who are certainly the best natured set of people in the world, and they look upon their wives' gallants as favourably as men do upon their deputies that take the troublesome part of their business off of their hands, though they have not the less to do, for they are generally deputies in another place themselves. In one word, 'tis the established custom for every lady to have two husbands, one that bears the name, and another that performs the duties; and these engagements are so well known, that it would be a downright affront and publicly resented if you invited a woman of quality to dinner without at the same time inviting her two attendants of lover and husband, between whom she always sits in state with great gravity.

J. B. S. MORRITT

The dances in vogue here are the walses, and English country dances, so Heaven be praised we need not, as in France, torture our legs into cotillons, or have a dancing-master to teach us to hold up our heads. The walse, however, we have not yet dared to attempt ... In doing it the other day as part of a country dance I gave my partner such a kick that we were very near both falling together. They dance them so well here that I assure you it was a great subject of lamentation to us that we could not join in them. The night after we were at another ball, which was given in a *superbe bosquet* [arbour] in the middle of Prince Lichtenstein's garden, but which, choosing unfortunately to be *vastly rural*, was extremely cold. What with a German play and Battel [supper] given in an alley of the garden, all lighted with

A street scene in Vienna, 1733

lamps, it was very magnificent, but we were obliged to teach the natives to dance Country Bumpkin by way of keeping ourselves warm. Besides the plays in German, and an Italian opera, there are more public places of resort, and more frequented, than in any town I have seen. There are lounges for every hour of the day, almost equal, I think, to Bond Street. In the different public walks and drives of the Prater and Schönbrunn there are great public saloons and coffee-rooms, where people of all ranks breakfast, dine, or sup, and where there are *traiteurs* [restaurants], and refreshments of ice, etc., at all hours. You here meet everybody, for the weather has been uncommonly fine, and people here dare amuse themselves, because it is not thought vulgar. In London it would be certainly thought rather odd, but in a broad, open street like St James's Street I have seen women of fashion, and even princesses with a hundred thousand quarterings, sitting eating ice at a coffee-house door after ten o'clock at night.

The history of our day was in general this: After breakfast we went seeing sights, or playing tennis, or walking in the gardens, which occupations lasted till dinner ... At five go in our carriage to the Prater, the Hyde Park here, but much prettier, and walk about seeing our friends, or playing the fool in swings and merry-go-rounds, with which the place abounds. We afterwards go to the opera sometimes, or on the ramparts, where there are music, ices, and another assemblage of everything that is gay till ten o'clock, when, if we do not contrive in the course of the day to be asked to a ball or a supper, we march home, and shut up shop. The Emperor not being here there is no Court, so our bags [wigs] and swords are unemployed ... There is less form of that sort here than in any metropolis except London, and in most places, as in England, you cannot be too undressed to be genteel. Indeed, if an Englishman wore his shoes on his head I believe he would

The Schönbrunn Palace in Vienna, by Bellotto

have imitators here, as we are in high vogue and received with great cordiality.

After Vienna, Dr Burney took himself through Bohemia to Prague and then on to Saxony to visit Dresden. Both had suffered much at the hands of Frederick the Great in the Seven Years War that had ended in 1763. At Prague, 'A great part of the town is new, as scarce a single building escaped the Prussian batteries, and bombardment during the blockade, in the last war. A few churches and palaces only, that were strongly built, and of less combustible materials than the rest, were proof against their fury; and in the walls of these, are still sticking innumerable cannon balls, and bombs.' The same applied to Dresden, a foretaste of its devastation in 1945. Frederick had been Britain's ally during the War.

The city itself has suffered so much in the last war, that it is difficult for a stranger to imagine himself near the celebrated capital of Saxony, even when he sees it from the most favourable eminence in the neighbourhood, so few of its once many cloud-capped towers are left standing; only two or three remain entire; of all the stately edifices which formerly embellished this city; so that here, as well as at Prague, the inhabitants are still repairing the ravages of the Prussians; of whom it is remarkable, that though, during the last war, they ruined many a noble city, they never took one by a regular siege.

They were in possession of Dresden three years: it was taken from them during the absence of the king of Prussia, by the prince of Deux-ponts, who commanded the army of the empire. In 1760, that monarch invested it again, and did incredible damage by his batteries, and bombardments, till it was relieved by General Lacy.*

The river Elbe divides the city into two parts, which are called Old and New Town; these have a communication by one of the finest bridges in Europe ... There is a rule observed in passing this bridge, worthy of imitation; one side being appropriated to the use of those who are going to the Old Town, and the other to those who are going to the New; so that each passenger moves without interruption, and has his right hand constantly next the parapet wall ...

Everyone here is in the utmost indigence ... most of the nobility and gentry are too much impoverished, to be able to afford to learn, or to let their children learn music.

The Saxons of old, so remarkable for patience, industry, and probity, are now reduced to knavery and chicane, beyond the inhabitants of any other country. Dresden is at present a melancholy residence; from being the seat of the Muses, and habitation of pleasure, it is now only a dwelling for beggary, theft, and wretchedness. No society among the natives can be supported; all must retrench; the court is obliged to abandon genius and talents, and is, in turn, abandoned by them!

The horses in this Electorate have had no corn allowed them, nor the soldiers powder for their hair, these three years; but though every species of economy seems now put in practice, yet, it is thought with little effect, as to restoring the inhabitants and state to their ancient affluence and splendour.

During the reign of Augustus III this city was regarded by the rest of Europe, as the Athens of modern times; all the arts, but particularly those of music, poetry, and painting, were loved and cherished by that prince, with a zeal and munificence, greater than can be found in the brightest period of ancient history; but, perhaps, some part of the late and present distresses of this country, have originated in this excessive magnificence ...

The school singers who frequent the streets, not excepting the little boys, wear a black undertaker-like uniform, and large grizzle wigs; and as every house pays annually something towards their support, the ambassadors generally give them a crown a quarter, for *not* singing at *their* doors.

* Frederick incurred great odium for his bombardment because it was commonly held that he knew he did not have the time to take the city. As Boswell said, 'I hated the barbarous hero. He was under no necessity to bombard Dresden.'

Armed with the necessary letters of introduction, but without quite the proper wardrobe, Boswell visited a number of the small courts of Germany: Brunswick and then Coswig can stand as examples.

Sunday, 12 August. I breakfasted with my worthy Baron de Pless, and then he conducted me to the Duke's Chapel, where I heard a psalm performed with magnificent music, eunuchs and other singers from the opera, an organ, a French horn, flutes, fiddles, trumpets. It was quite heaven. I adored my God, and I hoped for immortal joy. It was really grand to see the serene family of Brunswick at their devotions. After chapel was the levée of the Hereditary Princess, this day being her birthday. The Court was in grand gala. Unluckily, I did not think of this before I left Berlin, so had only with me two suits of silk clothes. However, I passed very well . . .

We had a prodigious company to dine at Court, and a most magnificent dinner. I sat by Madame de Boick, Gouvernante to the young princesses, an amiable, pleasant old lady. Grand music played in an apartment adjoining, and round the table was a vast crowd of spectators. I confess that I was supremely elevated. I had the utmost pleasure of contrast by considering at this hour is assembled Auchinleck* kirk and many a whine and many a sad look is found therein. But how shall I support it some time hence? I know not, and let it not disturb me at present . . .

After dinner we walked in the garden, then had a concert at Court, and then grand court in the Duke's bedchamber, where every Sunday he receives the compliments of his subjects. I played at whist. I was not invited to supper, and was weak enough to go home vexed a little. Such is a mind rendered too delicate by fine living. I however recollected that when there was such a crowd the Maréchal [of the Court] might easily forget me.

Monday, 13 August. There came into my room this morning the sweetest girl I ever saw, a *blanchisseuse* [laundress], eighteen, fresh, gay. I spoke German to her with unusual ease, and told her that I would not for the world debauch her to give myself a few days' pleasure, but if she would go with me to England and then to Scotland, I would be very kind to her. She was really innocent. Her beauty thrilled my frame. I thought that I might be an old patriarch upon occasions and could not see any harm in taking her with me. She refused to go, but promised to come back from time to time . . .

After dinner I was at the noble entertainment of rope-dancing, at which was the Duke and all the Court. I have omitted in this my journal to

* Boswell's Scottish home.

The ramparts at Dresden in 1750, an etching by Bellotto

mention that one day last week we had a ball at Court, where I danced most agreeably. I asked to dance a minuet with the Hereditary Princess. She graciously consented, but we had just made our reverence when the fiddles struck up a country dance which the Hereditary Prince was to begin. So we were stopped. Oh, I was a mortified gentleman. This evening was again a ball. No sooner did the amiable Princess perceive me than she came up to me with a smile celestial and said, 'Mr Boswell, let us finish our minuet.' Accordingly I danced with Her Royal Highness, who danced extremely well. We made a very fine English minuet – or British, if you please, for it was a Scots gentleman and an English lady that performed it. What a group of fine ideas had I! I was dancing with a princess ... with the sister of George III, my sovereign.

Monday, 24 September. About noon I arrived at Coswig, the residence of the Prince of Zerbst, who is a strange, wrong-headed being.* He has got his troops, forsooth, to the number of 150 foot and 30 horse, and, during the last war, he took a fancy that the King of Prussia was coming to attack him. So he put in readiness his little battery of cannon, and led out his 180 to

* He was the last of his line. His greatest claim to remembrance is that he was the brother of Catherine the Great of Russia.

make head against the armies of Frederick. He was not here at present, but at Vienna, as he has a regiment in the Austrian service. So I had no opportunity of paying my court to him. The appearance of his little dirty town, his castle, and his sentinels with sentry-boxes painted in lozenges of different colours, like the stockings of Harlequin, diverted me a good deal. I walked about, and, to have a little German talk, I asked every sentry, '*Vie veel troepen hebt der Furst?*'* One soldier, whose head resembled that of his prince, had marked me with serious political attention, and, dreading that a foreign spy had got into his Highness's dominions, and that a conspiracy was forming against the state, followed me close, and at last when I came to the grenadier before the Castle-gate, he laid hold of me, charged the sentry with me and, bringing a party, conducted me to the main Guard. I was heartily entertained with this adventure, and marched with all the formal composure of a state prisoner. When I arrived at the Guard, there was a hue and cry around me as if I had entered a kennel of dogs. I could not explain myself well enough in German, and stood for some time like the stag at bay. At last a blackguard dog of a soldier said, '*Dominus forsitan loquitur Latine.*'† I told this fellow that I was a stranger, a gentleman of Scotland, and that I had asked the number of his prince's troops to amuse my curiosity, and that I supposed I had done no harm. He repeated this in German, and most of the troops seemed content. But my foolish fellow of an accuser would see more into the matter, and so away they carried me before the Burgmeester, while I laughed and cried 'Beast'. My interpreter repeated my defence to the Burgmeester, and this judicious magistrate smiled at the fellow and dismissed me immediately.

A high point of Dr Burney's researches into German music was his attendance at a recital on the flute given by Frederick the Great, but Burney very nearly did not make it to Berlin to hear the royal woodwind. On the last stage his postilion lost his way in a storm at night and drove his wagon, 'the worst and most defenceless that I had hitherto mounted', into a bog. There it and they remained from eleven at night until six the next morning. It then took three hours to clear customs.

I was carried thither‡ between five and six o'clock in the evening, by an officer of the household, a privileged person, otherwise it would have been impossible for a stranger, like myself, to gain admission into a palace where

* 'How many troops does the Prince have?'
† 'Perhaps my Lord speaks Latin.'
‡ The palace of Sans Souci.

Frederick the Great playing the flute at Potsdam, by Menzel. Quantz is on the extreme right, while C. P. E. Bach is playing the harpsichord

the king resides; and even with my well-known guide, I underwent a severe examination, not only at going out of the gates at Potsdam, but at every door of the palace ...

I was carried to one of the interior apartments of the palace, in which the gentlemen of the king's band were waiting for his commands. This apartment was contiguous to the concert room, where I could distinctly hear his majesty practising *Solfeggi* [scales] on the flute, and exercising himself in difficult passages, previous to his calling in the band ...

The concert began by a German flute concerto, in which his majesty executed the solo parts with great precision ... I was much pleased, and even surprised with the neatness of his execution in the *allegros*, as well as by his expression and feeling in the *adagio*; in short, his performance surpassed, in many particulars, anything I had ever heard among *Dilettanti*, or even professors. His majesty played three long and difficult concertos successively, and all with equal perfection ...

M. Quantz [the King's music tutor] bore no other part in the performance of the concertos of to-night, than to give the time with the motion of his hand, at the beginning of each movement, except now and then to cry out *bravo!* to his royal scholar, at the end of the solo parts and closes; which seems to be a privilege allowed to no other musician of the band. The cadenzas which his majesty made, were good, but very long and studied. It is easy to discover that these concertos were composed at a time when he did not so frequently require an opportunity of breathing as at present; for in some of the divisions, which were very long and difficult, as well as in the closes, he was obliged to take his breath, contrary to rule, before the passages were finished.

As the Tourist finally headed for a Dutch or Channel port he might, like William Beckford, look in on the fashionable watering place of Spa, which give its name to the whole breed. Amsterdam elicited praise from the Rev. William Coxe, bear leader to Lord Herbert, writing to his mother Lady Pembroke in 1777, but Dr Burney was critical of the Dutch taste for carillons and chimes.

WILLIAM BECKFORD

Next morning a zigzag road brought us, after many descents and rises, to Spa. The approach, through a rocky vale, is not totally devoid of picturesque merit; and, as I met no cabriolets or tituppings on the *chaussée*, I concluded, that the waters were not as yet much visited; and, that I should have their romantic environs pretty much to myself. But, alas, how widely was I deceived! The moment we entered, up flew a dozen sashes. Chevaliers de St Louis, meagre Marquises, the ladies of the scarlet order of Babylon, all poked their heads out. In a few minutes, half the town was in motion; taylors, confectioners, and barbers, thrusting bills into our hands, with manifold grimaces and contortions. Then succeeded a *grand entré* of *valets de place*, who were hardly dismissed before the lodging-letters arrived, followed by somebody with a list of *les seigneurs* and dames, as long as a Welsh pedigree. Half an hour was wasted in speeches and recommendations; another passed, before we could snatch a morsel of refreshment; they then finding I was neither inclined to go to the ball, nor enter the land where Pharaoh reigneth [go gaming], peace was restored, a few feeble bows were scraped, and I found myself in perfect solitude. Taking advantage of this quiet moment, I stole out of town, and followed a path cut in the rocks, which brought me to a young wood of oaks on their summits. Luckily, I met no saunterer: the gay vagabonds, it seems, were all at the assembly, as happy as billiards and chit-chat could make them. It was not an evening to tempt such folks abroad. The air was cool, and the sky lowering, a melancholy cloud shaded the wild hills and irregular woods at a distance. There was something so importunate in their appearance, that I could not help asking their name, and was told they were skirts of the forest of Ardenne ...

254

All languages are chattering at the Table d'Hôte, and all sorts of business transacted under my very windows. The racket and perfume of this place make me resolve to get out of it to-morrow ... 'Indeed, Sir, no *Monsieur comme il faut* ever left Spa in such dudgeon before, unless jilted by a Polish princess, or stripped by an itinerant Count. You have neither breakfasted at the Vauxhall, nor attended the Spectacle, nor tasted the waters. Had you but taken one sip, your ill-humour would have all trickled away, and you would have felt both your heels and your elbows quite alive, in the evening.' – Granted; but, pray tell your postillions to drive off as fast as their horses will carry them.

WILLIAM COXE

Lord Herbert continues very well. I have read with him occasionally about the constitution of the United Provinces; and when there is no time for that I have desired him to read while his hair is dressing which he never fails doing ... As we passed along the Canals it was a curious sight to see an universal flat below water level consisting of rich meadows covered with inumerable cattle and interspersed thick with villages on every side. The Town of Amsterdam is of itself a wonderful instance of how human industry will arise superior to all the disadvantages of situation. It lies upon a soil so marshy that all the Houses are built upon piles. The air is unwholesome, the water bad, and the stench of the Canals in summer is intolerable, and yet it contains near 300,000 inhabitants. The taxes are perhaps higher than in any other Government, and the necessaries of life exhorbitantly dear, but the surprising industry and steady perseverance of the people makes amends for all these disadvantages, and tho' these provinces produce neither *corn wine nor oil* yet Amsterdam is the great mart of all the productions of the universe. I cannot say that I should like to be an inhabitant of Holland; the inhabitants have mostly a sallow look, and both men and women in general very bad teeth, which I should think a proof of their unhealthiness. What pleases me most in these provinces is the universal toleration that is established. Calvinism is the reigning religion: but Lutherans, Catholics, Jews, Greeks, Armenians, etc., have their separate Churches and are tolerated without reserve. I would that their liberal principal were more universal.

CHARLES BURNEY

[The blind organist of the Oude Kerk – Old Church – in Amsterdam] was deprived of his sight, at seven years old, by the smallpox; and this misfortune first suggested to his friends the thought of making music, which hitherto

The Oude Kerk in Amsterdam during the seventeenth century, by de Witte

had afforded him no pleasure, his profession; and it afterwards became his darling amusement ...

He is married, and has children; and though not young and totally blind, he runs up and down the narrow steps of the organ loft, as nimbly as if he were but fifteen, and had the perfect enjoyment of his sight: he likewise pulls out, and puts in the stops of the organ himself, with wonderful dexterity, which, from their being so numerous, would be a difficult task, and require practice, in one that could see ... the touch of this instrument is the heaviest that I ever felt, each key requiring almost a two pound weight to put it down ... He had very much astonished me on the organ, after all that I had heard in the rest of Europe; but in playing those bells, his amazing dexterity raised my wonder much higher; for he executed with his two hands passages that would be very difficult to play with the ten fingers ...

He began with a Psalm tune, with which their High Mightinesses are chiefly delighted, and which they require at his hands whenever he performs, which is on Tuesdays and Fridays; he next played variations upon the Psalm tune, with great fancy, and even taste: when he had performed this task, he was so obliging as to play a quarter of an hour extempore, in such a manner as he thought would be more agreeable to me than psalmody ...

But surely this was a barbarous invention, and there is barbarity in the continuance of it: if M. Pothoff (the performer) had been put into Dr Dominicetti's hottest human cauldron* for an hour, he could not have perspired more violently than he did after a quarter of an hour of this furious exercise; he stripped to his shirt, put on his night cap, and trussed up his sleeves for this *execution*; and he said he was forced to go to bed the instant it was over, in order to prevent his catching cold, as well as to recover himself; he being usually so much exhausted, as to be utterly unable to speak ...

Besides these *carillons à clavier*, the chimes here, played by clockwork, are much celebrated. The brass cylinder, on which the tunes are set, weighs 4,474 pounds, and has 7,200 iron studs fixed in it, which, in the rotation of the cylinder, give motion to the clappers of the bells. If their High Mightinesses' judgment, as well as taste, had not failed them, for half the prime cost of this expensive machine, and its real charge for repairs, new setting, and constant attendance, they might have had one of the best bands in Europe: but those who can be charmed with *barrel music*, certainly neither want, nor deserve better ...

This is truly the country of chimes; every quarter of an hour a tune is played by them at all the churches, but so indistinctly, on account of the confluence of sounds, that I was seldom able to discover what was played ... There is scarce a church belonging to the Calvinists, in Amsterdam, without its chimes, which not only play the same tunes every quarter of an hour, for three months together, without their being changed; but, by the difference of clocks, one has scarce five minutes' quiet in the four and twenty hours, from these *corals* [babies' teething rings] *for grown gentlemen.*

* In Boswell's *Life of Johnson*, 26 October, 1769, Dr Johnson condemns Dominicetti and his 'medicated baths', which had been established in Cheyne Walk, Chelsea, in 1765.

Conclusion

Return to England brought with it either a yearning for the foreign parts and manners so recently left behind, or a new appreciation of the good points of the old country. Gray, having quarrelled with his travelling companion Walpole in Italy, got back a week before him in 1741 and wrote regretfully to their mutual friend John Chute, still in Florence. When Walpole returned he also wrote to Florence, to Horace Mann, but without regrets, as did Lady Mary Wortley Montagu to an Italian friend, the savant Abbé Antonio Conti, in 1718. Fynes Moryson had the satisfaction of being unrecognised when he returned in 1595.

THOMAS GRAY

If this be London, Lord send me to Constantinople. Either I, or it are extremely odd. The Boys laugh at the depth of my Ruffles, the immensity of my Bagg [wig], and the length of my Sword. I am as an Alien in my native land, yea! I am as an owl among the small birds. It rains, every body is discontented, and so am I. You can't imagine how mortifieing it is to fall into the hands of an English Barber ... If my pockets had any thing in them, I should be afraid of every body I met. Look in their face, they knock you down; speak to them, they bite off your Nose. I am no longer ashamed in publick, but extremely afraid. If ever they catch me among 'em, I give them leave to eat me. So much for dress, as to Politicks, every body is extreme angry with all that has been, or shall be done: even a Victory at this time would be look'd upon as a wicked attempt to please the Nation ... Now I have been at home, and seen how things go there, would I were with you again ... Omit nothing, when you write, for things that were quite indifferent to me at Florence, at this distance become interesting.

HORACE WALPOLE

I have not brought over a word of French or Italian for common use; I have so taken pains to avoid affectation in this point, that I have failed only now and then in a *chi è là?* to the servants, who I can scarce persuade myself yet

258

are English. The country I own delights me: the populousness, the ease, the gaiety, and well-dressed everybody amaze me. Canterbury which, on my setting out, I thought deplorable, is a paradise to Modena, Reggio, Parma, etc. I had before discovered that there was nowhere but in England the distinction of *middling people*; I perceive now that there is peculiar to us, *middling houses*: how snug they are!

LADY MARY WORTLEY MONTAGU

I cannot help looking with partial eyes on my native land. The partiality was certainly given us by nature to prevent rambling, the effect of an ambitious thirst after knowledge which we are not formed to enjoy. All we get by it is a fruitless desire of mixing the different pleasures and conveniencies which are given to different parts of the world and cannot meet in any one of them. After having read all that is to be found in the languages I am mistress of, and having decayed my sight by midnight studies, I envy the easy peace of mind of a ruddy milkmaid who, undisturbed by doubt, hears the sermon with humility every Sunday, having not confused the sentiments of natural duty in her head by the vain inquiries of the schools, who may be more learned, yet after all must remain as ignorant. And after having seen part of Asia and Africa and almost made the tour of Europe I think the honest English squire more happy who verily believes the Greek wines less delicious than March beer, that the African fruits have not so fine a flavour as golden pippins, and the *beccaficbi* [small birds] of Italy are not so well tasted as a rump of beef, and that, in short, there is no perfect enjoyment of this life out of Old England. I pray God I may think so for the rest of my life, and since I must be contented with our scanty allowance of daylight, that I may forget the enlivening sun of Constantinople.

FYNES MORYSON

At London it happened, that (in regard of my robbing in France [see p. 51]) when I entered my sisters house in poore habit, a servant of the house upon my demaund answered, that my sister was at home: but when he did see me goe up the staires too boldly (as he thought) without a guide, hee not knowing mee, in respect of my long absence, did furiously and with threatning words call me backe, and surely would have been rude with me, had I not gone up faster then he could follow me, and just as I entred my sisters chamber, he had taken hold on my old cloake, which I willingly flung of, to be rid of him. Then by my sisters imbraces he perceived who I was, and stole backe as if he had trodden upon a Snake.

Biographical Notes on the Writers

ROBERT ADAM 1728–92
Son of William Adam, the Scottish architect. Educated at Edinburgh University, he worked in his father's practice until he had accumulated enough money to go on a lavish Tour in gentlemanly style, though his aims were highly professional. He set out in 1754 with the brother of Lord Hopetoun on whose house he had been working. He set up his own practice in London and from 1760 to 1780 was the most fashionable architect in England, assisted by his brothers James and William. He replaced the Palladianism promoted by Lord Burlington with the delicate and refined Neoclassicism of the Adam style, to be seen at Syon and Osterley near London, at Kedleston in Derbyshire and the New Town in Edinburgh, in particular. His furniture and interior schemes of decoration are as important as his architectural exteriors. The passages by him quoted here are from his letters home included in John Fleming's book, *Robert Adam and His Circle*.

JOSEPH ADDISON 1672–1719
Son of the Dean of Lichfield, he became a Fellow of Magdalen College, Oxford in 1698. In 1699 he went on Tour with a government pension in expectation of later becoming a diplomat, returning to England in 1703. In 1705 he became an Under-Secretary of State and in 1708 an MP. Other offices followed. He was a close friend of Swift and Steele, and wrote regularly for the *Tatler* and the *Spectator*, in which he created the character of Sir Roger de Coverley. His tragedy *Cato* was produced in 1713.

WILLIAM BECKFORD 1760–1844
Son of a Lord Mayor of London, hugely wealthy thanks to West Indian sugar, he toured first from 1780 to 1781, then wrote his oriental novel *Vathek* in French before going on Tour again in 1782. In 1783 the first printing of his book on his travels, *Dreams, Waking Thoughts and Incidents*, was suppressed as a result of pressure from his mother. Driven abroad by accusations of homosexuality in 1785, he only returned permanently to

England in 1796. He built Fonthill Abbey in Wiltshire, a huge gothick pile, to house his collections.

JAMES BOSWELL 1740–95

Son of a Scottish judge, he studied law before coming to London in 1762, where he met Dr Johnson. He continued his studies in Holland and then set out on Tour in 1764, which included a visit to Corsica. Seduced by Rousseau's long-standing lover Thérèse Le Vasseur on the journey back to London in 1766, once there he set himself up as the champion of Corsican liberty. He practised law in Edinburgh and London, married a cousin in 1769, and, in 1773, toured Scotland with Dr Johnson, whose *Life* he published in 1791.

PATRICK BRYDONE 1736–1818

Son of the minister of Coldingham in Berwickshire. After university he went to Switzerland where he conducted electrical experiments. In 1767 he went on Tour as bear leader to Mr Beckford of Somerby in Suffolk, and two other young men called Glover and Fullarton. His book, *A Tour Through Sicily and Malta* (1773), described a trip he made with them in 1770, and went through seven editions in his lifetime. From 1779 he held the Comptrollership of the Stamp Office.

CHARLES BURNEY 1726–1814

Studied the organ as a child and was taken up by the composer Thomas Arne. He was organist at King's Lynn from 1751 to 1760 before setting up as a teacher, performer and composer in London. His daughter was the diarist and novelist Fanny Burney. He went on Tour in 1770 and 1772, collecting materials for his *History of Music*. He also published accounts of his travels, *The Present State of Music in France and Italy* (1771) and *Germany* (1773). Arthur Young was his brother-in-law; he was a friend of Mrs Thrale and was unofficial sponsor of her second husband, the musician Gabriel Mario Piozzi, on his arrival in England in 1776.

THE EARL OF CORK AND ORRERY 1706–62

John Boyle became 5th Earl of Orrery in 1731 and 5th Earl of Cork on the death of his cousin, the Earl of Cork and Burlington, in 1753. He was a friend of Swift, Pope and Johnson, although the last said of him that he 'did not keep up the dignity of his rank. He was so generally civil, that nobody thanked him for it.' He translated the letters of Pliny the Younger (1751). He set out with his second wife and ten-year-old daughter on Tour in 1754. His *Letters From Italy* were published afer his death, in 1773.

THOMAS CORYATE *c.*1577–1617

Son of the rector of Odcombe in Somerset, after Oxford he drifted in London, becoming a licensed eccentric at Court and one of the circle round Ben Jonson. He set out on his Tour in 1608 but his book, *Coryat's Crudities, Hastily gobled up in Five Moneths Travells* ... , did not appear until 1611. In 1612 he set out overland to India where he died at Surat.

JOHN EVELYN 1620–1706

His great family wealth was derived from the manufacture of gunpowder. Educated at Oxford and the Inns of Court, his first trip abroad was to Holland in 1641, before his main Tour commenced in 1643. He only returned in 1647, having married the daughter of Charles I's ambassador in Paris. He was involved in the foundation of the Royal Society in 1659–60 and had many other interests, particularly gardening and trees; his book on the latter, *Sylva*, appeared in 1664. His *Diary* was published in 1818.

EDWARD GIBBON 1737–94

After Oxford he was sent to Lausanne for five years to remove him from Catholic influences, before returning to serve in the Hampshire Militia from 1759 to 1763, when he left for his Tour. In 1772 he settled in London and began writing *The Decline and Fall of the Roman Empire*. The first volume appeared in 1776.

THOMAS GRAY 1716–71

His mother kept a milliner's shop, but he went to Eton, where his uncle was a master, and then to Cambridge. He accompanied Horace Walpole, son of the Prime Minister, on Tour in 1739, though they quarrelled towards the end and returned separately in September 1741. In 1742 he went back to Cambridge to continue his studies, and it remained his headquarters for the rest of his bachelor life. The quarrel with Horace Walpole was patched up in 1744. His 'Elegy in a Country Churchyard' was published in 1751.

LORD HERBERT 1759–1827

Only son of the erratic 10th Earl of Pembroke, he was sent off on a Grand Tour in 1775, which lasted for five years. He was accompanied by the Rev. William Coxe to look after his morals and mind, and Captain John Floyd to supervise his physical education, particularly everything to do with equitation (a subject on which his father was an acknowledged expert). In 1779 his father wrote to him, 'Pray keep a journal and give it me, when your travels end in repose and a rich wife at home, sans quoi you, and I and Co, shall end in Newgate.' He fought in Flanders in 1793 and inherited the earldom in 1794.

SIR HORACE MANN 1706–86

Son of the Deputy Treasurer of Chelsea Hospital, he was British Envoy at the Court of Tuscany in Florence, where one of his main tasks was to monitor the activities of the Jacobites in Italy. He was a distant relation of Horace Walpole and the two became firm friends when Walpole arrived in Florence in 1739. Their correspondence continued until Mann's death in Florence over forty years later.

LADY MARY WORTLEY MONTAGU 1689–1762

Daughter of the Earl of Kingston, she was intellectually ambitious and taught herself Latin, before marrying against her father's wishes. In 1716 her husband was appointed Ambassador in Constantinople and her letters written from there are justly famous, as is her advocacy of the Turkish habit of inoculation against smallpox. Back in England she took an active part in literary and political life, fighting with her erstwhile friend Pope and defending Sir Robert Walpole. Her marriage was not a lasting success and in 1736 she became infatuated with Francesco Algarotti, a cosmopolitan homosexual littérateur. In 1739 she pursued him to the Continent, only for her passion to cool once she finally caught up with him. She remained abroad until the last year of her life.

J. B. S. MORRITT 1772–1843

Son of the squire of Rokeby Park on Teesside in Yorkshire, which he inherited in 1791 whilst still at Cambridge. He set out on Tour with a tutor and friend called Robert Stockdale in 1794, going to Constantinople via Vienna, then to the site of Troy, Mount Athos, Athens and the Peloponnese. From the Ionian Islands they sailed to Naples. They then escaped the advancing French armies and arrived home in 1796. Morritt was later a Tory MP and counted Sir Walter Scott and Sir Humphry Davy among his friends. His letters from the Grand Tour to his family were published in 1914.

FYNES MORYSON 1566–1630

Son of the MP for Grimsby, he became a Fellow of Peterhouse, Cambridge in 1584. He left England in 1591 and his wanderings lasted until 1595. However, before that year was out he set off again with his brother for Jerusalem. The brother died near Antioch and Fynes came home once more in 1597. He became secretary to Sir Charles Blount, Lord Deputy of Ireland, in 1600. His *Itinerary* was not published until 1617.

SAMUEL SHARP *c.* 1700–78

He trained at St Thomas's Hospital in London and became surgeon at Guy's Hospital in 1733, both lecturing and running an extensive practice. He has been called the link between the old and the modern surgery. He retired in 1765 and went on Tour to help his asthma. His *Letters From Italy* appeared in 1766.

TOBIAS SMOLLETT 1721–71

Son of a Scottish laird, after Glasgow University he became a surgeon, and then joined the Navy in 1741, before starting to practise in London in 1744. His novel *Roderick Random* appeared in 1747 and *Peregrine Pickle* in 1751, and he sought to augment his meagre income by all kinds of hack literary work. His *History of England* (1757–8) at last brought him financial security. In 1763 his magazine, *The Briton*, had failed, his only daughter had died, and he was in ill health, so he went on Tour with his wife and household for two years. His combative and opinionated *Travels Through France and Italy* came out in 1766. In 1768 he retired to Italy where he wrote *Humphry Clinker* (1771).

LAURENCE STERNE 1713–68

An amorous and consumptive Yorkshire clergyman, son of a poor infantry officer. Publication of the first two volumes of his quirky novel *Tristram Shandy* in 1759 brought him rapid fame, the fruits of which he enjoyed to the full in London. Four more volumes appeared in 1762, but he and his family had to move to the South of France for his health. In 1765 he went on an eight-month Tour, incidents from which he put into *A Sentimental Journey* (1767), there lampooning the cantankerous Smollett as 'the learned Smelfungus'.

HENRY SWINBURNE 1743–1803

Fourth son of Sir John Swinburne Bt of Capheaton, Northumberland, the same old recusant family as that of Algernon Charles Swinburne, the Victorian poet. After an expedition to Spain with Sir Thomas Gascoigne (a Yorkshire baronet and like Swinburne a Roman Catholic at this time), he, his family and Sir Thomas moved to Naples in 1777. From there his expeditions to the south of Italy and Sicily were mounted, much facilitated by the fact of his religion. He published *Travels Through Spain* in 1779 and *Travels In the Two Sicilies* (2 vols) in 1783 and 1785. Via her sister the Queen of Naples, he became a friend of Marie Antoinette who gave him lands in the island of St Vincent in 1783. He died of sunstroke in Trinidad. His letters, under the title *The Courts of Europe* . . . , were published in 1841.

HESTER THRALE 1741–1821

Hester Salusbury came from an impoverished gentry family. A precocious linguist, she married the wealthy brewer Henry Thrale in 1763; it was no love match though she bore him twelve children. In 1764 the Thrales met Dr Johnson and in 1766 took him into their home when he was suffering a breakdown. In 1781 her husband died, she sold the brewery and, in 1784, she married her daughter's music teacher, Gabriel Mario Piozzi. This deeply shocked her family and the aged Dr Johnson. Her Tour with her new husband was both a long honeymoon and an escape from such disapproval. As she said of herself: 'My mind is an active whirling mind ... When I rattle, I rattle *on purpose.*' Her *Observations and Reflections in course of a Journey Through France, Italy and Germany* was published in 1789.

HORACE WALPOLE 1717–97

Third son of England's first Prime Minister. He set out on his Tour in 1739 with Thomas Gray, returning in 1741. He paid visits to France subsequently. An historian, connoisseur and, above all, indefatigable correspondent, the definitive edition of his letters fills dozens of volumes. He wrote with an eye to eventual publication, rightly expecting that his letters would be his most permanent memorial. His house, Strawberry Hill at Twickenham on the Thames, was one of the earliest and most important displays of the new gothick taste. He eventually inherited the earldom of Orford from his mad nephew in 1791.

EDWARD WRIGHT [dates not known]

He travelled as bear leader to Lord Parker, later Earl of Macclesfield, between 1720 and 1722. His book, *Observations Travelling Through France, Italy etc.*, was published in 1730.

ARTHUR YOUNG 1741–1820

Came from the Suffolk squirearchy. Never a successful farmer himself, he virtually founded the profession of agricultural journalism, writing a series of instructional books and descriptions of his tours of different areas of Britain examining the state of farming. His book *Travels during the years 1787, 1788 and 1789* is a marvellous eye-witness account of France on the brink of the Revolution. He moved on to Italy after the fall of the Bastille, returning home in January 1790. In 1791 Pitt offered him the secretaryship of the new Board of Agriculture, which allowed him to shine in society until, desolated by the death of his daughter in 1797, he turned to religion.

Further Reading

The standard editions of the letters or journals of the likes of Horace Walpole or James Boswell have not been listed here, neither have the titles of the eighteenth-century travel books given in the Biographical Notes on the Writers.

WILLIAM BECKFORD, *The Grand Tour of William Beckford* ed. Elizabeth Mavor, 1986. This is the most accessible selection from his travel writing. For the full text of *Dreams, Waking Thoughts and Incidents* see *The Travel Diaries of William Beckford* ed. Guy Chapman, 1928

JEREMY BLACK, *The British Abroad*: The Grand Tour in the Eighteenth Century, 1992

J. MORDAUNT CROOK, *The Greek Revival*, 1972

JOHN FLEMING, *Robert Adam and His Circle*, 1962

BRINSLEY FORD, Various articles on different aspects of the Grand Tour in *Apollo* xcix, June 1974, and cxiv, December 1981

JOHANN WOLFGANG GOETHE, *Italian Journey*, translated by W. H. Auden and Elizabeth Mayer, 1962

FRANCIS HASKELL AND NICHOLAS PENNY, *Taste and The Antique: The Lure of Classical Sculpture 1500–1900*, 1981

LORD HERBERT (ed.), *The Pembroke Papers* (1734–80): *Letters and Diaries of Henry, 10th Earl of Pembroke and his Circle*, 1942

CHRISTOPHER HIBBERT, *The Grand Tour*, 1987

JAMES LEES-MILNE, *The Earls of Creation*, 1962. (On the aristocratic leaders of taste in the first half of eighteenth-century England.)

SIR HORACE MANN (ed. JAMES DORAN), *'Mann' and Manners at the Court of Florence*, 2 vols, 1876

J. B. S. MORRITT, His letters home were reissued in paperback under the title *A Grand Tour, 1794–96* in 1985

J. H. PLUMB, 'The Grand Tour', an essay included in *Men and Places*, 1963

PETER QUENNELL, *Four Portraits*, 1945, but reissued several times since. Excellent essays on Boswell, Gibbon, Sterne and Wilkes

GEOFFREY TREASE, *The Grand Tour*, 1967

— *The Treasure Houses of Britain: Five Hundred Years of Private Patronage and Art Collecting*, 1985. (The catalogue of the exhibition at the National Gallery of Art, Washington, which includes essays by Francis Haskell, Brinsley Ford and others.)

An extensive bibliography of the subject will be found in the recent book by Jeremy Black, above.

Index